"An engrossing and informative
experience... thoroughly researched"
- *The Hon. Linda Burney*

# A Soldier
# A Sailor

# &

# *Arabanoo*

# PETER STEWART

A Soldier, A Sailor and Arabanoo © 2024 Peter Stewart

All Rights Reserved. No part of this book may be reproduced in any form or by any electronic or mechanical means including information storage and retrieval systems, without permission in writing from the author. The only exception is by a reviewer, who may quote short excerpts in a review.

This book is a work of creative non-fiction. Some parts have been fictionalized to varying degrees, for various purposes, with some names, dates, places, events, and details changed, invented, and altered for literary effect or to protect the privacy of the people involved.

Printed in Australia

First printing: July 2024

JPR Creative

Paperback ISBN 978-1-9231-7159-6

eBook ISBN 978-1-9231-7160-2

Hardback ISBN 978-1-9231-7161-9

Distributed by IngramSpark

*JPR Creative acknowledges the traditional owners of the land and pays respects to the Elders, past and present.*

 A catalogue record for this work is available from the National Library of Australia

"An engrossing and informative experience... thoroughly researched"
- *The Hon. Linda Burney*

# A Soldier A Sailor

# &

# *Arabanoo*

# PETER STEWART

For Australia's First Nations Peoples and Eliza and Madeleine so their generation may understand Australia's true history.

**Cultural Advice:** Please be advised and warned that some content within this book may be confronting or unsettling to our First Nations Peoples.

Content relating to the murder and massacres of First Nations Peoples is contained in this book. Aboriginal and Torres Strait Islander Peoples are advised and warned that this work contains the names of Original First Nations People of the land who have passed away and are living in the dreaming.

This book also contains Men's Business and Sorry Business.

# Foreword

*A Soldier, a Sailor and Arabanoo* presents an engrossing and informative experience for readers wishing to know more about the true history of this country, particularly regarding the early stages of the British colony here.

The book is a work of fiction; however, the foundation of the story is based very closely on historical facts, which Peter has thoroughly researched.

Peter takes the reader on a journey through the early days of the Sydney colony, including the troubled relationship between the colony and native Australians, a dramatic sea voyage stricken by storms and scurvy and a deadly smallpox outbreak.

When reflecting on this nation's history, it's important to put truth-telling at the forefront of the narrative. While this book may be at times confronting for First Nations Australians, it diligently recalls significant historical events with accuracy.

Each of the key characters in this book puts forward an interesting perspective of the time, and there is a diverse range of them, including the morally conflicted marine Captain Watkin Tench, the master mariner Captain John Hunter, the gentle and trusting Arabanoo, the perpetually abrasive Major Robert Ross and the morally driven Lieutenant William Dawes.

To ensure the credibility of Arabanoo's version of the story, the author has relied on the input of highly respected First Nations Holders of Knowledge Aunty Tracie Howie and Aunty Trish Levett.

I recommend this book to anyone interested in expanding their knowledge of Australia's history. Historical knowledge and an understanding of the wrongs of the past are essential to ensure we remain firmly on the path towards reconciliation.

The Hon. Linda Burney
Minister for Indigenous Australians
Canberra
April 2024

# Author's Note

This book is a work of fiction. It should not be considered anything else. It is, however, very factually based. Although I have read and referred to numerous other works and resources (listed in the references below) in writing this book, I have depended very heavily on the works of Captain Watkin Tench and the journal of Captain John Hunter. Readers will note I have provided numbered footnotes at the end of most chapters or sections of this book. These refer to the pages of the works on which I have based the particular piece of fiction that I have written. The reader will find that these refer almost exclusively to the works of Tench and Hunter, but there are also a few references to other works that I have relied on in particular chapters. My aim in doing so is to facilitate the reader's fact-checking on this fascinating period of our history, because I am very aware that the real interest and power in a historical story of this nature lies in its truth, not in anything a writer can invent.

When writing a book like this about the 'Colvasion' (colonisation/invasion) of this country, it is understandably very difficult to get inside the heads of eighteenth-century British marine and naval captains. The fact that we have at our disposal their written works does at least give us some insight into their characters, their thoughts and their actions. We also have various other primary source documents that reveal what other people thought of them at the time. I have therefore attempted to be as faithful as I can be in the way I have interpreted these historical characters.

In the case of Arabanoo, however, it has been much more difficult. Trying to get into the mind of an eighteenth-century Gamaragal

Warrior is virtually impossible for me. We have only what Tench, Hunter and others said about him.

I have therefore been greatly indebted to both Gundungurra Elder Aunty Trish Levett and Aunty Tracey Howie, Elder of the Garigal/Walkaloa clans, for their wonderful assistance. Their contribution has given much greater depth and perspective to the characters of Arabanoo and his colleagues and to their culture. In regard to the attitudes and conversations of the Original First Nations Peoples regarding the arrival of the First Fleet, I have relied largely on Muruwari descendant Jane Harrison's play, 'The Visitors'. This powerful play was extremely helpful in providing me with ideas about portraying the point of view of our First Nations Peoples.

Although all characters in this book are real historical figures, I do not pretend that I have provided accurate portrayals of their characters. In the case of many of the key figures, I have relied on what others have said about them or what they may have revealed in their own writings. In the case of minor characters, I have simply used their names when there is nothing on the historical record (that I could find, anyway) about their actions or characters. This is all the more reason to view this book as fiction. The one proviso to that is, of course, that all the significant events described in this book actually happened and these were the people involved.

I also apologise for any offence that may be caused by some of the language used in this book. As I am attempting to tell the story from the points of view of eighteenth-century men and women, I have used the language that they used. An example of this is the fact that in his books, Tench refers to Australia's First Nations People as 'Indians', an apparent hangover from his time in the Americas. I therefore have often used 'Indians' when Tench is speaking.

I believe that it is important to note here, however, that although some eighteenth-century sensibilities were different to ours today, there were a wide range of attitudes at that time, just as there are now. Just as there are racist or sexist and extreme political views held today, so there were at that time. On the other hand, just as there are tolerant, enlightened people today, the same was the case in the eighteenth century. Just as we believe we live in an enlightened age, so did they in the eighteenth century. Numerous documents support that this was very much the case and included attitudes to race, slavery, women, etc. I hope you find this book shows some of the range of attitudes that existed at the time.

I hope you find it interesting and informative and enjoy reading it as much as I have enjoyed researching and writing it.

# Chapter 1

# Sydney Cove, December 1790

Captain Watkin Tench strode across the small bridge over the Tank Stream, which divided the colony, and up the hill towards the governor's residence, wondering why on earth he had been summoned. He had been given no information whatsoever, other than being told the governor wanted to see him immediately. Although he enjoyed a good relationship with the governor, recent events in the colony made Tench quite nervous, and as he arrived at the Government House, the largest building in the new colony, he had a strong feeling that whatever the governor had to say to him, he wasn't going to like it.

When Tench entered Governor Arthur Phillip's office, he was sitting at his large oak desk, rubbing his balding head rather firmly. The lines on his face, a legacy of his years at sea, masked an expression that was a combination of anger, sadness and frustration. At first, he didn't look up as the thirty-two-year-old marine captain entered the room. Despite his immaculately tailored red uniform with its elaborate silver bullion epaulettes, bright magenta sash and smart pewter buttons, Tench looked anything but a British marine. His fine features, deep brown eyes and fair hair prematurely greying at the temples ensured he looked far more like a distinguished English gentleman than a hardened war veteran.

Tench stood in silence for a moment before he uttered an almost hesitant, 'Good morning, Excellency.'

'Oh, good morning, Captain,' murmured Phillip, motioning to the chair in front of his desk.

Tench sat in silence and immediately mopped the beads of sweat that had formed on his forehead as a result of the warmth of the morning, his heavy uniform and his brisk walk to the governor's residence.

'Captain, I'm afraid to say that with this tragic business with McIntyre, we simply have to respond, for I am advised the man will most certainly die as a result of his wounds... We can't just allow the natives to attack our people on every occasion we need to go into the bush.'

'Yes, Excellency,' Tench responded. He had quietly feared this was the reason for his summons.

'As this is a particularly sensitive and difficult matter, I wish to discuss it directly with you, without any of the other officers present.'

'Yes, sir. I appreciate that.'

'Well, you may not like what I have to say, but I have decided on the action we are to take, so I'll come straight to the point,' Phillip said bluntly.

Tench nodded before Phillip continued. 'As you know your way around the bushland areas here better than most, and I know I can trust you, I want you to lead a large party against the Bideegal tribe at Botany Bay...'

The governor paused, but Tench sat in silence, fearing what he may say next.

Phillip looked directly at Tench, leant forward on his oak desk and continued solemnly, 'You are to execute ten of them and bring their heads back to me. You will be provided with hatchets and bags for this purpose. You are to capture two of them and destroy all weapons of war that you can find, and in particular, you are to make every endeavour to capture or kill this Pemulwuy fellow.'

Phillip paused again while Tench continued to sit in stunned silence.

'You are not, however, to injure any women or children or destroy their huts. In exercising this duty, you are not to show any sign of amity or friendliness to lure them to you. Doing so would be an act of treachery and only develop a sense of mistrust amongst them that would give them reason to distrust every future act of peace and friendship on our part. You are also not to speak to any of the natives who are known to us and with whom we usually communicate. Is that clear?'

'Yes, sir.' Tench nodded, but he shifted uncomfortably in his chair.

'Now, Captain, I wish to explain why I believe it is necessary to adopt measures of such severity.' Phillip had by this point stopped rubbing his own brow and had started stroking the head of his favourite greyhound, which sat beside him. The dog was pure white, except for a brindle patch on its left ear, and it had a particularly docile nature. Although Tench quite liked dogs, Phillip's obsession with this particular greyhound had always irritated him, never more so than now. Here was Phillip, gently stroking the head of an animal while ordering him to go and kill human beings.

The irony was not lost on Tench, but again, he responded, 'Yes, sir.' He was a British marine, after all.

'In the time we have been in this country, no less than seventeen of our people have been killed or wounded by the natives, and it is this Pemulwuy and this Bideegal tribe living on the north arm of Botany Bay who are the principal aggressors.'

Phillip paused yet again, but Tench said nothing. Totally oblivious to the fact that Tench's silence did not mean consent, but rather was due to the disciplined captain nearly biting his tongue off, Phillip continued, 'My observation of the natives is that they do not fear death individually, but they value the strength and security of their whole tribe. It is therefore essential that we strike a decisive blow against this tribe. We must convince them of our superiority and infuse in them a universal terror that will operate to prevent further mischief.'

Tench nodded hesitantly. 'Yes, Excellency.'

'Captain, although you say *Yes, Excellency*, your countenance reveals reluctance on your part. You don't agree with me?'

Tench paused while he got his emotions under control, and

although his mind was racing, he spoke slowly and deliberately. 'Well, Excellency, I understand McIntyre was hunting game for you and you had a lot of time for the man.'

'Yes, I did, but my thoughts on him have nothing to do with the fact that we cannot just allow the natives to wantonly attack our people like that.'

'I understand, sir, but my point is that many have the view that McIntyre may have brought this upon himself. You must know full well the accusations against the man.'

'Enough,' Phillip responded, raising his hand. 'I don't want to hear about that, and knowing the man as I do, I don't believe any of them.'

Tench said nothing, and Phillip continued, 'Captain, it is my belief that previous attacks by the natives have resulted from them receiving some injury from us, or from some misapprehension. But despite what you suggest, in this case, the reports I have clearly state McIntyre has been most wantonly attacked and that it was entirely unprovoked. I have questioned the sergeant and the two convicts who accompanied him at the time of this attack, and they all have the same short, simple account of the matter. Whatever the malicious rumours about his previous behaviour... to which, as I have said, I attach no credence anyway... there is no doubt that, on this occasion, he had put down his weapon before this Pemulwuy leapt onto a fallen log and speared him.'

Phillip and Tench again sat in silence briefly before Phillip continued, 'You obviously still don't agree with me, do you?'

'I'm sorry, sir, but from my knowledge of the natives and the fear that those we know held of McIntyre, it seems apparent that it was a case of "payback", which we are now aware is a key aspect of their system of law and justice. I believe a response like this is excessive in the extreme.'

Phillip looked directly at Tench. 'Alright, I respect your views. What would you suggest is an appropriate action, given the situation in which we find ourselves? And before you provide me with your answer, you should understand that I won't accept anything less than clear, decisive action.'

Tench pondered for a moment. As he did, he fidgeted with the white diagonal strap of his uniform, which crossed his chest down to his waist, where his sword hung. He ran his thumb and forefinger up and down the strap before replying, 'Well, sir, may I respectfully suggest that rather than immediately killing and beheading ten of them and capturing two, we may find that an alternative action could better achieve our objectives?'

'Go on.'

'What if we were to capture six of them and bring them back? Out of this number, we could then set aside a number for retaliation, and the others, having witnessed the fate of their comrades, could be released to advise their tribe of the punishment that awaits them should they offend again in such a manner.'

'Hmm. I see. Yes, there could be some benefits to that approach.' Phillip continued stroking the head of the greyhound. 'Alright, we'll capture six. If six cannot be taken, let this number be shot and beheaded. Should you find it possible to take that many, I will hang two and send the rest to Norfolk Island for a certain period, which will cause their countrymen to believe we have killed them secretly.'

Tench nodded. 'Yes, sir.'

'And, Captain, I wish to ensure you have more than sufficient men to accomplish your goals in this mission, so you are to take fifty, including three officers and two surgeons. Also, take Lieutenant Dawes and, to guide you, Sergeant Young, who was with McIntyre when he was speared.'

'Sir, that is all fine with me, but I am quite sure that Lieutenant Dawes will want no part of such a matter.'

'Well, that is unfortunate, but he is to go,' Phillip replied flatly.

Tench hesitated for a moment, but knowing full well how opposed his friend would be to such a mission, he ventured, 'Excellency, Lieutenant Dawes has particularly–'

Phillip cut him off and flew back, 'He's a marine, Captain. He doesn't get to pick and choose what missions he undertakes.' He paused. 'And advise him that if he doesn't accompany you, he will be court-martialled for disobeying a direct order.'

'Oh! Yes, Excellency,' replied a rather stunned Tench, who was becoming concerned that defending his friend was damaging his good relationship with Phillip, at least in the short term.

Phillip calmed down almost instantly and added, 'So, Captain, given the fact you are a friend of Lieutenant Dawes, I would encourage you to persuade him to join you. The last thing this colony needs is an officer of Lieutenant Dawes's stature and importance being court-martialled.'

'I will most certainly do my best to persuade him.' Tench got to his feet before adding, 'And when would you wish us to leave, sir?'

'As soon as you can organise the detachment.'

'Yes, sir, I will. We will depart before dawn tomorrow.'

*Ref. 1*

\*\*\*

Tench hurried down the hill, away from the governor's residence, and through the streets of the young colony. His mind was again racing as he passed the motley collection of crude houses built of clay brick and wood, with thatched roofs and windows of woven sticks. He loathed the idea of such a mission, particularly as his friendship with some of the local tribespeople had grown to a level of genuine, mutual respect. Apart from that, the last thing he wanted to do was push Dawes into joining him when he knew his friend would be betraying his core beliefs to undertake such a mission.

He strode into the marines' quarters, briefed Lieutenant Poulden on the mission and began organising the detachment. An hour later, he headed up the hill to the west. As the colony's astronomer, engineer and surveyor, Dawes had his own hut, which was somewhat larger and better-made than most, and it sat perched on the colony's highest point, some distance from the quarters shared by the rest of the marines. The point rose majestically above the blue waters of the harbour on a clear, sunny day such as this, and unlike so much of the natural bushland areas surrounding the diminutive colony below, it was not covered in tall trees. By contrast, it was covered in low, scrubby bushland, which allowed unimpeded vision of the spectacular views both up and down the harbour to the east and west. The few large trees that had been growing there had been felled to allow Dawes clear vision of the night sky.

'Will,' Tench called as he approached his friend's hut.

Dawes emerged from the hut, accompanied by an attractive young Aboriginal woman, Patyegerang, whose shy smile Tench always found most endearing. Dawes gently motioned for her to stay inside the hut before he walked towards Tench. Dawes, at just twenty-eight, had the look of an academic, which matched his gentle nature. He pushed his wavy dark hair away from his soft face as he approached Tench – his skin seemed to have endured the extended exposure to the sun and salt much better than most of his colleagues'. Unlike Tench, there was no sign of premature greying, nor did he wear sideburns, which were fashionable at the time. This was due less to a matter of personal choice than the fact that his kind face was almost hairless.

'Good morning, Watkin,' he said glumly, and immediately identifying the expression on Tench's face, he added, 'You're here to tell me about this massacre you've been ordered to undertake.'

'How did you know?'

'As you know well, news travels fast in this little colony, but before you ask, I am not going to have any part of it,' Dawes replied flatly.

'Before you adopt that position, you should be aware that I have managed to convince the governor to moderate our actions somewhat.'

'How, precisely?' questioned Dawes, with a hint of hope creeping into his tone, as the two friends turned and began walking together towards the end of the point.

'Well, he had originally determined that we were to take a detachment down to Botany Bay and murder ten of the native men, behead them and bring the heads back here.'

'Yes. That's what I'd heard.'

Tench responded, 'I've convinced Phillip that we can achieve his objectives for the mission without such extreme and horrific actions.'

'Go on.'

'He has agreed that we are to capture six and bring them back here.'

'And what shall happen to them then?'

'Phillip says he will hang two and send the rest to Norfolk Island for a period.'

Dawes retorted, 'That's nearly as bad.'

'Well, it's nowhere near as extreme as murdering and beheading ten of them!' Tench hesitated to tell Dawes what Phillip's orders were if they couldn't capture any.

'We are supposed to be British marines, not a bunch of headhunters from some Pacific island,' Dawes spat in disgust.

'I did advise Phillip of your feelings on such matters, but he had no sympathy at all.'

'I wouldn't expect he would.' Dawes looked at the ground, shaking his head.

'Look, Will, I share your feelings, but if we do capture them and bring them back here, we can hopefully persuade him not to hang them. Besides, Phillip has threatened to have you court-martialled if you disobey a direct order.'

'What?' replied a stunned Dawes. 'He wouldn't dare do that over a matter of conscience like this… would he?'

'I don't really know, but I think it may be best if you don't test him on the matter,' Tench advised calmly.

'I thought we wouldn't have to put up with that sort of bullying behaviour since Phillip sent Major Ross to Norfolk Island.'

Tench smiled gently at his friend's agitation before replying, 'I just think we shouldn't ostracise Phillip over the matter at this stage.'

Dawes ignored the comment. His mind was elsewhere as he ran his fingers through his hair in frustration before replying, 'Watkin, I was talking to Patye about this just yesterday, and I asked her, *Why are the black men so angry with us white men? Why won't they come and talk to us?* And do you know what she said?'

'What?'

'She said, *They just want your people to go away...* That says it all, doesn't it? It's their country, their land. They just want us to go away and leave them alone, because when they retaliate to the abuses of a low-life like McIntyre, Phillip justifies murdering them.'

'I agree with you completely about McIntyre, but frustratingly, though, Phillip didn't want to hear anything about his reputation for murdering them and ill-using their women. When I tried to give him details about those accusations, he just told me he didn't want to hear any of it, as he simply didn't believe it of McIntyre.'

'How naïve can he be?' Dawes muttered. 'Anyway, the fact the man was such a despicable low-life is all the more reason my conscience will not allow me to go on such a mission.'

Tench hesitated and now stopped beside his colleague. He put one hand on Dawes's shoulder as the pair turned to each other. Tench looked closely at his friend as he thought of a different approach. 'Alright, I understand it is a matter of conscience, so why don't you go and discuss the matter with Reverend Johnson and find out if he sees any benefit in having yourself court-martialled?'

'Hmm.' Dawes nodded slowly. 'Perhaps I could do that, but I can't make you any promises.'

'Please do... Oh, and just be careful with Patye. She is wonderful, but I would hate for Phillip to ever find her here.'

'Phillip wants to know about their language and customs. That's what I'm doing.'

'He might not be convinced if he sees how attractive your teacher is.'

The two men smiled at each other and were about to turn away when Tench added, 'Will, the last thing I want is to be undertaking this repugnant mission without you beside me, so please be there for me tomorrow morning.'

*Ref. 2*

# Chapter 2

# Sydney Cove, 14 December 1790

At 4 a.m. the next morning, it was black beneath the sliver of a new moon when Tench entered the yard to meet the assembled detachment.

'Good morning, Captain,' said Lieutenant Poulden as he walked up to Tench.

'Good morning, Mr Poulden,' Tench replied.

'I have the sacks, sir–' Poulden advised before Tench cut him off.

'Sacks, what sacks?' Tench replied.

'The sacks for the heads, sir,' Poulden replied, oblivious to his captain's attitude to the mission. 'And I've distributed the hatchets amongst the men.'

Without replying, Tench walked over towards the detachment and noted that Dawes was there, standing alongside surgeons Worgan and Lowes, in front of the marines.

'Delighted to see you with us this morning, Lieutenant.'

'Thank you, Captain,' replied Dawes.

Tench smiled at Dawes. 'Good morning, Mr Worgan, Mr Lowes.'

The two surgeons returned the greeting, and the detachment was called to attention by Sergeant Young as Tench turned towards them. Tench gave a cursory glance up and down the two lines of slightly weary men, standing bolt upright with their Brown Bess muskets against their shoulders – the seventeen-inch bayonets of which were slung by their sides.

Shortly afterwards, the marines, led by Sergeant Young, wound their way through the sleeping streets of the tiny colony and onto the well-worn track to Botany Bay. It was a track that for thousands of years had been softly worn into the earth by the naked feet of the local tribal groups. Now, though, the land of the Eora nation groaned beneath the heavy tread of the British boot as the tracks became eroded into the landscape.

Tench and Dawes walked side by side, chatting quietly. They had their orders to capture or massacre the native people, but they were the last ones in the colony who would wish to follow such orders. Although they were aware that it was the first time in the colony's short history that such orders had been given, they were unaware that it would not be the last.

***

The sun bathed Botany Bay in the warm light of a summer morning as Tench and his party trudged across the elevated land, heading towards the north shore of the bay.

'Still no sign of any natives, sir,' Young told Tench.

The detachment soon arrived in a small clearing in the eucalypt forest, where a roughly built hut stood. It was used by the colony's hunters to stay in overnight so they could hunt kangaroos and other game at sunset and sunrise. Tench paused as he looked down the track to where a fallen tree lay across the path.

'That's where the attack happened, sir,' said Poulden.

Tench nodded as he took in the scene of the attack and replayed the incident in his mind. 'Thank you, Mr Poulden. Well, all we can do is keep moving and hope we come across some Indians. Do you know where any of their camps are?'

'Sir, there are a few that I know of. One is down closer to the bay, further to the east.'

'Ok, well, let's see what we can find around here and then head that way.'

Phillip's party of avengers wound their way along the tracks of the peninsula like a gigantic red snake – or so they would have appeared to the large white sea eagle that cruised amongst the pale puffs of cloud in the sapphire sky above.

After a couple more hours of fruitless wandering, Tench paused with Sergeant Young and Lieutenant Poulden. 'Alright, gentlemen, where would you like to go now?'

'Let's head along the foreshore of the bay. That's where another camp is,' replied Young, brushing a fly from his sweating face.

'Lead the way,' requested Tench.

Dawes walked up and joined Tench as the sergeant led the party off.

'Well, Watkin, how do you think it is progressing so far?' Dawes suppressed a smile.

'I would say it's going splendidly, just splendidly, don't you think?'

Dawes allowed the smile to crease his face. 'Yes, I'd have to agree with you. If it wasn't so damned hot, I would be almost enjoying the walk.'

'Yes, but it's the damned humidity that's so oppressive. Anyway, let's keep trying,' was Tench's reply.

The detachment proceeded down to the shores of the bay through the low coastal scrub before following it to the north-west... still without success. Again, they paused.

'Where to now, Sergeant?' Tench asked Young, who had now taken over the role of the party's sole guide.

'Let's head north for a while, sir, away from the bay,' replied Young, as sweat continued to trickle down his face.

'Certainly. We'll follow you.' Tench turned to Dawes. 'Actually, Will, it gets more splendid by the hour.'

Dawes put his head down and chuckled quietly to himself.

At five o'clock in the afternoon, Phillip's redcoats stopped for the evening near the edge of one of the estuaries that fed into Botany Bay.

Tench joined Dawes, who was sitting a little away from the detachment, as the men readied the camp for the night and prepared the evening meal.

'Well, that was a successful day.' Tench smiled as he unhitched his sword, dropped it to the ground and slumped down next to Dawes.

'Yes, highly,' replied Dawes, pulling off his boots.

Tench did the same before saying, 'You haven't told me about your conversation yesterday with Reverend Johnson. Obviously, he said something that changed your mind.'

'He really just helped me calm down a little and look at the whole situation more objectively. To try to look at the big picture for Patye and her people. As you said, how do they benefit if I'm court-martialled? Anyway, I lay on my bunk, looking at Patye asleep beside me, and I thought, well, I'm just not going to be involved in killing her people, but I can still obey the order and go for a walk with you. So, I'm just here for the walk, Watkin. I will not be involving myself in shooting or capturing the natives. And besides, I've got the utmost confidence in you being a thoroughly incompetent hunter of natives.' Dawes smiled.

Tench returned the smile before replying, 'That's fine with me. The way things are progressing, I don't think any of us will be shooting or capturing too many of the Indians anyway.'

The two friends kept talking as the sun gently slid beyond the bushland to their west, casting a pink and mauve tinge on the fine clouds scattered across the horizon. Their meal of salted pork rations, along with a mug of tea, was brought to them as they continued their conversation. Although the pair had only met in the months leading up to the fleet's departure from Portsmouth in May of 1787, their friendship felt to both of them as if it had been of much longer duration. That feeling was probably due to the fact they had so much in common – they were both marine officers, both had served in the American Revolutionary War and, most importantly, both were similarly intelligent and well educated.

It had been a long time since they had had the opportunity of such a lengthy chat together. Their varying duties back in the colony, with Tench often being stationed at Rosehill and Dawes's duties as engineer and surveyor during the day, along with his night duties studying the stars and learning the local tribal language from Patyegerang, meant such opportunities were exceedingly rare. The only thing that disturbed the flow of the conversation was the plague of mosquitoes and sandflies intent on feeding on their once-soft English skin. The fact that that skin had now been hardened somewhat, more so in Tench's case, by long periods at sea and under the southern sun was no deterrent to the insects.

The sun had been set for some time, and the nocturnal noises of the detachment were now in full cry, but Tench and Dawes were enjoying their conversation far too much to consider sleep.

'Something I have been meaning to ask you, Watkin, is about your book. What did you call it again?'

'*A Narrative of the Expedition to Botany Bay.*'

'And have you heard how it's selling?'

'Yes, I understand it's selling exceedingly well.'

'Really? That is pleasing, but not surprising for a talented writer like you.'

'Thank you, Will.' Tench nodded. 'The publishers are so pleased they now have me working on another one.'

'Sounds promising. You may make good money from it, then.'

'Ahh, you know with us writers, it's not about the money. It's about the glory.'

Dawes laughed. 'Well, knowing you, I'm sure you'll enjoy the attention of many young ladies in London society when you return, as I believe there will be many trying to meet the famous writer Captain Watkin Tench.'

Tench joined Dawes in his mirth. 'Oh, if only that were true. If only that were true.'

The conversation between the two paused, and Tench's mind drifted back to London and to young women dressed in their finery. The subject of women was a favourite topic for the officers, given that those who had wives were not allowed to bring them to the colony.

The Colonial Office had considered the marine officers should always be 'battle ready' while in the colony and wives would only be a distraction. The lower ranks of the marines were, however, allowed to bring their wives, but as those who were married were in the minority, there was only a small number of non-convict women in the colony.

'Ahh, London,' murmured Tench, beginning to verbalise his thoughts.

'Hmmm.' Dawes had been sitting up but now lay back and looked to the night sky. 'Have a look at that. It's just magnificent, isn't it?' he uttered in wonder. 'It's as if the Lord has scattered thousands of tiny diamonds across a black velvet rug... so beautiful.'

'That is rather poetic for an astronomer.'

Dawes smiled. 'I may marvel at the science involved, but that doesn't mean I'm incapable of admiring the beauty of it too. Now, honestly, Watkin, where would you rather be – here, gazing up at this spectacular sky, or in hustling, bustling, crowded, smelly London?'

'I agree the fresh air and the absence of the Thames's stench is refreshing, but sorry, it's still no contest. I don't have someone like Patye to share my nights with, so I'd like to be in the arms of one of those young London ladies that you mentioned a moment ago. I'd just be helping her remove her finery right about now.' Tench stopped, slapped the side of his own face and added, 'And I wouldn't be getting eaten alive by damn insects.'

'Yep, they're just awful, aren't they? Not as bad as the Americas, but still terrible... But what about Gooreedeeana? I thought you were quite interested in her.'

'Hmmm, yes, but I've just discovered she is married.'

'Oh, no. You didn't mention that.'

'Well, apart from the fact I am an English gentleman and wouldn't do that sort of thing–'

Dawes interrupted, 'You mean sleep with a married woman or sleep with a native?'

'You have me there, Will... or perhaps you don't, because as I think about it, perhaps it's only the first, but allow me to take both issues separately.'

'Go ahead. This should be fascinating, and I have absolutely nothing else to do but listen to your ruminations.' Dawes smiled.

Tench knew his friend was having fun with him but was quite happy to go along with it.

'The first question is, would I, as an English officer and gentleman, sleep with a married woman? To that I would have to say no, probably not, but it may depend, to some degree, on the circumstances and happiness of the marriage. However, when the woman concerned is a married native woman, I would say definitely not. And I must confess a significant part of the reason is that I like to be able to sleep at night, and if my conscience didn't keep me awake, I know my fear definitely would.'

Dawes chuckled quietly.

'Yes, I'd be terrified that her husband would creep into my room and cut my throat while I slept,' admitted Tench.

'Aah, Watkin, you must remember that the natives here are far more broadminded about such things than we conservative Englishmen, and in various circumstances are prepared to lend their wives to respected visitors.'

'I know, you've explained that, but if you think I would be prepared to try to negotiate the complexities of the native culture to determine when it is acceptable to sleep with a married woman and when you're going to get your throat cut, you're mistaken, my friend.'

'And what about the second question? Would you sleep with a native woman?' Dawes asked, propping himself up on his elbow to look at Tench.

'When I first arrived here, the answer to that question was definitely no, because, as you know, I tended to have an extremely low opinion of them. However, as I have grown to know and understand them and their extraordinary culture—'

Dawes interrupted, 'And seen how attractive some of the women are.'

'Yes, I have to agree some are very attractive, particularly their form, and particularly Gooreedeeana... and Patye, of course.'

'So, after all that qualification and rambling, the answer to question two is yes!' Dawes smiled again.

Tench nodded and chuckled quietly. 'Yes.'

The pair lay back in silence for a moment, staring up at the sky, before Dawes spoke.

'Have you thought about how tragically ironic it is that we are sitting here talking about beautiful young London ladies, attractive native women and the magnificence of the universe when we are supposed to be undertaking this horrific mission?'

'Mmmm, horribly ironic!' Tench murmured before adding, 'I must admit, Will, I fear what tomorrow may bring.'

*Ref. 3*

# Chapter 3

# Botany Bay, December 1790

Watkin Tench woke to the gentle warbling of a group of magpies as they pecked at the ground near the marines' camp. He rolled onto his side and watched them as they searched the soil for a tasty morning morsel. He lay there, admiring how nature had provided such a plain-looking bird with such a soft, melodious tone. A moment later, though, he snapped himself from his trance-like state and jumped to his feet. Shortly afterwards, he had his men on the move again, and as they marched eastwards along the foreshore, they each shielded their eyes from the morning sun's first rays, which danced across the waters of Botany Bay. It was another muggy summer morning, and after a solid two-hour march eastwards through the low coastal scrub, the march had become a trudge under their heavy packs and thick uniforms soaked with sweat. Finally, Sergeant Young called them to a halt above an ocean beach. All were pleased for the break and the chance to soak in the cooling north-easterly breeze. Tench walked up beside Young.

'It seems that we have missed any camps,' Tench remarked without annoyance.

'I'm sorry, Captain. I thought that track we were on would take us to one.'

The two marines stood in silence briefly as they admired the magnificent view of the Pacific Ocean, with its white-capped waves gently caressing the warm sands below. At that moment, five Aboriginal tribesmen walked out of the bush and onto the beach.

'Look!' Young grabbed Tench's arm and pointed.

'Yes, Sergeant. It looks like we have finally found some Indians. So now we will just have to take this quietly.' Although they were exactly what Tench's men had been looking for, their fruitless search so far meant he was caught rather by surprise. His stomach knotted slightly.

Young immediately turned to the detachment and ordered their silence as Lieutenant Poulden came forward to join them.

Tench ordered, 'Lieutenant, take the sergeant and twenty of the men and head through the bush towards the far end of the beach. Leave ten men partway along your path, and then, when you are in position, we will have them surrounded and we'll move in.'

'Yes, sir,' replied Poulden as he turned to organise his men.

'And, gentlemen, just remember we are trying to capture them, not kill them. Shooting is to be an absolute last resort.' Tench thought for a moment and then added, 'So don't shoot unless you see my party do so first. And tell your men that.'

'Yes, sir.'

Young hurried off, leading his twenty men through the lightly wooded scrub at the back of the beach.

Dawes now hurried up to join Tench.

'What are you going to do, Captain?' Dawes asked anxiously.

'What I've been ordered to do. Try to capture them.' Tench paused and looked at his friend to see the lines of worry, bordering on panic, stretching across his face. 'Don't worry, Will, I've told Poulden and Young not to shoot unless my party shoot first… and we won't be shooting.'

Dawes shook his head, said nothing and walked away while Tench ordered his men to slowly move forward. They did so before crouching behind large grass tussocks overlooking the beach. Tench and his men waited in silence for Young's group to get into place. As Tench looked down on the scene unfolding below, he wrestled with conflicting emotions. Did he really wish to capture these natives, knowing the fate Phillip had planned for them?

Such thoughts vanished from his mind as he saw the tribesmen suddenly start running across the beach. They must have seen Young's men. Tench jumped to his feet and led his men charging down the hill after them. Young's men, who were at the bottom of the hill, had also spotted the fleeing tribesmen and were giving chase. Young yelled for them to stop, but it was futile, as the fleet-footed locals quickly disappeared into the thickening bush away from the beach.

Tench and his party soon joined Young's group on the edge of the bush.

'Should we keep chasing them, Captain?' Young queried between gasping breaths.

'Do you think you can catch them?' replied Tench, fully aware of the answer.

'No, sir, not with our packs and weapons and everything.'

Tench turned and strode away and met Dawes, who was walking slowly down the hill.

'That was close, Captain.'

'Not even remotely close, Mr Dawes. We have no chance of outrunning them.'

'At least none were shot.' Dawes's face revealed his relief.

'Well, they were my orders, but I'm not sure what I'll do if we can't capture some soon... If we can find any more, that is.'

After a brief discussion between Tench, Poulden and Young, the detachment of redcoats headed quickly south-west, aiming for another Aboriginal camp that Young knew of. A short time later, as they drew close to where Young believed the camp to be, they halted, removed their heavy packs and dropped them to the ground.

Tench asked Dawes and a couple of the men to remain with the packs, while the remainder of the detachment moved slowly forward. As they drew close, Young and Tench halted and directed the men to surround the small camp, which consisted of just five huts.

Within a few minutes, they had the huts entirely surrounded.

'On my signal, Sergeant,' Tench ordered, before dropping his raised arm.

The redcoats charged out of the bush and into the camp, muskets raised at the ready. They quickly checked the huts and the immediate surrounds before Young turned to Tench.

'No-one here, sir. It's deserted,' he advised, with disappointment evident in his voice.

'Look, sir,' called a young corporal.

Tench looked where the marine was pointing to see three canoes full of tribespeople frantically rowing for the opposite shore of the bay.

'Will we fire on them, sir?' Young asked, raising his Brown Bess musket.

'No! Put that down,' Tench ordered, grabbing the barrel. 'You can see they're well out of range. There's no point.' Tench was not entirely sure if they were out of range or not, but he wasn't going to allow Young to find out.

A frustrated Young reluctantly lowered his musket.

\*\*\*

A short while later, after Tench's redcoats had regathered their packs and were following the shore of the bay back towards the east, they spotted a native tribesman in waist-deep water, a considerable distance from shore. He stood motionless, his fishing spear poised above his head.

Tench brought his detachment to a halt as Dawes walked up to join him and Young.

'What do you think, Captain? Can we capture him?' Young queried.

'I don't see how we can, Sergeant. Can you? He's nearly two hundred yards from shore. We can't send men out wading waist-deep in water. That native would be off and gone before our men got anywhere near him. What do you think, Mr Dawes?'

Before Dawes had a chance to answer, the tribesman saw the redcoats on the beach, and rather than looking to avoid them, he immediately started walking towards them.

'He's coming this way, sir,' a confused Young muttered.

'Hmmm, yes, I can see that, Sergeant.'

Tench looked at Dawes and shrugged.

'Will we shoot him when he gets close enough, sir?' Young was about to raise his musket.

'No, certainly not.'

'Why isn't he running away, sir? Like the others?' asked Young.

The local tribesman continued striding towards them, with the sun glistening on the water surrounding him and a speared fish wriggling helplessly on the point of his spear.

'Hey!' the tribesman called and began waving to them. 'Hey, Captain!'

Tench looked at Dawes as they both said simultaneously, 'Oh, it's Colbee.'

'Who, sir?' inquired Young.

'Colbee! One of the natives from the colony.'

'Who's he, sir?'

'You know Bennelong, don't you?' responded Tench.

Young was almost offended. 'Yes, of course, sir.'

'Well, last year, when the governor had Bennelong captured, Colbee was captured with him.'

'Really! I didn't know that, sir.'

'Yes, well, that is probably due to the fact the governor only held him prisoner for a week before he escaped his leg irons and went back to his people,' Tench explained patiently. 'Since then, though, he has been a regular visitor to the colony, particularly to the governor, with whom he often dines at the governor's residence.'

'Oh, really, sir?'

Tench and Dawes were now waving back to the grinning tribesman as he drew nearer.

'Colbee,' Dawes called.

'Captain,' Young said somewhat hesitantly.

'Yes, Sergeant.'

'Sir, do you think we should capture him now, while we have the chance?'

'Pardon?' replied Tench despite the fact he had heard the question quite clearly.

'Sir, just so the mission isn't a complete failure, we could capture him now.'

Tench looked at Dawes and shook his head before turning to Young. 'Sergeant, if the governor wanted Colbee captured, he could capture him any time he likes... in his own dining room!' Tench had raised his voice slightly at the end of the statement. It was not from anger but rather for effect and for Dawes's amusement.

Dawes put his head down and chuckled quietly as Colbee walked out of the water and up the beach, his white teeth gleaming beneath his dark, smallpox-scarred skin. He threw his arms around both Tench and Dawes, who responded warmly.

The conversation that followed was a mixture of Colbee's broken English and Dawes's broken Dharug, but revealed that Colbee had been in the colony just the previous day and had heard about Tench's mission. He had dined with the governor, who had tried to persuade him to stay rather than head down to Botany Bay, which he had explained was his intention. Colbee explained in the most animated manner how the governor had kept providing him with more and more food in an effort to get him to stay, but when Colbee had had more than his fill, he thanked the governor and was on his way to Botany Bay.

At that point, Tench broke into the conversation and asked, 'Colbee, do you know where Pemulwuy is? Pemulwuy, where?'

'Captain, him gone long, long way down dere,' Colbee replied, pointing to the south. 'Many, many days, far.'

'Hmmm,' murmured Tench as he glanced at Dawes.

The naked Colbee then joined the detachment of redcoats as they found an area where the low, scrubby trees provided a little shade from the heat of the midday sun. The fatigued marines dropped their packs onto the sandy soil and reclined against them as they began gnawing unenthusiastically on their tasteless salt beef rations. Colbee, on the other hand, cooked up his large, freshly speared snapper and, as was the custom of his people, shared some with his friends Tench and Dawes.

'Oh, thank you, Colbee,' the invaders responded gratefully, before Tench offered Colbee some of his salt beef. Colbee's reaction was simply to screw up his nose as if it were dried rat droppings.

'Well, you can't blame him there, Watkin.' Dawes chuckled.

'Hmmm.' Tench nodded.

The stilted conversation between the three continued quietly for a short time before it was shattered by the cry of 'Snake!' from one of the marines seated a short distance away.

The marine and all those around him immediately jumped to their feet. Tench, Dawes and Colbee hurried over to see a large snake nearly eight feet long and as thick as a man's wrist with a heavily patterned black and yellow skin wriggling across the hot sandy soil. Without saying anything, Colbee calmly walked over and picked the snake up by the tail. As it swung around in an attempt to bite him, he flicked it like a whip to make it miss its target. He lowered it to the ground, and it immediately began to try to slither away from its tormentor. As it did so, Colbee swiftly put his foot on the back of its head, pinning it to the ground. Colbee turned to Tench and pointed to the sword that hung from Tench's waist as he said, 'Captain.'

Tench immediately withdrew his sword from its scabbard and handed it to Colbee, who used it, with a skill that surprised all, to behead the snake. They all watched the body of the now-headless snake twist and writhe in its death throes. Tench looked at the Gadigal warrior standing there, British marine officer's sword in one hand and dead snake's head in the other, and a sliver of a thought flashed through his mind. There was something about the whole scene he found rather ironic.

When all had resumed their seats to rest further before the next leg of the expedition, Tench and Dawes began asking Colbee about the different snakes in his country. Colbee explained that the snake he had just killed, and which now lay on the ground beside him, was harmless and 'good tucker'.

'It must be some sort of python,' Dawes commented to Tench.

Tench nodded. 'Hmmm.'

'But dem brown fellas,' Colbee explained, 'dem bad fellas, bery bery bad fellas.' He put both hands around his own throat and made a strangled 'KKcckkkk' noise.

Dawes looked at Tench. 'Well, I think we can safely assume that brown snakes are deadly.'

'Indeed,' replied Tench. 'That is handy to know.'

***

By early afternoon, having bid a warm farewell to Colbee, who wandered off with his dinner slung around his neck, the marines resumed their hunt for his countrymen. They were now headed westward in search of another Aboriginal camp that Young knew of. They had been walking for a few hours when they came to a swamp, the strange and offensive odour of which immediately struck Tench's nostrils.

'By Jove, this is just such an unpleasant piece of landscape, isn't it?' he remarked to Dawes beside him.

Sergeant Young walked up to them and advised, 'We need to follow around the edge of this swamp, Captain.'

'Certainly. Lead the way.'

Late in the afternoon, after hours trudging beneath the afternoon sun, the exhausted, sweating redcoats arrived at the bank of a small estuary that flowed into the bay.

Young called the relieved marines to a halt.

'Now, where exactly is this other camp?' Tench inquired.

'It's just a couple of miles the other side of this small river, sir.'

'Low tide is due about two in the morning, so if we cross this creek then, we should be able to raid the natives' camp at dawn.'

'Yes, sir.'

\*\*\*

At exactly 2 a.m., after a sleep regularly broken by biting, stinging insects, Tench and the bulk of the detachment set out to cross the river. Dawes had volunteered again to stay behind with six of the detachment and guard the packs so the others would be unencumbered by them during their raid.

The new moon glistened on the wet mud, providing the only light as Young led the way into the creek, which was about sixty yards across from bank to bank. Tench was close behind him, with the rest of the marines following in pairs. At first, the group strode easily across the mud, their heavy black boots just breaking the surface. As they approached the middle of the creek, though, Tench felt his boot suck into the mud. He paused and looked down to see that his entire foot had disappeared beneath the surface. As he pulled it out, he called to Young, 'Sergeant, are you sure that it's safe to cross here?'

'Not sure, sir. I've never done it, but...' Young stopped. He and Tench locked eyes on each other as, suddenly, both of them sank knee-deep into the mud. Tench turned to see the same fate quickly befalling those closest to them.

'Men, tie your ammunition pouches to your heads.' Tench turned back to Young. 'Alright, now what do we do? We're halfway.'

Tench felt his leg becoming further entrapped in the slush, so he didn't wait for an answer. 'Let's get moving quickly, Sergeant,' he ordered, as with considerable effort, he pulled one leg and then the other from the morass and made for the far bank.

As he did so, though, he heard a panicked voice behind him call, 'I'm stuck, sir.'

It was quickly followed by another. 'So am I, sir!'

Tench and Young both stopped and turned to see several of their men crotch-deep in the mud and really struggling to pull their legs out of the mire, making forward progress virtually impossible.

'You men at the back,' Tench called. 'Go to the bank, don't come any further. Try to find another place to cross.'

Those at the back of the detachment quickly returned to the safety of the bank, where they hurried along the shore until they found another point to cross, closer to the bay, that was far sandier and less muddy.

Those still in the creek with Tench and Young were in increasingly serious difficulty.

'Help, sir,' called the heavily set Private King, who had now disappeared almost to his ample waistline. 'Help! I'm sinking.'

'Hold on, Private,' Tench called as he strained every sinew, trying to head back towards the private, who, along with two others, was trapped in a particularly treacherous section near the middle of the creek.

As he battled towards them, Tench's mind was racing, struggling to find a solution, when he heard Poulden's voice behind him, calling to the men who now appeared on the other bank. 'You men, cut some tree branches, quickly.'

'Aha, good idea, Lieutenant,' a relieved Tench responded.

The men on the bank quickly set about chopping off tree branches with their hatchets.

'And get those ropes also,' called Tench.

'Help, sir!' called the now totally panic-stricken Private King, as he remained engulfed to his waist.

'Quickly, men, quickly!' Tench called as the men on the bank entered the creek armed with branches and rope. They threw the branches to the stricken marines and one end of the rope to Private King.

'Now, Private,' called Poulden, 'tie that under your arms and around your chest.'

Private King quickly disposed of his musket, which to this point he had been protecting by holding it above his head. He frantically tied the rope around himself as the voracious mush encompassed his waist. Several of the rescue party then took a firm grip on the long rope and began heaving as they reached the solid land of the bank. Slowly but surely, the private was dragged from the dark brown mire as his companions used the branches to extricate themselves and complete the crossing, where they were shortly joined by Tench and Young. The exhausted marines slumped and hunched together, trying to recover themselves. Their once-red coats were now covered with thick brown mud, making them a rather amusing sight to the dark eyes that had been watching the action from the cover of some nearby trees.

After allowing them several minutes to recover, Tench was on his feet.

'Alright, men. Let's go!' he ordered.

The marines were quickly but reluctantly on their feet and setting off into the darkness. After winding their way along a rarely used track through the bush for a couple of hours, Young called the detachment to a halt. The sun had now begun to creep above the eastern horizon as Tench, Poulden and Young began dividing their detachment into three groups. Tench gave the directions for a coordinated attack on the camp that lay less than sixty yards in front of them.

They spread out to the three different points from which they would launch the attack, and Tench's stomach knotted as he crouched in the scrub. He was a proud British marine who would be embarrassed to return to Phillip with his mission a complete failure, but his heart and conscience said it was a mission they should not be on in the first place. He was still wrestling with these thoughts when he realised it was time to attack. He rose to his feet, gave the signal and began running without ever having made the conscious decision to do so. He was still in a trance-like state as the Aboriginal huts appeared in front of him. His heart pounded in his chest. His muscle memory from years of training and combat raised his musket to his shoulder as all three groups of marines simultaneously burst into the camp to be greeted by... silence. Nothing. Not a soul. The natives had fled during the night.

Tench suddenly realised his deepest feelings as a tidal wave of relief engulfed him.

*Ref. 4*

# Chapter 4

# Botany Bay, December 1790

It was late on another rapidly warming morning when Tench's marines returned to where Dawes and his group were guarding their gear. They'd had to make a quick dash back across the rising creek before they were cut off for the day from their supplies and food. They had, of course, chosen to cross closer to the bay, where the creek bed was sandy.

Dawes watched as they trudged into the makeshift camp. What an almost comical sight. Their tops were wet from sweat, which saturated their heavy red coats. Their midriffs were brown with mud from their altercation with the mire of the creek, while from the thigh down, they were soaking from their dash through its rising waters.

Although Dawes was momentarily distracted by the oddness of their appearance, his first thought was to quickly check each man in the group to see if any were carrying a canvas sack that may contain a native's head. Once he had ascertained there weren't any, he relaxed enough to ask Tench, as he suppressed a smile, 'What happened to you lot?'

Tench collapsed to the ground beside Dawes and took a large swig from his canteen before answering, 'Anyone who said Botany Bay was a suitable place to establish a colony hasn't ever been here.'

Dawes chuckled quietly. 'Yes, it's most curious that Cook and Banks thought it was so ideal.'

'Yes, curious indeed. I'd say it was quite ridiculous, actually. The place is nothing but swamps, bogs, mangroves, sand and scrubland,

and as we've discovered, even the Indians don't linger for long around here.'

'It does have some nice beaches on its western shore, though.' Dawes smiled.

'You can't build a colony on a beach, Will,' responded Tench with mock annoyance.

'No luck, then, on your native-hunting expedition?'

'None at all,' Tench replied, before adding quietly, in case any of the marines nearby were listening, 'thankfully.'

'Oh, well, that is pleasing,' Dawes responded equally quietly.

Tench half-smiled as he pulled off his sodden boots and examined his feet, which were covered in bunions and blisters – an occupational hazard. He nodded. 'Hmmm, I can't help but think that Colbee's presence in the area may have had something to do with the disappearance of Pemulwuy and his mob, as well as all the other Indians.'

'That must have been why he was in a hurry to escape the governor's hospitality, which is so unlike him,' observed Dawes.

'Speaking of the governor's hospitality, I'm hungry,' said Tench, as he opened his pack and pulled out some rations.

'I think I'll join you,' responded Dawes.

The pair chatted while they chewed grudgingly on their salted pork. Tench then lay back on his pack to rest. His brain didn't rest, though, and it wasn't long before he sat up again and turned to Dawes. 'How did it get to this point, Will?' He paused before adding, 'And where do we go from here?'

'You mean with the natives?'

'Exactly... and the whole colony too, I suppose,' responded Tench.

'Well, as we have discussed with David Collins, there are major issues around the whole legality of the colony under international law.'

'I'm sorry to interject straight away, Will, and yes, we have discussed it with David, and yes, he is our legal expert, and yes, he put forward a most compelling case, but whether or not it is illegal doesn't explain the issues with the Indians. After all, they wouldn't have any idea about international law. And Phillip's orders from the Admiralty are that we are supposed to be living peacefully with them.'

'Standard orders,' responded Dawes dismissively, as he was somewhat frustrated that Tench had cut him off before his story had even started.

'Yes, yes, I know they are the standard orders when establishing a colony, but I believe that was why Phillip refused to seek revenge when he himself was speared at Manly Cove,' responded Tench.

Dawes interjected, 'But he knew that was clearly a case of payback, which even he understands is such an important part of their culture. And…'

Dawes paused as Lieutenant Poulden and Sergeant Young approached.

'Yes, gentlemen, what is it?' asked Tench.

'Sorry to interrupt you, sir,' said Poulden, 'but the sergeant and I have just been discussing the situation with a couple of the men, and they have reminded us about another camping place the natives use at times that I had completely forgotten about. It is a little further south from here.'

'Really!' responded Tench.

'Yes, sir. It seems they only use it at certain times of year, but we believe they should be there now.'

'Hmmm, interesting,' responded Tench. It was the last thing he wanted to hear. He glanced at Dawes and paused for a moment.

Poulden continued, 'Sir, if we want to reach their camp by sunset, we will need to leave very soon.'

Tench hesitated again before replying, 'Alright. Mr Poulden, Sergeant, let the men know. We leave in five minutes.'

'Yes, sir,' responded Poulden and Young as they turned and hurried back to the rest of the marines.

Dawes looked at Tench, who was now staring at the ground in front of where he sat, leaning forward with his arms on his knees.

'So, you're really going to continue with this horrific mission?' questioned Dawes.

Tench continued looking at the ground in front of him. The burden of command was not something that usually weighed heavily on him. Suddenly, he felt as if a lead-laden pack had been dumped on his shoulders. He had thought the mission was over. He had thought he was going to be able to return to Phillip and say he had failed to capture or kill any natives but had tried his best. If he stopped now, though, that wouldn't be true. He ran his thumb down the inside of the white diagonal strap of his uniform and, without looking at Dawes, replied.

'I am afraid I still have to follow orders. We must continue the mission.'

'Watkin, how can you possibly say that?' responded a frustrated Dawes. 'You've tried. You don't have to keep going. Why keep going?'

If Dawes was frustrated, Tench was doubly so. Not by Dawes, but by the situation in which he found himself. He returned his gaze to the ground in front of him as he reflected on how it had all come to this. How, when they had arrived believing there would be no issues with the local natives, due to their small numbers and nomadic lifestyle, had he ended up in this situation – trying to hunt down those natives, the fellow tribesmen of a dear, departed friend?

Finally, he turned to Dawes and replied almost regretfully, 'Because I'm a marine, Will, because I'm a marine!'

He pulled his boots back on and pushed himself grudgingly off the ground, before looking again at Dawes.

'I'm sorry, Will,' he murmured, and he turned and strode over to the detachment reclining nearby.

'On your feet, men!' he yelled.

*Ref. 5*

# Chapter 5

# Leith, East Coast of Scotland, 1746

Excitement swelled in young John Hunter like the incoming tide on a full moon as he ran up the gangplank and onto the ship. He felt he had been waiting the entire nine years of his life to go to sea, and finally, now he was actually going on the ship on which his beloved father was shipmaster. His family were pushing him towards a career in the church, but he was only interested in a life of adventure on the high seas. And although this was only a short trading trip, they were going to Scandinavia, the land of the Vikings, so the thrill of a first voyage was greatly magnified.

John stood beside his father, beaming, as the trading barque sailed away from the docks of his hometown and towards the rising sun, which danced across the water in front of them.

'Could I have a look through your telescope, please?'

William Hunter smiled down at him and handed him the telescope.

John raised it to his eye, as he had done many times in the front yard at home, but this was so different. Despite the relative calm of the sea, compared to dry land, the ship was rolling quite significantly, and John found it difficult to fix on the distant sail of the ship ahead of them.

'Father, it's hard to see the ship.'

'Don't hold it so tightly against your eye, son. Hold it just a wee bit away.'

John did so, and immediately, the distant sail became clearer.

'Is that better?' William Hunter asked.

'Aye, much better. Thank you.'

The lessons continued as the ship sailed out into the North Sea, where the rolling rapidly became more dramatic. John was thrilled and fascinated, staring up at the sails of the ship as they were filled with the strengthening southerly breeze. He thought the sail on the foremast looked ready to burst. The further they travelled into the open sea, the stronger the wind became and the bigger the waves grew as the bow of the ship crashed through them.

'How are you feeling, son?' his father asked, looking down at the boy as he wrapped his scarf more tightly around his neck.

'Wonderful, just wonderful.' John beamed back.

'How is your stomach?'

'Good, good. It's fine, really. I love the smell of this air.'

'Ahh, you're born to it, my boy.' William Hunter smiled as he proudly patted his son on the back.

The three-masted barque ploughed on through the waves on its way to Norway, with John learning all he could from his father and the other crew. By the time the sun set, young John was exhausted both physically and mentally. Despite his small bunk in the cramped quarters below deck, the creaking timbers and the rolling of the ship, he was asleep with his head filling with dreams of 'sailing the seven seas' almost as soon as he hit the pillow.

He had no idea how long he'd been asleep when he was suddenly woken by the sound of yelling.

'Quick, John, quick, get up on deck.' He heard his father's voice and felt himself being dragged from the bed. His head was still engulfed by the fog of sleep as his father pushed him up the ladder in front of him. 'We're about to hit some rocks, son. Hurry!'

As John emerged onto the deck, he was hit by the full ferocity of a North Sea storm. Lightning lit up the sky as bitter wind and rain bit at his face, and a moment later, a wave crashed across the deck, nearly knocking him off his feet.

'Grab the rail, son! Grab the rail!'

Terrified, John flung himself forward and grasped the rail, and the instant he did, he felt the whole ship shudder as the sound of splintering timber rose above the roar of the storm.

'Just hold on, son. Don't you let go,' his father ordered.

John clung desperately to the rail as his father and the captain staggered around the shaking ship, yelling orders to the panic-stricken crew. As each wave struck the windward side of the ship, it was pushed further onto the rocks. John looked over the side of the rail to see pieces of the ship's hull slowly breaking away beneath the waves.

Then his father was back beside him. 'Just stay calm, son. Don't panic. It will take a while for the ship to break up and sink. We just need to work out how we can make it to the shore. Look how close it is.' His father pointed across the ship.

John nodded. 'Aye, father.' He wasn't panicking at all. It had happened so fast he really hadn't had time to. It hadn't occurred to him that he and his father could die here on these rocks, shipwrecked like countless sailors before them. It hadn't occurred to him that he could die on his very first voyage to sea. He had a child's faith in his father. The darkness of the thoughts racing through his beloved father's mind just hadn't occurred to him.

'Now let's get you across to leeward.' His father grabbed him by the arm as the two of them battled across the deck.

As they reached the leeward side, they heard one of the crew yell, 'Look!'

Father and son looked up and desperately strained their eyes, attempting to see through the gloom of the night and the blinding rain. There, outlined against the white sand of the nearby beach…

'There, there, there!' William Hunter pointed frantically.

There, there were people moving. A group of fishermen pushing their boats into the water. A moment later, they were rowing towards the stricken ship.

'It'll be alright, son, they'll save you. You'll be alright, you'll be alright!' William Hunter threw his arm around his son and hugged him tightly as tears of relief streamed down his face.

*Ref. 6*

# Chapter 6

# Chester, England, 1770

Young Watkin Tench sat at his desk, daydreaming, as he looked out the leadlight window to the River Dee flowing past the southern boundary of the boarding school that his parents ran. Although a good student, twelve-year-old Watkin had had enough of studying for the day and was staring longingly at his favourite fishing spot on the riverbank beside the large ash tree. It looked so inviting on this pleasant summer evening.

'Watkin.' It was his mother Margaritta's voice. He turned as she entered the room. 'How's your study going?' She smiled.

'Oh, it's going well,' he assured her.

'I'm pleased to hear that. What have you been working on?'

'My French,' he replied as he held up his textbook.

'Good, but don't forget you have your Latin exam next week.'

Watkin smiled. 'I haven't forgotten, but to be honest with you, although I appreciate the benefit of studying French, I just don't understand the need to study Latin.'

'Well, you know your father says it is essential for a proper, well-rounded education, and you know if you are to follow in his footsteps and become an academic, you need your education.'

'Mother dear, you know only too well I have no desire to be an academic. I want to be a marine and see the world and serve our king and country.'

'I do wish you would give up on that idea, my son. I don't want you being killed in a war in some distant land.'

Young Watkin stood up and gave his mother a brief hug. 'Neither do I, but if I can stay alive, it will be a wonderfully adventurous career. And girls do love the uniform.' He smirked.

'Behave yourself, young man.' Margaritta gave him a gentle smack on the shoulder. 'Now come downstairs. Your dinner is nearly ready.'

# Chapter 7

# Kai'ymay, Gamaragal Land, 1772

Young Arabanoo was awake as the first rays of Grandfather Sun began creeping amongst the distant clouds on the horizon behind his clan's camp. He had barely slept the night before and was awake even before the kookaburras and cockatoos began their morning commotion. He had been preparing for this for weeks, and this evening, he and his friends Bennelong and Colbee were going fishing. This time, though, they weren't going to be fishing from the safety of the shore with lines or light spears. They were going out with the men in canoes, and they were going to be using large spears and harpoons. And to make it even more exciting for the twelve-year-old boy, his father, a respected Elder and Knowledge Holder in the clan group, said it was that time of year when the dugongs were active in the warm currents of their waters, and they were hoping to spear one.

It was all part of the preparation for their initiation into manhood, and although the three of them were from different clan groups, they were all preparing together. Arabanoo was Gamaragal, Bennelong was Wangal and Colbee was Gadigal, but as they were all part of the Eora Nation, they had spent the previous few weeks learning together – crafting their own spears from wood and making the pointed tips by binding sharpened bones and stingray barbs to their ends. It was a slow and somewhat tedious process, but Arabanoo had enjoyed every moment of it, because not only was he working with his father and friends, but it was all leading up to the big evening of fishing. Besides, learning to throw them was just plain fun, even if it was serious men's business. While he and his friends had been making their spears with stalks from the grass tree plant, Arabanoo's father and the other men of the mob had been making harpoons, in case they were lucky enough to get a dugong or even a large stingray. The harpoons were larger and heavier than the spears, and they had a woven rope made from fibres of a tree on the end, which was attached to the arm of the thrower.

For the preceding few days, the men had been teaching the boys how to use their spears to hunt fish in the shallows of the bay, rather than the much lighter, multi-pronged fizgigs. They had been taught to wade into the thigh-deep water and then to stand as still as a tree trunk until the fish that had been scared off by them walking into the bay gradually returned to nibble on the sea grass. It was an activity that suited Arabanoo's quiet, passive nature. He was happy to pretend to be a tree for as long as he needed to. His father had taught him that this was also vitally important when hunting kangaroos. He had explained to Arabanoo that he'd had to learn to creep up ever so slowly while the kangaroos had their heads down eating, and as soon as the hypervigilant roos put their heads up – stand still as a tree. That way, the roos would think you were a tree and not a hunter.

Being a tree held no interest, though, for the rather impatient Bennelong. The result was that on their first day, Arabanoo managed to spear two fish and Bennelong only one, despite him being, arguably – and the two friends did argue about it – a better spear thrower than Arabanoo. As for Colbee, he speared three fish. He was patient and a good spear thrower, and being a little older than his friends, he had more experience.

Finally, the big night arrived, and as the Grandfather Sun was painting the low clouds in the western sky a gentle crimson, the men took the three boys down to the beach of the inner harbour. They loaded the five canoes with several spears each and a few harpoons and clubs. The canoes were somewhat larger than the ones the women often fished from but were made in the same way – a large piece of bark cut in one piece from a tree was made pliable by the heat of a fire before being tied together at each end with vine. In the middle, a straight piece of timber was placed to hold the sides apart and give it some support. They were, nevertheless, rather flimsy and sat low in the water.

Before the men pushed the canoes into the water, they told the three boys to sit on the sand and listen. It was Arabanoo's father who spoke.

'Boys, you must remember the importance of safety while we are out there. Although this is all very exciting for you, you must be careful at all times. Make sure you have your feet set apart and you are well balanced before you throw a spear, or you will tip your canoe over and end up in the water. Just do as we have taught you on the beach.'

The boys all nodded enthusiastically before Arabanoo's father continued.

'Most importantly, though, if we see any large sharks, just sit down carefully in the canoe and stay still. They will be active at this time of the evening in the warm waters. So, if you see any, don't paddle. The splashing will only attract them. Just sit still. Is that clear?'

'Yes, yes.' The boys nodded as Bennelong jumped to his feet and started heading to his canoe.

Arabanoo's father ignored him and looked to Arabanoo and Colbee, saying, 'Alright, let's go.'

In a few moments, they had all five canoes in the water, with two occupants in each. The three boys were with their fathers, and four young men were in the other two canoes. It was a calm, warm evening without a hint of breeze, as the north-easterly off the ocean had now dropped and they were sheltered in the small bay of the inner harbour. They paddled out towards the point where it opened up into the full expanse of the harbour. Just around the next point was the open ocean. Thousands of years of cultural knowledge that had been passed down told Arabanoo's people that this was a prime fishing spot at this time of year, and an area where dugongs were likely to be, as they swam into the warm waters of the sheltered bay to feed on the sea grass.

No sooner had they reached the point than a school of large snapper cruised under the canoes as the fishermen scattered burley across the surface. The three excited boys jumped to their feet as their fathers balanced the canoes. Bennelong immediately threw his first spear but missed. Arabanoo and Colbee, though, stood patiently, waiting for some of the snapper to pass near their canoes, just below the surface. Colbee threw his spear, and it pierced a good-size fish. His father quickly grabbed the end of the spear before the wounded fish could struggle for freedom. He lifted the speared fish into their canoe.

'Well done, son,' he said as Colbee beamed with pride.

Arabanoo continued to stand patiently with the spear raised above his shoulder. Then he saw a huge snapper appear near the surface. He thrust his spear into the top of its head and clung to the end of his weapon. The fish struggled to break free as it shook desperately beneath the surface. Just as Arabanoo sat down and adjusted his grip on the spear to lift the large fish into the canoe, he heard his father yell, 'Shark!'

In that same instant, he saw the open mouth and the rows of jagged teeth of the sea's most feared creature. Although it only took a moment, Arabanoo remembered every detail of that moment for the rest of his life. The shark's massive jaw and jagged teeth latched onto the snapper at the end of his spear and wrenched the spear from his grasp as its huge dorsal fin flashed past the side of the canoe. The shark disappeared from sight as Arabanoo's father touched him reassuringly on the shoulder.

'Are you alright, son?'

A trembling Arabanoo hesitated before replying. 'Yes, yes. I think so.'

The next moment, the pair of them heard Bennelong's voice. It was a mixture of excitement and fear.

'There it is. I'll get it!'

Arabanoo looked over to see Bennelong quickly get to his knees and raise one of the harpoons above his head. The shark had resurfaced and was cruising between the canoes. Although fear overtook his entire body, Arabanoo, the artist, saw for a moment the stunning beauty of the creature as its dorsal fin cut through the crimson glass of the water's surface and turned towards Bennelong's canoe.

'Sit down, son. It's too big!' Bennelong's father yelled.

'I've got it,' Bennelong called as he launched the harpoon at the fast-approaching shark. The harpoon brushed its massive flank but didn't pierce its skin. Bennelong's father quickly pulled his son back down as the shark turned suddenly, hitting the side of the canoe with its tail. The flimsy canoe began to rock violently from the force. Panic-stricken, Bennelong looked to his father for reassurance.

'I'm sorry,' he pleaded.

'Just hang on.'

His father clung to the sides of the canoe, trying to stop it from rocking and taking on any water – a small amount of which would cause it to sink. Gradually, its rocking began to ease, as the eyes of all the fishermen scanned the surface for any sign of the beast returning. They sat motionless in their canoes, watching and watching.

Nothing. The shark was gone.

# Chapter 8

# Atlantic Coast of America, 1776

John Hunter now stood in his father's place as master of a ship. This, however, was no small trading ship sailing around the North Sea. This was the HMS *Eagle*, a sixty-four-gun ship of the line, the flagship of the British Navy, which was under the command of Vice Admiral Lord Howe, the commander-in-chief in the Atlantic. And this was not some trading mission – it was war! The American Revolutionary War was what the British called it. To the Americans, it was the American War of Independence.

Over the next four years, Hunter would show himself to be an immensely competent sailor who could hold his nerve under fire while enduring great physical pain. He would navigate the HMS *Eagle* up a river the Americans would only dare send a pilot boat along. And, when the *Eagle* reached the American position, it was able to fire the entire line of guns, causing major casualties that forced the enemy to abandon their position.

The young Scottish lad who had been shipwrecked on his first voyage as a nine-year-old had grown into one of the most respected sailors in the British Navy. Despite his love of the ocean and his experiences with his father, the navy was not actually his first choice of careers. His first choice was to be a professional musician, having developed a love of music and art as a teenager, when he studied under celebrated musician, composer and historian Dr Charles Burney. Having been discouraged from that option by his uncle, with whom he was living, Hunter had attended university and ultimately chosen a career in the navy over the other options that were presented to him – a career in the church or the army.

Although he retained his love of music and art, he enthusiastically embraced his career in the navy. He was steady, reliable, amiable and brave. More importantly, by the time he returned to England from America in October of 1779, he had the patronage and support of Lord Howe, one of the most influential people in the British Navy. It was that patronage that would see him rise to first lieutenant on the one-hundred-gun HMS *Victory*. It was a prestigious appointment to be second in command, under Lord Howe, of a ship that, at two thousand, one hundred and sixty-four tons, was one of the largest in the British Navy.

# CHAPTER 9

# ASSATEAGUE ISLAND, ATLANTIC COAST OF AMERICA, 8 JULY 1778

The HMS *Mermaid* was in dire trouble. She was outnumbered and outgunned, and now she was being outmanoeuvred by the American ships *Sagittaire* and *Fantasque*. She had just twenty-eight guns to their combined total of one hundred and fourteen. It was a hopeless situation.

Nineteen-year-old Marine Lieutenant Watkin Tench listened intently as the ship's captain and master animatedly discussed their options. There were only two. Either surrender and allow the Americans to capture the ship, as well as all the crew, or beach the ship on the adjacent island and just hope they could get away to continue the fight.

The captain grabbed the wheel and spun it dramatically, turning the ship towards the island's long beach. It only took a few moments for the Americans to realise what the *Mermaid* was doing and quickly follow. Tench watched nervously as the *Mermaid* was grabbed by the Atlantic swell and pushed towards the beach. He then looked back to see the Americans launching their longboats as their ships swerved away from the island.

Tench ordered his men to grab their packs and supplies. 'Whatever you do, men, keep your weapons dry or we'll be defenceless when we hit that beach.'

The captain steered the frigate bow-first into the beach, trying to minimise the amount of water the men would have to cross to reach it. Suddenly, the *Mermaid* shuddered as the hull hit the sand. Longboats, ropes and rope ladders were dropped over the side as the crew and marines desperately sought a safe and dry method of reaching the beach.

Just before he climbed onto a rope ladder, Tench had a quick look to determine the Americans' positions. He was horrified to see they already had several longboats in the water, rowing towards either end of the beach, and in a very short time would have the British forces surrounded. He looked down at his men as they battled for the land. Some staggered up the beach as they were knocked over in the waves, their muskets and powder soaked.

Tench cursed aloud. He knew it was futile. They would have no option but to surrender.

## CHAPTER 10

## INDIAN OCEAN, 16 NOVEMBER 1787

The delicate white clouds scattered across the sky peered down on eleven insignificant little vessels struggling across the vastness of the Indian Ocean. From above, their progress over the huge expanse of water appeared almost indiscernible, like ants trying to cross a desert. On board those tiny ships, though, it was a vastly different picture. With a good westerly breeze behind them, they were slicing their way through the choppy, white-capped waves. All on board felt they were moving at a very solid pace, which only made it even more depressing to awaken each morning to more and more endless sea without even a hint of land anywhere in sight. It was just ocean, ocean and more ocean.

Below deck on the HMS *Sirius*, Captain Arthur Phillip and Captain John Hunter sat in the captain's cabin. Phillip was the commander of the fleet and soon-to-be first governor of the penal colony in New South Wales, which was the largest and most ambitious undertaking in the history of colonisation. Hunter, the captain of the *Sirius*, had been appointed due to the patronage of Lord Howe.

The two men were trying to decide on the most efficient way to overcome the vastly different sailing speeds of the ships in the fleet. Phillip believed he had the solution. 'Captain, I think the best option may be for me to change ships and go aboard the *Supply*. I can have the faster transports accompany me, and you can remain with the slower vessels. Without the encumbrance of those slow transports, like *Lady Penrhyn*, I would estimate that I can get to Botany Bay a good fortnight to three weeks before you and the rest of the fleet. That way, we'll be able to identify the best location for the colony and we should have time to do some of the essential building works before you arrive with the remainder of the convicts.'

'Aye, sir, that should be quite achievable, particularly if you sail south into the higher latitudes to pick up the stronger winds.'

'I don't know that I shall bother with that. The winds are perfectly strong enough at our current latitude.'

'Very well, Captain. Whatever you think.' Hunter nodded. 'And who do you wish to take with you?'

'Well, of course, I shall need to take Major Ross, but I'll take Lieutenants Dawes and King as well.' Phillip paused before adding, 'And I'll take the three fastest store ships and sufficient numbers of skilled convicts and materials for the buildings.'

'Aye, that sounds perfectly logical, sir. So, if there is nothing else you require at this time, I shall go and start making arrangements to have the necessary men and equipment transferred between ships.'

'Thank you, Captain.'

*Ref. 7*

# Chapter 11

# Indian Ocean, 25 November 1787

Captain John Hunter stood on the deck of the *Sirius*, looking towards the horizon under a slowly darkening sky. Next to him were Lieutenant Bradley and the helmsman at the wheel of the fleet's flagship. Hunter raised his telescope and peered through it as his father had taught him so many years before. He was watching the tiny specks that were the *Supply* and the three store ships, *Friendship*, *Scarborough* and *Alexander*, as they gradually disappeared beyond the horizon and into the night.

Hunter lowered his telescope. 'Alright, Mr Bradley, they're gone. Let's take this fleet south.'

Lieutenant Bradley immediately passed the order to the helmsman, who spun the wheel dramatically to the right before Bradley looked across at Hunter and smiled. 'You've been waiting for that moment, haven't you, sir.'

'Aye, I certainly have, Mr Bradley.'

'And you didn't feel you could take us south until they were out of sight?' queried Bradley.

'Well, I didn't feel it would be appropriate, as I had no desire to be disrespectful to the commodore.'

'Mmmm.' Bradley nodded. 'And do you think we can beat them to Botany Bay, sir?'

'Well, without the *Lady Penrhyn* slowing us down, I'm given to believe we could, but even with her, I tend to think that we will surprise our commodore with how close behind him we are, even if we can't beat him there. That is, of course, given the usual winds above the fortieth parallel.'

'Captain, it sounds to me like the race is on.'

Again, Bradley smiled. There was nothing he enjoyed more than a good race, and as he greatly admired the skills of his captain, he was hoping to find someone on board who enjoyed a little wager.

'Where's Tench when you need him,' mumbled Bradley to himself.

'I beg your pardon, Lieutenant?' inquired Hunter.

'Sorry, sir. Nothing really. I was just thinking aloud. Captain Tench is still on board the *Charlotte*, isn't he, sir?'

'Aye, I'm given to believe that's correct, but why do you ask?'

'Oh, no reason, sir.' This time, Bradley's smile was inward only. He hesitated for a moment before adding, 'But next time the wind drops, I may take the longboat and pay him a visit, with your permission, sir… Just to check on how all is going aboard the *Charlotte*, of course.'

'Aye, of course,' replied Hunter, oblivious to Bradley's real intentions.

*Ref. 8*

## CHAPTER 12

## KAI'YMAY, GAMARAGAL LAND, JANUARY 1788

Arabanoo lay delicately balanced across his canoe about one hundred yards from the shore of the cove. On one side of the canoe, his feet dangled in the water, while on the other side, his face was submerged just below the surface. Beside his face were the tips of his multi-pronged fizgig. For well over a minute, he had been lying motionless, waiting for that school of fish to swim up close enough for him to strike. Just as he was about to pull his face out of the water to draw a quick breath, the fish turned and swam towards him.

*Gotcha*, he thought, as he launched the fizgig straight into the side of the closest fish. He quickly pulled the struggling fish out of the water on the end of his spear, sat up and ended its struggles before dropping it to the bottom of the canoe. He then immediately resumed his awkward position, facedown in the water.

\*\*\*

Arabanoo strolled back into his camp and lay the four fish he had caught on a large coolamon next to the community fire, ready for cooking. He then walked over to Weereweea, who smiled up at him and immediately handed him their new baby daughter. He sat down, crossed his legs and gently nursed the infant child. He stroked her curly dark hair with the soothing touch of a loving parent. Weereweea stopped grinding grass seeds on the grinding stone in front of her, briefly rested her head on her husband's shoulder and joined him in admiring the newest addition to their small family.

Although their marriage had been arranged by the Elders when they were children and they were from different clan groups, they had spent considerable time together as they grew up and knew each other well. Consequently, they had developed a very strong mutual affection. She admired his gentle, quiet, even-tempered ways and the fact he could always make her laugh. He admired her strength and, for one so young, her wisdom. Most of all, though, he admired her kindness.

Arabanoo kissed his wife's forehead. 'She is beautiful. She looks just like you.'

Weereweea looked up at him, smiled and responded, 'Well, thankfully she doesn't look like you, Boo.'

Arabanoo smiled at her and then motioned to their two-year-old son, who was playing nearby with his friends. 'But our handsome son does.'

'Yes, he certainly does,' was her smiling reply.

It was early evening, and the warm summer sun was drifting leisurely beyond the distant horizon as the smell of fish and shellfish on the fire wafted around the camp, which was home to thirty of Arabanoo's people. The camp consisted of ten rudimentary shelters, built of thick bark and branches on a relatively flat area that was on the side of a hill rising gently above the small cove whose waters provided so much of their diet. The shelters were placed just a short distance from a large cave, to which the Gamaragal people could retreat when it rained heavily. From all parts of the camp, filtered views of the cove below were visible through the canopy of scattered gums further down the hill. It was an idyllic location and Arabanoo's favourite of the various campsites they used as his people moved around their native soil during the different seasons.

# Chapter 13

# Botany Bay, New South Wales, 20 January 1788

Hunter had brought his fleet up the coast of New South Wales, and when he determined they were eight miles from the entrance to Botany Bay, he slowed them under an easy sail to avoid attempting to enter the unknown bay in darkness.

At first light on a cloudless morning, Hunter stood next to Lieutenant Bradley and the helmsman as they sailed past the sheer sandstone cliffs that marked the southern entrance to the bay, before sailing through its heads on a gentle south-easterly breeze. As they did so, Bradley asked the helmsman to step away from the wheel and motioned for Hunter to take it.

'Congratulations, Captain. After a journey of thirty-six weeks, we have made it. The wheel is yours, sir.'

Hunter smiled, nodded, and took the wheel. If ever there was a man who looked the part of a British naval captain, it was John Hunter. He was now fifty-one years old and looked every day of it, with his grey hair marching higher on his forehead and his skin deeply lined from constant exposure to salt and sun. He had inherited his father's strong jawline, which, combined with his broad shoulders, made him an imposing-looking character. It was a look that belied his amiable nature.

'Thank you, Mr Bradley, and thank you for your invaluable assistance throughout the voyage.'

'Sir, it is an honour to serve under you.' Bradley paused before inquiring, 'Do you think Captain Phillip will have beaten us here?'

'Aye, I would certainly expect so. I should think we would have seen them as we sailed up the coast otherwise.'

'What if we passed them in the Southern Ocean, Captain?'

'Hmmm, well, I suppose that is possible, but I would think it is highly unlikely, given the fact we had to wait for the *Lady Penrhyn* the entire time.'

Bradley nodded without saying anything. When the *Sirius* led the fleet into the Bay, Bradley's question was quickly answered, as he and Hunter saw the *Supply* and the three transports anchored not far inside the bay's entrance, near the northern shore.

'That was lucky,' mumbled Bradley under his breath.

'I beg your pardon?'

'Oh, nothing, sir.'

'Mr Bradley, you've been doing a lot of mumbling recently,' remarked Hunter.

'Sorry, sir.' Bradley paused before continuing. 'Well, actually, what I said was *That was lucky*.'

'And I assume you're going to explain why you would say that.'

'Yes, Captain. I wanted to have a wager with Captain Tench that we would beat Captain Phillip and the *Supply* to Botany Bay.'

'Really?'

'Yes, but he refused to accept. He said he had far too much respect for you and your navigational skills to be betting against you.'

'That is very kind of him, but I wonder how many days they have beaten us by.'

'In the wager I was trying to arrange with Captain Tench, I wanted three days start, sir. You know, just to be on the safe side, in case they beat us narrowly.'

As the two sailors were chatting, they noticed a group of the local Aboriginal men gathered on the southern shore, who began waving and gesticulating with their spears and pointing them towards the ships.

'Look, sir.' Bradley pointed to the group. 'They don't look too pleased to see us.'

'Aye, they certainly don't, Lieutenant.' Hunter frowned.

'What are they yelling, sir?' inquired Bradley, straining to hear the raised voices from the shore.

'It sounds like *Warra, warra, wai!*'

'What does that mean, sir?'

Hunter paused and looked directly at Bradley for a moment before replying, 'I have absolutely no idea, as I am totally unfamiliar with the language of the natives of New Holland, but I would suggest to you that it doesn't mean *Hello, welcome!*'

'I think you're probably right there, sir.' Bradley smiled.

'Cook and Banks were quite sure the natives wouldn't provide any problems for us, though, as they said the whole place is very sparsely populated.'

'I hope they're right, sir.'

\*\*\*

Shortly afterwards, Hunter and Bradley joined Phillip aboard the *Supply*.

'Welcome aboard, Captain.' Phillip smiled as Hunter climbed over the ship's rail and onto the deck.

'Thank you, sir,' replied Hunter.

'I must say, though, I am quite shocked to see you so soon. That's extraordinary seamanship, given how heavily some of those transports sail. How did you get here so quickly?'

'Well, Captain, we sailed a little further south to pick up the stronger winds.'

'Hmmm,' said Phillip. 'Which, of course, you recommended I should do with my fleet as well.'

Hunter nodded almost reluctantly. 'Aye, sir.'

'And I ignored you, didn't I, Captain?'

'You are the fleet commodore, sir, so that was entirely up to you. But may I ask when you arrived?'

'On the afternoon of the eighteenth, Captain. Less than two days ago.'

'Less than two days!' Hunter turned to Bradley, who had now joined them on the deck. 'Looks like your friend Captain Tench is a wise man, Mr Bradley.'

Bradley smiled as Hunter addressed Phillip. 'And sir, have you had the opportunity to form an opinion of the country around the bay yet?'

'From what I've seen so far, I am not in the least impressed. It looks quite unsuitable for our colony. The soil appears generally very sandy, and the southern shore appears to be mangrove swamps, but I am shortly going ashore to explore further and would like you to join me. Firstly, though, can I assume from your countenance and your manner that the remainder of the fleet have all made it safely?'

'Aye, they have indeed, sir, and therefore, may I congratulate you on that wonderful achievement? Eleven ships with fourteen hundred souls on a ten-thousand-mile voyage, the first time in the history of navigation, so I think you can be justly proud, particularly to have lost so few.' Hunter smiled as he firmly shook Phillip's hand.

'Thank you, Captain. So, there has been little loss of life amongst your fleet since we separated?

'Very little, sir. I believe only about twenty-five or thirty.'

'That would make the total for the entire voyage less than fifty, then.'

'Aye, sir, so that is an excellent outcome.'

'Thank you, Captain. That is pleasing. Obviously, your assistance has been essential. Unfortunately, though, the voyage may well have been the easy part. Establishing a colony and growing sufficient food to feed everyone is going to be the real challenge.'

'I agree, sir. Especially being in such a remote location.' Hunter glanced towards the entrance of the bay to see the *Charlotte* emerge from behind the southern headland. 'Here is the first of the remainder of the fleet, sir.'

Phillip turned to watch the three-masted, square-rigged *Charlotte* entering the bay, where on board, Captain Watkin Tench stood on the foredeck alongside Surgeon General John White, indulging in the moment and enjoying the warm morning air as the gentle breeze caressed their faces.

'So, this is Botany Bay about which we have heard so much, Captain,' observed White, stating the obvious.

'I believe it is indeed, Mr White.' Tench paused then added, *'Heavily in clouds came on the day, this great important day, which I hope the foundation, not the fall, of an empire will be dated from.'* He paused again. 'Excuse me for being a bore, but I couldn't help myself on such an historic occasion.'

White looked at him and smiled. 'Not at all, Captain, but which of the classics are you quoting this time?'

Tench smiled back. 'Why, Addison's *Cato, a Tragedy*, Mr White, about the Roman Empire but a literary inspiration for the American Revolution.'

'Ah, yes, of course. Liberty or death.' White smiled.

'Correct. You do know the classics, after all.' Tench smiled again. 'Let's just hope the British Empire finds this colony behaves itself a little better than the Americans.'

'Well, there are no clouds today, Captain, so hopefully that is a good sign.'

'Hopefully, Mr White, hopefully.'

At that moment, Tench looked beyond White's shoulder to see a large group of the local tribesmen running along the southern headland of the bay, yelling, 'Warra, warra, wai!'

\*\*\*

Later that same morning, Phillip and Hunter led a party of marines to explore the south-eastern shore of Botany Bay. Shortly after they landed the longboat, they observed a group of ten Aboriginal men standing back in the tree line on the edge of the beach. They made no sign of approaching or aggression, and so, Phillip had his party begin exploring for fresh water and fertile soil while the locals watched from a distance.

A few hours later, though, after their search discovered little fresh water, poor, sandy soil and more mangrove swamps on the southern shore of the bay, Phillip's party were walking back towards their boat when the local tribesmen approached.

'Warra, warra, wai,' several of them called as they began waving their spears in a menacing manner.

'They obviously want us to leave, Captain,' observed Hunter.

'Yes, that would seem apparent,' replied Phillip, 'but let's just see if we can communicate with them and show them we don't intend any harm.'

The entire British party held their breaths and tightened their grips on their weapons.

'Nobody move,' ordered Phillip as he stepped forward, holding his hands out to indicate he had nothing in them and was not threatening the natives.

The British watched on, motionless except for their jangling nerves, as an older tribesman with greying hair and beard stepped forward and said something totally unintelligible to them. Hunter had one of the sailors hand him a mirror and some beads, and stepping forward himself, he passed them to Phillip, who held them up towards the tribal Elder. The old man hesitated for a moment and then stepped further forward and accepted the trinkets from Phillip. He looked into the mirror and, apparently impressed, handed it to his colleagues. They took turns looking at the mirror and began laughing and holding it up to each other.

As the British began to breathe a little more easily, Hunter observed to Phillip, 'It works every time, sir.'

'It certainly does, Captain.' Phillip smiled back.

The tribal Elder turned back to Phillip and Hunter and again began talking to them. What he said was also unintelligible to the

British, until he grabbed his own naked groin and began pointing to their groin areas.

'I think he wants to know what sex we are, Captain. They are obviously confused by our clothes,' commented Phillip.

'Aye, and perhaps our shaven faces also, sir. They all have beards,' responded Hunter.

'Yes, well, we need to show them,' said Phillip, turning to the nearest sailor and adding, 'Lower your trousers and show them your manhood, sailor.'

The sailor hesitated momentarily, looking around at his amused colleagues.

'Better you than me,' one of them whispered before adding with a snigger, 'but I don't think they'll be impressed by your wee todger.'

The sailor reluctantly pulled down his pants and held up his shirt, displaying his rather insignificant genitals to the Elder and his people, who had now also moved closer. This caused them even greater amusement than the mirror. For a brief moment, the British and the land's custodians shared a joke while the sailor's face flushed. Shortly, though, a more earnest expression returned to the Elder's face, and waving his hand dismissively, he said, 'Warra warra,' before turning and walking back across the beach, with the men, to where the women and children watched from within the tree line.

*Ref. 9 & 10*

## Chapter 14

## Port Jackson, 21 January 1788

Having decided that Botany Bay was a most unsuitable location for a colony, Arthur Phillip determined to explore other options and now sat with John Hunter in the first of three longboats that sailed northward along the coast. It was a coastline of rugged cliffs standing as menacing, silent sentries guarding the handful of warm, welcoming beaches sprinkled in between.

Beneath an azure sky, the three small British boats sailed across the placid sea until they reached a point where the massive cliffs parted and invited travellers to enter. Some eighteen years prior, Captain James Cook had declined the invitation, believing it to be just a large open bay that would not provide safe harbour for ships. Like so many other landmarks along the coast, however, he had named it. Port Jackson, he had called it, in honour of Admiralty Secretary Sir George Jackson, but for many thousands of years before that, it had been known as Birrabirragal to the First Nations clans of the Eora Nation who inhabited its shores. Its various coves and inlets had been known by a variety of names, including Warrane, Walla-mulla, Gomora and Kai'ymay.

John Hunter sat in silence alongside Phillip as the longboats cruised between the heads on the small swell driven by the morning's gentle nor-easterly breeze. From a distance, Hunter had been inclined to agree with Cook's view that it was just a large open bay. That view began to rapidly change, though, as soon as they passed inside the heads. Hunter looked to the north to see two large but separate expanses of protected water with small coves scattered amongst them. He felt a tinge of excitement rising in his chest at the sight of them. As they sailed deeper into the waterway and cleared the southern headland, he looked to the south to see a massive expanse of sheltered water stretching before them.

Phillip was still absorbing the view to the north, so, without saying a word, Hunter tapped him on the shoulder and pointed. Phillip immediately turned and Hunter was almost sure he heard the governor utter an audible gasp but dismissed it as just the splash of the swell on the bow of the boat. Veteran British naval men like him and Phillip didn't gasp at such things. They didn't gasp at anything, in fact.

Phillip looked at Hunter as a smile creased his weathered face – a face that hadn't seen a smile since they had arrived in Botany Bay. Phillip ordered the crew to sail to the south. They were now in quite sheltered water, protected almost completely from the ocean swell by the southern headland, with little breeze to fill the small sail. Some of the men therefore picked up their oars and began to row to hasten the journey. As they navigated south, though, they could not see the extent of the waterway to the west, due to a very large headland that projected from the northern shore and completely blocked their view.

Several minutes later, they cleared the headland, and as Hunter and Phillip looked to the west, this time Hunter was sure he heard an audible gasp from the governor. There in front of them was a vast expanse of completely sheltered blue water stretching away to the west, bejewelled on both shores by a variety of sparkling coves, bays and beaches. To complete the sublime setting, a number of timber-covered islands adorned the centre of the waterway.

'Look,' Phillip announced to all in the boat, trying to suppress the excitement in his voice.

The sailors, who had been focussed either on rowing or trimming the longboat's sail, now sat up and looked in wonder at the mass and variety of waterways that surrounded them.

Hunter turned to Phillip and extended his hand. 'Congratulations,

Captain. It would appear you have discovered one of the world's finest harbours.'

'It certainly looks like it. Thank you,' Phillip enthused before quickly resuming his more usual measured tone and adding, 'Yes, it certainly is magnificent, but unfortunately, as you well know, we need a lot more than a good harbour to ensure the viability of this colony. We need fresh water and fertile soil and substantial quantities of both.'

'Well, sir, let's hope we can find both here somewhere.'

'And let's hope that somewhere amongst all these coves, there is a deep one that will enable us to get the ships in close to the shore.'

'Aye, sir, but there certainly be plenty to choose from,' Hunter replied.

Phillip nodded before announcing, as the excitement returned to his voice, 'Alright, men, let's explore the shores of this harbour and see what we can find. Let us start at the start and go back to that cove inside the northern headland. Then we can decide from there where else to explore.'

*Ref. 11*

# Chapter 15

# Birrabirragal, Gamaragal Land, 21 January 1788

On that same summer morning, Colbee, Bennelong, Arabanoo and a group of twenty Gamaragal, Wangal and Gadigal men and traditional lore holders, Elders, stood atop the northern head inside the harbour entry. They were gazing intently down on the three strange canoes that had just entered the glistening waters of their beautiful harbour. They had assembled to discuss the fact they had heard that eleven huge canoes with white sails had entered Kamay a few days before. Their clan groups knew very well that a single such huge canoe had been seen in Kamay many years before, when Colbee, Bennelong and Arabanoo were just young boys. That canoe had contained white 'ghost' people. Fortunately, it only stayed a few days and then left and never returned.

Colbee's expression reflected the deep concern he felt as he strained the perfect vision of his brown eyes to discern every detail he could of these strange canoes and their occupants. Colbee was a highly respected warrior and was expected to soon become a traditional lore holder himself.

'Who do you think they are?' asked Arabanoo hesitantly.

Colbee thought deeply before replying, 'They must be from the same place as that giant canoe in Kamay all those years ago, but I have no idea where that may be.'

'What do you think we should do?' Arabanoo asked.

Again, Colbee thought carefully before replying, 'Well, let's just watch them for a while and see what they do. They may just stay a few days and go away, like the other one did.'

'They look like giant pelicans drifting across the water, ready to gobble up everything in front of them,' observed Bennelong. 'They must be more of those white ghost people, so we should call all the mobs together and just drive them away.'

Colbee didn't look at Bennelong as he answered but instead just kept his eyes fixed firmly on the strange canoes. 'We can do that later if we need to, but I think we should just keep watching them for now and see what we can learn about them and what they want. And we should remember that if they come from the same place as those who visited Kamay, they may have the same weapons.'

The others nodded, fully aware of the stories of the weapon that made a loud bang and put a hole straight through one of their shields.

The whole group stood in silence for some time, watching as the Berewalgal sailed further and further into the harbour. Bennelong's jaw clenched as he tightened his grip on his spear.

Eventually, after navigating their way deep into the harbour, the strange canoes finally turned and headed back towards Kai'ymay.

'Look!' called Arabanoo. 'They're turning. They are heading back this way.'

The group watched closely for many minutes before Colbee said, 'Alright, I believe we should go down and meet them if they land on the beach. We should talk to them and find out what they want and how long they want to stay. We can then decide if we wish to invite them onto our land, the same as we would do with any other visitors, but we show no fear.'

'But these people are not like any other visitors,' replied Bennelong. 'They are different. They are white, just like the ones that visited Kamay. They're ghosts.'

'Yes, they may be white and different, but I don't think they are ghosts, and they may not have any evil intentions towards us and our peoples,' Colbee replied.

Arabanoo thought for a moment before adding, 'I agree with Colbee. Let's go down and find out what they want.'

'Alright, we'll meet them, but we show them no fear,' Bennelong conceded.

The group turned to the holders of knowledge, who nodded their approval, and immediately, the young men set off to run down the hill towards Kai'ymay. By the time they reached the beach, the three strange craft were approaching the shore.

'Let's leave our spears and weapons here and show them we mean them no harm,' Colbee urged. 'We'll go out to greet them and yarn to them. We show them no fear.'

With that, the tribal group left their weapons at the edge of the beach and walked across the warm white sand of the cove and into the water as the strange people rowed into the shallows.

'Hallo,' Colbee called, raising his arm. 'Welcome.'

Arabanoo and the others did the same as they waded up to the boats, in which the occupants stopped rowing and allowed the boats to cruise in amongst them. The visitors' leader was wearing a strange blue costume and headdress, even stranger than the rest of them, but he spoke quietly and held his hands out flat, showing he was unarmed. He said something unintelligible to the locals as they took hold of the sides of the big canoe in the shallow water. He then turned and took some things from one of the people in the canoe and offered them to Colbee and Bennelong, who stood at the front of their group of locals. Colbee and Bennelong took one each.

'What are they?' Arabanoo asked.

Colbee looked at it closely and replied, 'It's the same as when you look into a pool of still water. I can see myself. Look!'

Colbee held it up in front of Arabanoo's face, and Arabanoo immediately burst out laughing, as did his colleagues when he showed them.

The leader of the people in the boat said something, but the locals ignored him for two reasons; firstly, they were all too interested in these strange things that looked like water but were hard, and secondly, they had no idea what he was saying.

'Will we pull their canoes into the beach and let them get out on our land?' Arabanoo asked.

'I think so,' Colbee replied as he turned to the others, who nodded their agreement. Several of the locals then took hold of the sides of the other two big canoes as well and dragged them onto the cove's sandy beach, where the Elders had just arrived.

The leader of the visitors jumped out of the canoe, onto the sand, and immediately nodded to Colbee, Bennelong, and Arabanoo. He put his hand in a hole in the side of his costume and pulled out some shiny beads. He held them up and handed them to Colbee, who nodded.

'Thank you.'

Colbee inspected them briefly before handing them to Bennelong, who was standing beside him. Bennelong immediately put them around his neck and turned to the others with a broad smile.

'How good do I look in these?' He laughed.

'They'll look better on Barangaroo.' Arabanoo smiled back.

The leader of the strangers spoke to a man with a strong jaw and grey hair who was standing beside him, and he handed the leader some more beads, which were distributed amongst the traditional lore holders of the clan. Although they were moderately amused by them, they were more focussed on the crucial question that Colbee now asked.

'What do you want?' he asked the leader of the strangers, who made no reply. 'What are you doing here on our land?'

Still no reply.

'How long do you wish to stay?' he persisted.

The leader of the visitors made a brief reply that they couldn't understand, but he started pointing to the beach they stood upon before waving his right arm in a circular motion and pointing to Colbee and the Elders.

Colbee turned to the others and asked, 'What do you think he is trying to say?'

Arabanoo spoke up. 'Do you think he is asking if we belong to this land?'

'Hmmm.' Colbee nodded. 'That might be it.'

'Tell him to go away,' interjected Bennelong.

Colbee ignored Bennelong and nodded to the leader of the visitors. 'Yes, we belong to this land,' he said as he motioned to the surrounding area and then pointed to himself and the traditional lore holders.

Some of the other strangers started getting things off the big canoes while the leader continued trying to talk to them.

'What are they doing?' asked Bennelong.

Colbee got the attention of the leader and pointed to the strangers who were getting the strange things off the big canoe. The leader of the visitors motioned between his hand and his mouth.

'They want some food,' said Bennelong. 'We're not giving them any tucker. Tell them to go away!'

'Calm down, Bennelong,' Colbee replied. 'They're getting their own tucker out of their canoes.'

The leader of the strange visitors pointed towards the other end of the beach, then to himself and the others with him, and repeated the eating movement.

'Aah,' said Colbee, 'they want to eat some of their tucker on the beach. Is that alright with everyone?'

The traditional lore holders murmured their agreement before Bennelong added, 'How ugly are they with that horrible white skin? No wonder they cover it up with those costumes.' He paused before adding, 'I don't trust them. Send them away.'

'I agree they are very ugly, but we can't send them away because of that,' Colbee replied before turning to the leader of the visitors and nodding. 'Yes, you can stay on the beach while you have some tucker.'

The leader of the visitors nodded before saying something else in their tongue and leading them a short distance up the beach, where they sat down and began preparing some tucker, as the local traditional mobs watched on from a short distance away.

## CHAPTER 16

## PORT JACKSON, 21 JANUARY 1788

It was late afternoon by the time Phillip and Hunter were back in the longboat as it was rowed away from the beach of the cove.

'Captain,' Phillip said, 'I think we should head across to the southern shore to one of those sheltered little coves we saw earlier and camp for the night. We can explore further tomorrow.'

'Aye, certainly, sir. It will be most interesting to have a look further down the harbour and see what else we can discover,' Hunter replied. 'By the way, what did you think of that group of natives?'

'I must say I found them extremely impressive, really. They are very strongly made and showed no fear of us whatsoever,' Phillip observed.

'Aye, I agree they are strong and athletic and appear very different to the way Cook described them.'

'They were very manly in their look and their behaviour, so I think that would be an appropriate name for this cove – Manly Cove. What do you think?'

Hunter smiled and nodded. 'Sounds like a very suitable name, sir.' He paused for a moment before adding, 'One thing that has surprised me is just how plentiful the natives are. They appear on almost every shoreline as we pass.'

'Yes indeed. I agree. They are far more plentiful than I expected.'

With that, the two men fell into silence as they sat back to take in more of their newly discovered harbour. The nor-easterly breeze had picked up considerably since the morning and began to rapidly fill the sails of the longboat as they left the shelter of Manly Cove. The sailors swung their oars out of the water and joined their commanders in sitting back to enjoy being the first to sail Port Jackson.

*Ref. 12*

# Chapter 17

# Botany Bay, 22 January 1788

Watkin Tench was delighted that finally, he was going to get his chance to set foot on the shores of the famous Botany Bay. Up until this point, his duties had confined him to the *Charlotte* while he watched others set off in longboats to explore the various parts of the bay. Now, as he was rowed onto a sandy beach on the south-eastern shore, he could feel excitement rising in his chest. He focussed on keeping a relaxed exterior, though, as sitting next to him in the boat was young Edward Dwan, the seven-year-old son of Sergeant Dwan, who sat opposite him. Young Edward had become quite attached to Tench on the voyage out, and Tench found him to be a polite, amiable child with an endless list of questions that always amused the educated captain.

Shortly after they pulled their longboat onto the sand, the party of marines and sailors were walking along the beach towards the south when they observed a group of a dozen Aboriginal men striding towards them. They were all armed with spears and clubs, and young Edward immediately attached himself to Tench's hand.

'You'll be fine, Edward. They won't hurt us,' reassured Tench as he gave the boy's hand a gentle squeeze. Although his voice was perfectly calm and assured, Tench couldn't help but feel a degree of tension replace the excitement of the landing. 'Now, men, just keep your weapons lowered by your side and don't do anything that may cause them any offence.'

The two groups approached each other slowly and cautiously, with both the locals and the visitors keeping their weapons by their sides and making no attempt to do anything even slightly threatening.

'Hello,' said Tench with a half-smile as he raised his bent arm beside his face and stopped about seven yards from the local group.

The locals responded with something unintelligible before pointing at young Edward, who still held Tench's hand.

Tench looked down at the boy. 'Do you want to meet them, Edward?'

Edward nodded before adding, 'Yes, Captain.'

'Is that alright with you, Sergeant?'

'Certainly, Captain. Edward's not scared, are you, Edward?' assured Sergeant Dwan as he stepped forward, behind his son.

'No, Father,' responded Edward with just the slightest hint of hesitation creeping into his voice.

Tench and young Edward stepped forward, and as they did, an old man with a long grey beard and a pointed bone through the septum of his nose moved forward, away from his group. He smiled down at Edward, revealing a missing front tooth. He placed his hand gently on the boy's felt hat. He bent down, bringing his face close to Edward's, and spoke quietly in his unintelligible language before taking the sleeve of the boy's shirt and rubbing it between his fingers. He turned to his mob and said something that caused them some amusement, before he turned to Tench and motioned to touch the sleeve of his bright red coat. Tench held up his arm for the old man to feel, which he did, before he again turned to his people and said something that seemed to cause them even more hilarity.

'I think they find our heavyweight uniforms singularly unsuitable and rather amusing in this climate in the middle of summer,' Tench murmured to Dwan.

'I'd have to agree with him there, sir, but I think their nakedness is a little much,' Dwan replied.

Tench smiled at Dwan without replying before turning his attention back to the old man and young Edward. He realised the natives who had been standing some distance behind the old man had now moved closer. At that moment, he began to feel beads of sweat forming on his brow, but he was unsure if it was due to his sudden awareness of just how hot his marine uniform was or due to the proximity of the armed natives.

He looked again at the old man, who now motioned to Tench to open his coat, but given the complexity of such a task, Tench bent down to Edward and undid a couple of buttons on his shirt before pulling it apart to reveal the whiteness of the boy's skin. This caused even more amusement to the locals, who began talking animatedly amongst themselves. The old man gently touched the boy's skin and looked at Tench with something akin to wonder.

Tench felt Edward grip his hand more tightly and looked down at the boy.

'Do you want to go back to your father?'

Edward nodded and quickly retreated the step back to his father. The old man smiled at Edward and made a waving motion to him, which caused Edward to reciprocate with both a smile and a wave. The old man then turned and led his people away across the beach.

Sergeant Dwan stepped up beside Tench's left shoulder. 'No wonder Edward became a little fearful, Captain. He's an extremely ugly old man.'

*Ref. 13*

# Chapter 18

# Botany Bay, 24 January 1788

Watkin Tench had risen at dawn after a sleepless night. Today was the day they were to leave Botany Bay and sail the short distance up to Port Jackson, which both Phillip and Hunter had described as the finest harbour they had seen anywhere in the world. They had also found a small cove with a good stream of fresh water, which would provide them with an excellent location to establish their new colony.

Tench was just finishing dressing in his small cabin belowdecks when there was a knock at the door and Sergeant Dwan burst through in a most agitated manner. 'A ship, sir!' he blurted.

Although Tench had heard Dwan perfectly clearly, he was unable to grasp the meaning of his statement, so he immediately replied, 'What, Sergeant?'

'A ship, sir!' Dwan repeated.

'You're joking, surely!' came Tench's stunned reply.

'No, sir. There's a ship outside the entrance to the bay.'

'Whose is it?'

'We don't know, sir. It's too far off to tell.'

Tench grabbed his coat and rushed past Dwan. As he climbed the ladder to the deck, a thousand thoughts rushed through his mind as to the identity of the ship and its reason for being in such a remote part of the world. Tench arrived on deck to discover it crowded and the crew in a general state of excitement and alarm as everyone gazed towards the open ocean and the rising sun, which was trying to push its way through the cloudy horizon.

'There's a second sail,' the lookout called.

'What?' was the almost universal response.

Tench climbed onto the rail of the ship and, balancing himself with a rope, could just make out two ships in the distance outside the bay with the aid of his telescope. Dwan joined him.

'Who do you think it could be, sir?' Dwan asked.

'I have no idea, Sergeant. I certainly hope it isn't the Portuguese, because the only reason they would be here is to claim the region for themselves, and I really don't feel like a fight today.'

Dwan laughed. 'Well, we have them greatly outnumbered if it is, sir. Do you think they could be store ships for us from England?'

'No, I certainly wouldn't think so, as there were no plans to send any supplies out at all at this stage,' Tench replied. 'I just hope it's not the darn French. I had enough of them during the American War.'

'But we're not at war with them currently, Captain, so they shouldn't be a problem.'

'How does one ever know, Sergeant? One year they're our enemy, the next year they're our ally. I don't know about you, but I can't keep up with it all. And how would we know what is happening at home now, anyway? We left England nearly eight months ago. Who is to say we aren't at war with the French yet again?'

'Hmmm, I see your point, sir,' replied a rather confused Dwan.

The two men shared the telescope. They kept looking out at the two ships in the distance for some considerable time, listening to the mutterings of conjecture on the deck, before they heard a voice behind them yell, 'It's the French!'

Tench and Dwan both turned quickly. 'What?'

'Captain Phillip says it's the French.' It was the voice of the ship's master, Thomas Gilbert, who had just been taken in the longboat across to Phillip's ship.

He continued as he climbed out of the longboat, up the rope ladder and onto the deck. 'He says it will be the two French ships under the command of Monsieur La Perouse that are on a voyage of discovery in the southern hemisphere.'

'Well, the commodore should know what is going on with the French,' replied Tench.

'Why do you say that, Captain?' Dwan asked.

Tench was well aware that Phillip had recently been an English spy based in France but was not about to share that information with Dwan.

'Please just trust me, Sergeant. He'd know.'

'Very well, sir.'

There was a brief pause before Gilbert added, 'So in the circumstances, Captain, Captain Phillip has decided to delay our departure for Port Jackson until he can confirm that's who they are and make contact with them.'

'Certainly sounds reasonable to me.' Tench smiled.

*Ref. 14*

# Chapter 19

# Botany Bay, 26 January 1788

John Hunter stood in light summer rain on the deck of the *Sirius* with Lieutenant Bradley, watching as the two French ships, the *Bousolle* and *Astrolabe*, sailed into Botany Bay. Hazardous winds and rain had prevented them entering the previous day. Now, however, with a change to a nor-easterly wind and the assistance of a British naval officer, ordered by Phillip and arranged by Major Ross, they were able to safely enter the bay despite the continuing wind and rain. Phillip had left the previous day on board the *Supply* to sail to Port Jackson. The rest of the fleet was to follow under Hunter's guidance as soon as the winds became more favourable.

'Well, that was rather considerate of Captain Phillip, wasn't it, sir?' ventured Bradley.

'You mean having the French guided into the bay?' replied Hunter.

'Yes, don't you think, sir?'

'Aye, indeed it was, Mr Bradley.' A broad smile creased Hunter's weather-beaten face.

Bradley looked quizzically at his captain. 'You don't seem to think so, sir.'

'No, I agree with you. It was very considerate of Phillip, but…' Hunter paused before adding, 'I am also very well aware that Phillip is only too pleased to show the French Botany Bay. The last thing he wants is for them to see Port Jackson.'

Hunter could almost hear the penny drop in Bradley's head. 'Ooh!' Hunter had to stop himself from laughing. 'Aye, Lieutenant, ooh!

In fact, in my discussion with Phillip yesterday, he expressed to me how concerned he was that, with the winds yesterday preventing us all from leaving Botany Bay and the French from entering, they may sail further north and discover Port Jackson for themselves. Then we'd be in a nice mess, wouldn't we?'

'Of course.'

'And that was why he was so determined to sail up there yesterday, despite the winds still being unfavourable.'

Bradley had now caught up with Phillip's thinking. 'Ahh, yes, so our commodore couldn't get the French into this bay fast enough.'

'Aye, exactly.' Hunter smiled.

Phillip had nevertheless had the British flag raised at Point Sutherland, just to make it clear to the French that the British had claimed the region.

'That's why he had Major Ross organise that they be piloted in here, but note he has had our flag erected, just so the French don't get any clever ideas. Anyway, now that the French are safely in, we should follow the commodore up to Port Jackson, despite those winds, which will still make it a wee challenge trying to get this entire fleet safely out of this bay. Let's weigh anchor, Mr Bradley, and get on our way.'

Bradley turned to the crew and yelled, 'Weigh anchor, men, we're on our way to Port Jackson!'

It was an order that was greeted by an enthusiastic cheer from the ocean-weary sailors and marines.

*Ref. 15*

## Chapter 20

## Birrabirragal, Gamaragal Land, 26 January 1788

Colbee, Bennelong, Arabanoo and the traditional tribal lore holders again stood on the northern headland opposite the entrance to the harbour. They stood in total silence, trying to come to terms with the eerie sight emerging through the misty rain, which was slowly clearing. The eleven huge canoes with white cloth hanging from straight tree trunks that they had heard were at Kamay were now coming into their harbour, Birrabirragal. One had arrived the previous day, and now, ten others were following. Some of them were even bigger than the first.

Even Bennelong was struck dumb, and Arabanoo felt a shiver run down his spine. He wasn't sure what caused it, though. Was it fear about what this meant for his family and his people, or was it sheer awe at the size and number of these huge canoes and the ghostly appearance of their white sails in the misty rain? He had never seen anything like it in his life. No wonder the Elders called them Berewalgal, 'people from the clouds'.

The group continued to watch in wonder before Bennelong finally muttered, 'I knew we should have told them to go away.'

The others ignored him and just kept staring at the ships.

'What should we do?' asked Arabanoo to no-one in particular.

'I have no idea at all,' murmured Colbee in reply. 'No idea at all. The Elders will decide.'

'We should get all the mobs together and drive them away as soon as they try to land,' Bennelong urged.

The Elders had now moved away from the younger men and were in intense discussion amongst themselves. The young warriors continued watching the Berewalgal while they awaited the Elders' decision. They watched as the giant canoes continued well beyond where they would turn to head into the beach at Kai'ymay that they had visited before. They watched as the strange canoes continued further down the harbour.

Colbee turned to the Elders and asked, 'Can we follow them and see where they go?'

As soon as they gave their consent, Colbee, Arabanoo, Bennelong and the young warriors started running down towards the cove, where their canoes lay on the beach.

\*\*\*

Having paddled across the harbour, Colbee, Arabanoo and Bennelong now watched the visitors from the point of the cove known to them as Warrane, in which all eleven of the giant canoes were now anchored. It was late afternoon, and the visitors had all begun gathering around an area at the head of the cove. Many of them wore bright red costumes, others dark blue, and others in a variety of costumes that looked incredibly old and battered. The ones in the old costumes had been doing all the work while those in the red and blue costumes stood around telling them what to do.

'What are they doing now?' asked Arabanoo.

'I don't know,' replied Colbee, 'but they are putting that piece of red, blue and white cloth up on that piece of wood.'

The local mob watched intently, trying to understand what the visitors were doing as they all stood around looking at the colourful piece of cloth. They then heard the sound of drums emanating from amidst the visitors before their leader appeared to speak to them.

'Hooray! Hooray! Hooray!' the visitors yelled in unison.

Arabanoo looked at Colbee, who shrugged. 'It must be some sort of corroboree.'

The next moment, the local mob watched in shock as a loud bang echoed around the previously peaceful little cove.

'What was that?' asked Bennelong.

'It's their firesticks. Look at the smoke,' replied an awestruck Colbee as smoke from the sticks drifted into the air.

A moment later, huge firesticks on the side of one of the giant canoes began firing blast after blast, causing the local mobs to quickly hide behind trees and bushes, seeking safety. Arabanoo covered his ears as he crouched, trembling, behind a tree. Although quite terrified by the sound, Arabanoo's dominant emotion was one of total confusion. Who were these people? What were they doing on his people's land? What did they want?

Finally, the earth-shaking blasts of the giant firesticks fell silent, and the strangers on the shore began cheering as the traditional owners regained their feet and looked at each other.

'What strange people,' said Colbee.

'That's why we must get all the mobs together and drive them away,' responded Bennelong.

'But they have very powerful weapons,' ventured Arabanoo.

'Let's talk to the Elders and see what they say we should do,' suggested Colbee. 'I think we should go and talk to these visitors and see what they want and how long they wish to visit our land.'

# Chapter 21

# Sydney Cove, 27 January 1788

Watkin Tench and William Dawes stood on the deck of the *Charlotte*, watching the hive of activity in the little cove, which had started as the first rays of the summer sun had begun creeping above the eastern horizon. One of the store ships had manoeuvred to the western side of the cove, where the almost vertical, flat-topped rocks rising out of a good depth of water allowed the ships to get close to shore, easing the task of unloading the stores.

A group of marines and convicts had already been disembarked to commence the task of preparing the area for the first boot print of the British Empire. In one area, a party was cutting down trees and clearing the undergrowth; another was setting up a blacksmith's forge, while elsewhere, a marine officer was pitching marquees with the assistance of convicts.

The noise of the numerous steel axe heads crashing into timber was heard for the first time in the ancient land and sounded like clanging cymbals amongst an orchestra of cicadas and bird life.

'What an amazing combination of sounds,' observed Dawes.

'Hmmm.' Tench nodded but was too absorbed in taking in the whole scene to say more.

The little cove was quite lightly wooded on its eastern shore, which ran up a hill, where the trees became larger and thicker. The western shore was much rockier where the ships were unloading, while between the two shores at the head of the cove, a pleasant little stream bubbled its way through a thicket of small trees and bushes and out into the cove beside a tiny beach.

'It certainly is a little piece of paradise, Watkin.'

As Dawes spoke, a large tree crashed to the ground, sending a dozen white cockatoos screeching into the air.

'What a ghastly noise they make,' commented Tench.

'They do, but they're an impressive looking bird.'

Both men fell into silence watching the activities on the shore. Another tree came crashing down, this time sending a small group of grey kangaroos bounding across a clearing and into the thick bushland near the top of the hill on the eastern side of the cove.

'Look, kangaroos.' Dawes pointed excitedly.

Tench finally shared his friend's excitement. 'Now they are amazingly strange-looking creatures.' He paused before adding, 'I wonder what they taste like? I could certainly do with some fresh meat.'

'I think we all could,' agreed Dawes. 'No doubt the governor will organise a hunting party as soon as possible, but really, Watkin, you are hard to please. It's only a few days ago you were longing for some fresh fish. Now you've had plenty of them at Botany Bay, you want fresh meat.'

'Yes, but can't a man have a little fresh meat as well? Can you blame me for being tired of salted pork dominating our diet?'

'No, not at all.' Dawes smiled in reply.

The two friends continued watching the activities onshore, waiting their turn to disembark with a variety of emotions competing in both their hearts.

'This really is going to be the most amazing experience,' observed Tench as a hint of excitement crept into his voice.

'You mean building this new colony or exploring this country?' Dawes replied.

'Well, both, but here we are with the opportunity of a lifetime to explore a new country and see things that no white man has ever seen before – only the local Indians know what is here.'

At that moment, Tench touched Dawes on the arm and pointed to a group of locals on the eastern point of the cove.

Dawes nodded. 'Mmmm. Did you notice just how many of them were on the shores all the way down the harbour?'

'Yes, and all just watching us,' Tench responded. 'Given their numbers, I wonder how much of a problem they'll be to our colony.'

Dawes thought for a moment before replying, 'Hmmm… or we to them.'

*Ref. 16*

## Chapter 22

## Sydney Harbour, 29 January 1788

Captain John Hunter sat in the stern of the six-oared longboat with Lieutenant Bradley beside him as they were rowed down harbour, accompanied by a smaller boat. Phillip had dispatched them in the early morning to spend a couple of days undertaking a survey of the harbour and exploring its extent.

After putting into shore at various points, they were met on each occasion by small parties of locals. On each occasion, the meetings were fairly brief and amicable. A couple also resulted in the groups imitating each other's actions, which caused much mirth for both. On one occasion, the locals performed a song, accompanied by small clapping sticks and dancing. When they invited Hunter and his men to join in the dancing, Hunter urged a couple of the sailors to do so. The fact the sailors looked rather silly caused great amusement to both the visitors and locals. Hunter couldn't help feeling that it provided a hint of a bonding experience for the two groups.

Shortly after, as they rowed further down harbour, Hunter commented to Bradley, 'Well, Mr Bradley, I must observe just how contrary the natives are to the view I had formed based on the observations of the Endeavour's crew.'

'Yes, Captain. I agree.'

'Aye, they are a most lively and inquisitive people, and they are well formed and athletic, but also, they are in far greater numbers than we were led to believe.'

'Yes, indeed, sir,' Bradley replied.

The pair sat quietly for a few moments before Hunter added, 'Although they seem very friendly, given their numbers and given the experiences of Monsieur La Perouse, we need to be on our guard at all times.'

'I'm sorry, sir, I am unaware of Monsieur La Perouse's experiences with them.'

'Ahh, I thought you may have heard. Captain de Langle of the *Astrolabe*, the second ship in his expedition, and twelve of his crew were brutally murdered by natives in the Pacific Islands.'

'Oh, really, sir? I hadn't heard. That is very worrying.'

'Aye. Obviously, they were a different people to these here, but we must be very careful with any of these natives.'

'Yes, sir. Most definitely,' replied Bradley as concern crept across his face.

\*\*\*

Early the next morning, the visitors continued their survey further up the harbour. It was the beginning of a warm summer day, and droplets of the rising sun trickled off the edge of the oars at each stroke. Hunter and Bradley again sat together in the back of the boat as Hunter directed the crew to pull into a prominent point on the southern shore. They were only a short distance from the shore when a large group of locals suddenly emerged from the trees.

Bradley looked nervously at Hunter. 'This is a much bigger group than we have encountered before, sir. What should we do?'

Hunter was thinking about his reply when the locals began shouting, 'Warra, warra,' and brandishing their spears.

'Well, we certainly won't be landing here, Lieutenant. Not only do they have us greatly outnumbered but we're out-armed as well,' said Hunter, aware that his group only had three muskets between them. 'We'll look to land further down the harbour.'

With that, Bradley ordered the crew to row away from the shore, out of the range of the natives' spears, and further down harbour. A short time later, as they neared another point, Hunter ordered that they row in towards the land. He and Bradley scanned the thick bush beyond the point for any sign of the natives. Having determined there were none, Hunter ordered them to land the boat. No sooner had the order been given than Hunter felt Bradley grip his arm.

'Look, sir.' Bradley pointed to the tree line, where again, a large mob of heavily armed locals suddenly appeared and began hurrying down the point towards the boats.

Hunter felt tension surge in the pit of his stomach. Bradley grabbed the musket that lay across his lap. As he did so, Hunter reached across and gripped its barrel with his strong hands.

'No, Mr Bradley.' Hunter shook his head and immediately ordered the crew to row away.

As the crew tried to turn the boat, the tribesmen reached the edge of the point within twenty yards of the boat, brandishing their spears and yelling, 'Warra warra!'

'We're not safe here, sir! A musket shot should scare them off,' Bradley urged.

'No, Lieutenant. Row, men, row,' ordered Hunter before turning to Bradley. 'If we fire at them and it doesn't scare them off, we'd be in a wee bit of trouble, wouldn't we? They would almost certainly launch their spears at us, and they have countless. We would be absolutely defenceless in this boat.'

Having seen the demonstration of the locals' spear-throwing the previous day, Hunter had been struck by just how quickly they could slot spears into their throwers and launch them. He had noted they were able to do so many times faster than the British could fire and reload their Brown Bess muskets. He was therefore determined to avoid any sort of confrontation with them.

As their boat now turned and rowed away, Hunter and Bradley had their backs to the tribesmen on the beach. Hunter knew how vulnerable they were and tensed his back, almost expecting a spear to pierce it at any moment. He looked over his shoulder to see the large mob on the point continuing to wave aggressively at them. He scanned the mob's weapons and quickly noted none of them had their spears mounted in throwers.

Hunter breathed a sigh of relief as he murmured to Bradley, 'It's alright, we're safe.'

*Ref. 17*

## CHAPTER 23

## PORT JACKSON, 31 JANUARY 1788

The next day was heavily overcast and particularly humid when Hunter and Bradley returned to the same part of the harbour to continue their survey. Despite the fact they had extra protection in the form of additional marines and weapons, Hunter's eyes darted from shore to shore and point to point, being careful to check as far into the tree line as light would allow. He couldn't help but be a little nervous at the prospect of a clash with the natives. He was very familiar with Phillip's orders from the Colonial Office, and Phillip had stressed those orders to him the previous day, when Hunter had advised the governor of his fears of attack on his first excursion down harbour. Hunter knew that such orders were standard from the Colonial Office when Britain established a colony, but if truth be told, they really hadn't worked effectively anywhere else in the world. Hunter could see no reason why they would be achievable here. After all, they were taking over prime parts of the natives' land. He understood the Colonial Office's attitude to be *It is a big country, so the natives shouldn't really have any problem moving somewhere else if they don't wish to embrace the British colony.*

As far as possible, Hunter wanted to avoid a clash with the natives. He didn't want to risk himself or his men being killed or wounded, and the idea of slaughtering the natives was not one that sat comfortably with him. If it came to it, though, he and his men were ready. This was particularly in the light of hearing about the death of La Perouse's colleague, Captain de Langle, and his men. That news had, in fact, put every man in the boat very much on edge, so that Hunter's eyes weren't the only ones darting from shore to shore.

As they rowed around the harbour conducting their surveys, it became apparent to Hunter that there were far fewer natives around than there had been on their previous survey. He did, however, consider the possibility that they may just be keeping out of sight as he ordered the crew to row into a point close to the one they had previously attempted to land on. When they arrived, Hunter immediately ordered two armed marines to stand guard up near the tree line to avoid any chance of a surprise attack. The crew then unloaded some supplies and food and began building a fire. While they were engaged in these activities, Hunter observed a small group of seven natives on the other side of the harbour, on a point about one hundred yards away.

'Look, Mr Bradley, we have company.'

'Yes, sir. So I see,' Bradley replied. 'What do you think we should do?'

'We'll call them over and be friendly, shall we not?'

With that, Hunter began walking towards the end of the point and waving to the natives across the harbour.

'Hey, hello,' he called and motioned for them to come across.

The natives immediately waved back, walked down the beach, climbed into two canoes and began paddling across the harbour.

Hunter turned to Bradley. 'Have one of the men get the presents out of the boat, please.'

Bradley did as ordered, and he and Hunter soon had an array of mirrors and beads. They were quickly joined on the point by two marines, but Hunter ordered them to put their guns back further down the beach. They did so and rejoined Hunter and Bradley as the natives' canoes reached the beach.

'Hello,' Hunter said a little nervously, focussing on the spears and throwing sticks the natives were carrying as they walked up the beach towards him. He held out his hands to show he was unarmed, and the others with him followed his lead.

The natives stopped and had a brief conversation, which Hunter could not understand, thereby further increasing his nervousness. It was with great relief, then, that he watched as the natives took the few paces back to their canoes, dropped their weapons in and turned to Hunter with broad smiles on their faces.

'Hello,' he repeated as the locals approached. 'Welcome, welcome.' He smiled, oblivious to the irony of welcoming them to their own land.

Hunter and Bradley held out their hands, unsure for a moment if the locals would shake them, so were presently surprised when they did so without hesitation.

Hunter looked at Bradley. 'Aye, that's interesting.'

While the pleasantries were being exchanged, Hunter observed the large, raised scars across the locals' shoulders and chests, and how each had a front tooth missing, similar to most of the other native men that he had seen. Several of them also had the septum of their noses pierced through with a bone, indicating they were traditional lore men who had been through the traditional men's business ceremony.

'I wonder why so many of them have a front tooth missing and a bone through their noses?' commented Bradley.

'I can only guess that they, along with the scars, have some cultural significance, but I have no idea what it may be,' responded Hunter.

Hunter and Bradley then held out the mirrors and beads, but before the locals accepted them, they pointed behind Hunter and Bradley and said something with rather concerned expressions. Hunter turned and saw five marines standing by the boats with their muskets held across their chests.

'Put the muskets down, laddies,' Hunter called. 'Put them on the sand but stand by them.'

As the marines obeyed the order, the locals smiled and accepted the trinkets, examining the mirrors with the usual combination of curiosity and mirth. After a short conversation consisting of sign language, gestures and monosyllabic words, Hunter invited the locals to join them at their fire for some food. The locals happily agreed. The visitors and locals then sat around the fire, communicating as best they could, and Hunter was quite surprised by how effective such communication could be. One thing was clear to him – the locals had no taste for navy rations, salted pork or alcohol.

Hunter was totally absorbed in the conversation when Bradley, who was seated next to him, suddenly grabbed his arm and pointed to the edge of the tree line where the two marines stood guard as a large group of heavily armed locals emerged from the trees.

'Captain!' one of the guards yelled at the top of his voice.

Hunter jumped to his feet, and Bradley quickly joined him.

'What should we do, Captain?' Bradley queried.

'Nothing for the moment,' Hunter replied before calling to the guards on the edge of the bush. 'Easy, men. Let them come down.'

Hunter had quickly realised they had no options as they were so heavily outnumbered. He turned back to the group of locals who they had been talking with, and they motioned for Hunter and Bradley to resume their seats. They did so in such a reassuring manner that Bradley and Hunter felt almost comfortable in doing so.

The new group soon joined them, and Hunter began inquiring about their shields and weapons, as he had done with the different group the previous day. This resulted in the locals providing the visitors with a demonstration of how the spear, which was about ten feet long, was placed into the thrower. A sharpened hook-type feature at one end, held in place by gum and binding, was inserted into the hollowed end of the spear. This provided extra power and accuracy, which made Hunter feel relieved that they weren't been thrown at him, especially when the locals demonstrated their accuracy up to about eighty or ninety yards. The locals also demonstrated the shield's effectiveness against a spear. They did this by digging a shield into the sand of the adjacent beach and throwing a spear at it from a distance of some forty yards.

The locals then urged Hunter and Bradley to demonstrate the

effectiveness of their weapons. Hunter summoned one of the marines to provide the demonstration. The marine slowly raised his pistol and fired. When the shot went straight through the shield, the locals reacted with a combination of shock and curiosity at how such a small object had been so powerful.

The two groups continued their disjointed conversation. Hunter observed a group of women watching from within the tree line and pointed them out to Bradley.

'Yes, Captain, as usual, their women are watching from a safe distance.'

'Aye, well, let's see if we can encourage this group to come forward,' Hunter replied.

With that, Hunter turned to their guests, or hosts – in his own mind, he was unsure who was fulfilling which role in this gathering on the harbour's edge. He produced some more gifts and indicated to the men of the group that they were for the women. At first, the tribesmen indicated that they would take them and give them to the women, but Hunter made it clear that the women had to come forward to receive the gifts themselves. The men finally agreed, and one of the Elders called the women forward. Following the women, though, was yet another group of heavily armed men. This group were also heavily painted with white and red streaks all over their bodies. The lines of white on their dark skin gave them a rather terrifying appearance, looking somewhat like moving skeletons.

Hunter and Bradley glanced at each other somewhat uneasily, as neither was now sure it was a good idea to insist that the women come forward. They nevertheless proceeded with presenting the gifts of beads and strips of white linen to the naked women. As they adorned themselves with the trinkets, the women giggled rather nervously.

The meeting between the two groups continued without incident for a few hours as they endeavoured to learn all they could about each other. After some time, however, it became obvious to Hunter that the locals were repeating the same question, which Hunter interpreted to mean, *How long are you going to stay here on our land?*

It was a question Hunter was not comfortable answering honestly, so he feigned ignorance and moved on to another subject. When it finally came time for Hunter's group to leave, they did so on the most polite and friendly terms.

*Ref. 18*

\*\*\*

Upon his return to the new settlement, Hunter reported straight to the governor's surprisingly grand portable canvas house, where Phillip was keen to hear about his latest excursion.

'Sit down, Captain.' Phillip motioned to the chair in front of his desk, which had been one of the first items landed from the fleet. 'Now, please apprise me of the details of your survey.'

'Well, Excellency, it was most interesting yet again. We did not proceed much further down harbour, as there are so many coves and inlets to be explored. It would appear, however, that there may be more than one river feeding into the harbour.'

'Oh, really?'

'Aye, it would seem so, sir, but those coves and inlets are of such varying sizes, it is impossible to determine just how many may be fed by rivers or streams.' Hunter paused briefly before continuing, 'You will be interested to be informed that the reason we didn't explore further on this survey was that we spent several hours amongst the natives.'

Phillip's interest increased even further. 'And what was the outcome of that?'

Hunter explained in considerable detail their interactions with the locals before adding, 'In general, then, sir, I would say the men are between five feet six inches and five feet nine inches tall. They are very straight and clean-made but quite thin. The women are not so tall or thin but are well-made, and we saw some who possessed quite attractive features. Most of the mature-aged men are heavily scarred on their chests and shoulders, which I believe to be some sort of ceremonial matter, as, it would also appear, is the removal of a front tooth. Many of the men have a bone through their noses. All of them smear their skin with dirt, sand, ash and even animal fat.'

'To what purpose, Captain?' Phillip inquired.

'As far as I could determine, sir, it would appear to protect their skin from the sun and insects. I should also mention to you that we encountered one group of their men who were painted in a white and reddish colour all over their bodies.'

'Like a type of war paint?' inquired Phillip.

'Aye, sir, exactly. And I must confess that when we were first confronted by them, I had some initial concern for our safety, but they offered no aggression whatsoever.'

'Well, that is pleasing. And were your other encounters with them similar in nature?'

'They were. In fact, they were all very amiable, except, of course, the group who chased us away from their beach two days ago. And I must confess I am unsure as to why they behaved so differently to the others. So, despite that, sir, I am disposed to believe it will be not too difficult a matter, in due time, to conciliate their friendship and confidence, for although they generally appear armed at first meeting, which is perfectly understandable, whenever we lay aside our weapons and make signs of friendship, they always advance unarmed and with a friendly spirit.'

'Captain, that is most pleasing.' Phillip allowed a slight smile to warm his face as he stroked the head of the greyhound that sat beside his chair. 'Perhaps, for the first time in British colonial history, we shall be able to live in harmony with the native people of the country.'

'Let's hope so, sir.' Hunter was about to stand to leave when he hesitated. 'Perhaps one wee matter that I should mention, though, sir, is the question each group of natives we encounter repeatedly ask – how long do we intend to stay here?'

'Hmmm.' Phillip nodded slowly. 'Firstly, I must observe that I am both surprised and impressed that you can understand them sufficiently well to know that is what they are asking you.'

'Sir, we have spent many hours with the various groups, and nearly four hours with that latest group. It is a recurring question, and it is perfectly apparent from their sign language, to both Lieutenant Bradley and me, that that is precisely what they are asking.'

'And how do you reply, Captain?'

'I simply give them the impression that I do not understand the question and change the subject.'

'Yes, well, let's hope they quickly learn to accept our intentions to stay here permanently.' The smile that had briefly appeared on Phillip's face had now vanished.

'Aye, we can only hope so, Excellency.'

*Ref. 19*

\*\*\*

That evening, the senior naval and marine officers joined Phillip at the large rough-hewn dining table that two of the carpenters had prioritised making for His Excellency as soon as they had landed.

Despite the relatively high humidity, it was a pleasant summer evening and the first opportunity the officers had had to share a meal together since they had left Cape Town. This, combined with the fact they were served with fresh-caught fish and their first taste of kangaroo, courtesy of the governor's greyhounds, ensured a congenial, relaxed atmosphere around the table. Although they found the kangaroo a trifle tough and overcooked, it was fresh meat and infinitely preferrable to salted beef or pork. With such an indulgence, combined with rum, brandy and some of the governor's wine selection brought from Cape Town, it wasn't long before the atmosphere became quite jovial.

'Gentlemen, gentlemen! A toast!' announced Phillip. 'To the colony.'

'To the colony!' all responded, raising their mugs.

The evening wore on, and spirits remained generally high until the inevitable issue of the local Aboriginal people was raised. Tench had been asking Hunter about his surveys and his contacts with the natives when Tench commented, 'Captain, it is certainly pleasing to hear that your interactions with so many of them have been similar to those encounters we have had with smaller groups.'

'Aye, they are certainly particularly curious about us, but they are quite peaceful, despite the fact that due to their vastly superior numbers, they could have inflicted on us any such harm as they wished.'

'We will see how long that lasts,' Major Ross responded.

'So, you don't hold much hope for a peaceful relationship with them, Major?' Hunter replied.

'Well, let's be honest about this,' snarled Ross. 'The fact is, they be ignorant savages and they can't be trusted. It be as simple as that.'

'Perhaps you prejudge them?' ventured Tench. 'Savages were certainly what I was expecting initially, but from my limited contact with them and Captain Hunter's extensive encounters, it would seem they are a curious and peaceful people.'

'They're savages,' scoffed Ross.

Tench wanted to avoid arguing with Ross, who, as head of the marines, was not only his commanding officer but also the colony's lieutenant governor and second in command behind Phillip. This was despite Hunter holding a dormant commission as governor should anything happen to Phillip.

Tench therefore changed the subject and quickly addressed his next comment to Hunter. 'And, Captain, did you hear about Monsieur La Perouse's men's huge haul of fish at Botany Bay – nearly two thousand of them in one day.'

'Aye, well, I be sorry to hear that.' Hunter smiled. 'Because that's even more than us, and I don't like being beaten by the French at anything. Not even fishing!'

It was a comment that drew chuckles of agreement from all at the table.

William Dawes allowed the mirth to subside before addressing Phillip. 'Perhaps, sir, given that we are trying to develop harmonious relationships with the natives, it may serve us well to be a little careful of depleting their food resources, particularly the fish stocks.'

Before Phillip could answer, Ross jumped in. 'You cannot be making a comment like that sincerely, surely, Mr Dawes. We have over a thousand people to feed in this colony, so the last thing we should be doing is concerning ourselves with protecting the savages' fish stocks. Besides, there are so very many fish in these waters, we couldn't possibly make any impression on their numbers.'

All at the table focussed their attention on Phillip.

'Mr Dawes, I'm sorry, but I have to agree with Major Ross. Feeding our people has to be our total priority, and I sincerely doubt that we are here in sufficient numbers to affect the natives' resources.'

Dawes nodded reluctantly before looking at Tench, who shrugged his shoulders and gave his friend a supportive half-smile.

*Ref. 20*

# Chapter 24

# Kai'ymay, Gamaragal Land, February 1788

Arabanoo had just returned from yet another excursion with the other young warriors watching the visitors and their huge canoes and now sat next to Weereweea, who was making a fishing hook from a piece of shell, as she and some of the other women from the mob were going fishing the next day.

As soon as Arabanoo sat down next to her, she asked him gently, 'So, what have the Elders decided to do about the strangers?'

'There was much discussion, but they decided to find out all they can about them first, so the various mobs are going and meeting with them when small groups of them move away from their camp.'

She nodded as Arabanoo continued, 'They are particularly trying to find out how long the strangers wish to stay on our land. From what we can see, it may be that they wish to stay a long time, because they are cutting down trees and clearing the bush and putting up strange huts in which they sleep. They also have strange animals with them.'

Arabanoo paused for a moment and gently stroked his baby's head as a cloud of concern descended across his face. 'The Elders are very worried about how many of them there are in such a small area and what the land can sustain. They are catching huge numbers of fish here in Birrabirragal and down in the Bideegal waters.'

The cloud of concern now creased Weereweea's face.

'So, our people will continue to talk with them to try to confirm if they are going to stay for a long time, and if they are, we will stop talking to them so they no longer feel welcome, because we all just want them to go away.'

Weereweea nodded. 'Yes, it would be wonderful if they just went away.'

# CHAPTER 25

# SYDNEY COVE, 6 FEBRUARY 1788

It was midmorning as Major Robert Ross and Tench entered Governor Phillip's canvas house. The red uniforms of both men were stained with sweat from the short walk around the cove.

'You wished to see us, sir?' inquired Ross.

'Yes, I did, Major. Please have a seat,' Phillip responded, motioning to the chairs in front of his desk. 'Now, as you are aware, we will be landing the female convicts tonight. So, we are going to need to ensure that it all runs smoothly and there are no opportunities for the convict men to... how should I express this?' Phillip hesitated for a moment before continuing, 'To get amongst the women! I'm sure you follow my meaning.'

'Aye, I certainly do, sir, but I'm not sure how you would like me to assist,' replied Ross, totally devoid of expression.

'Well, we will obviously need a large contingent of your men to guard the convicts and ensure they stay well away from the women, as we have nothing yet built to keep them apart, and–'

Ross cut Phillip off. 'I have already advised you, Excellency, that my men will not be guarding the convicts now they have landed. You know full well, sir, that my orders be for my men to guard the convicts on board the ships on the voyage out here. Protecting the colony is now our duty. My marines will not be acting as common gaolers, so–'

Phillip cut Ross off in return. 'Major, I am the governor of this colony, and you and your men are ultimately under my command.'

'Aye, sir, but we be British marines, not common gaolers, and my orders do not require my men to act as such. We be here to protect the colony, not to guard convicts.'

Before Phillip could reply, Tench offered, somewhat hesitantly, 'Perhaps, Major, you could make an exception in these highly unusual circumstances.'

Ross turned and glared at Tench. 'I don't recall addressing you, Captain, so I don't need your opinion.'

Realising there was no point objecting further, Tench fell silent as Ross continued to Phillip, 'Sir, if we guard the men this afternoon as the women are landed, what is going to happen tonight, or tomorrow, or tomorrow night?'

'Major, I think we deal with tomorrow tomorrow,' an irritated Phillip replied. 'My first priority is to land the women safely and without any unsavoury incidents.'

'Sir, I have made my position perfectly clear. And from what we have seen of the morals of some of these women on the voyage out here, it'll be the men who need protecting from them, so I repeat, sir, my men will not be guarding convicts this afternoon, tonight or any other time.'

Phillip was totally exasperated by the recalcitrant major, who he knew had a reputation for being difficult, but he had not experienced it personally to date. Up until the last couple of weeks, though, they had been at sea on different ships. Phillip put his head down and began to stroke the head of his white greyhound before waving Ross and Tench away.

'Will that be all, then, sir?' Ross asked, not satisfied with being dismissed by a wave of the hand.

Phillip looked up. 'Yes, that will be all, Major.'

Ross and Tench rose from their seats and walked out of the governor's canvas house. When they were back down the hill and well out of earshot, Ross swung around to Tench and drew his face to within inches of Tench's. Tench could see the veins in Ross's neck bulging and the red of fury spreading across his blotchy skin as he blurted, 'Don't you ever contradict me again in front of the governor, or you will regret it. Do you understand me?'

'Yes, sir, I do,' Tench replied calmly, and despite the fact he knew it was totally futile to disagree with Ross, he added, 'but I didn't contradict you, sir. I merely suggested a compromise.'

'You contradicted me, Captain!' Ross roared. 'And it's not to happen again. Do I make myself clear?'

'Yes, sir.' Tench nodded. 'Perfectly clear, Major.'

As the two marines walked back to their camp in silence, Tench thought that although there were many aspects of life in the new colony that he was going to find an exciting adventure, working under Major Ross was going to be a nightmare.

\*\*\*

Late in the afternoon on that same sweltering day, Tench and Dawes stood on the edge of Sydney Cove as boatload after boatload of women convicts were landed.

'This will be interesting,' remarked Tench.

Dawes nodded. 'Mmmm.'

What happened over the next few hours was a mixture of a riot and an orgy, although in the chaos, it was impossible to determine who of the women were willing participants, as Ross had suggested, and who were brutally raped. Sailors joined the convict men, some of whom had not seen a woman in over eight months, as they 'got to' the convict women. The chaos of the scene was only exacerbated by the violent thunderstorm that struck in the early evening. The ferocity of the tempest unleashed by the heavens failed to dampen the enthusiasm of the willing – neither did the furious thunder, nor the spectacular lightning that shattered the slate-grey sky, brilliantly illuminating their hedonistic activities for any bystanders to see.

Watching from the inadequate shelter of his tent, Reverend Johnson was horrified by the spectacle and half expected – or half hoped –

one of the lightning bolts would strike the sinners. Disgusted by the activities unfolding before him, he turned and knelt before the crucifix on the small table at the back of his tent and began praying frantically for all involved and for the morality of the colony.

Just as he did so, a huge bolt of lightning exploded amongst a group of sheep that were huddled together under a tree, killing five of them. A few moments later, another bolt crashed from the sky and struck a pig sheltering nearby, killing it instantly. All of the animals were crucial to providing breeding stock for the colony's survival, but all were the property of Major Ross.

*Ref. 21*

# Chapter 26

# Sydney Cove, Late February 1788

Watkin Tench and William Dawes were walking on the edge of the settlement when they approached a hastily erected enclosure that held several of the colony's remaining, and therefore especially precious, sheep. Standing on the other side of the enclosure were a group of Aboriginal men pointing at the strange animals and talking animatedly.

'What do you think, Watkin? I think we should attempt to converse with them,' Dawes suggested.

'Yes, most definitely,' replied Tench, turning at the end of the enclosure and walking slowly towards the group of local tribesmen.

Tench and Dawes leant their muskets and swords against the railing of the enclosure and held out their upturned hands to show they were unarmed and were not intending harm, while the locals did the same with their spears. This had become the standard practice whenever the two cultures met.

As the two groups approached each other, Tench and Dawes held out their right hands to be shaken, which they were, quite vigorously, by each of the tribal men in turn.

One of the locals then turned and gestured towards the sheep, saying, 'Kangaroo, kangaroo.'

Tench and Dawes looked at each other quizzically before Tench replied, 'Sheep,' and then, repeating more slowly, 'sheep.'

The tribal man again pointed to the sheep. 'Kangaroo,' he said with a broad smile.

'Just hold on a moment, Watkin,' Dawes interjected and pointed to a solitary cow that was also in the enclosure.

'Cow,' said Dawes, carefully.

The tribal man smiled again. 'Kangaroo.'

His colleagues nodded and repeated, 'Kangaroo.'

Tench and Dawes looked at each other again.

'Hmmm,' said Dawes. 'There seems to be some sort of confusion here.'

'Obviously, but…' Tench hesitated. 'I know, I know.'

He then turned to those he termed 'Indians' and, bending his arms up below his neck and allowing his hands to flop forward, he asked, 'What is this, then?' and immediately began hopping around, much to the amusement of all, particularly Dawes.

When the locals' laughter subsided, they all responded almost in unison, 'Patagorang.'

Again, Tench and Dawes looked at each other.

'What did they say?' queried Tench.

'I think it was patagorang,' replied Dawes. 'Do it again.'

Tench looked at his friend, smiled and again began hopping around.

'Patagorang?' Dawes questioned, pointing at Tench.

The locals nodded and smiled. 'Patagorang.'

A group of convict women who were working nearby were distracted from their duties by the laughter and the sight of a red-coated British marine captain hopping around as if he was in a children's pantomime on a London stage. They stood and watched and were immediately noticed by the Aboriginal men, who then ignored Tench and Dawes and began walking towards the women.

Tench tried to call them back, as he was determined to get certainty around what he immediately realised was a massive communication breakdown about the true name of one of the more unique animals on the planet, which was the subject of so much discussion in Britain. No matter how much he and Dawes tried to attract the attention of the locals, however, they ignored them and continued walking towards the women.

Dawes and Tench immediately felt the mirth and enjoyment they had both been feeling swamped by a sudden anxiety.

'Should we get our weapons, Watkin?'

'Probably best not to for the moment. We don't want to escalate the matter, but let's get over there.'

Tench and Dawes hurried off and were with the tribal men by the time they reached the convict women, who had not sought to walk away to return to their duties. The naked tribal men immediately began talking to the women quite animatedly.

One of the women, who held an eleven-month-old baby girl in her arms, turned to Tench and Dawes and asked, 'What are they saying?'

'I don't really have any idea,' replied Tench, and then, trying to reassure the women and himself, he added, 'but I think they seem to like you.'

She smiled. 'Mmmm, perhaps they do.'

Tench paused for a moment and looked closely at the attractive young convict with dark, curly hair falling across her shoulders, thinking that she could be no more than seventeen or eighteen years old.

'Do I know you?' Tench inquired, but before she could answer, he added, 'You do some work for Lieutenant Johnston, don't you?'

'Yes, sir.' She nodded. 'I milk his goat and do a little work for him.'

'Oh, yes, that's right. You're Esther. Esther Abrahams, isn't it?'

The young convict smiled. 'Yes, sir.'

'The lieutenant speaks glowingly of you.'

Tench noticed that Esther had blushed slightly at the compliment. He also knew that Esther's relationship with Johnston went well beyond 'milking his goat', as Johnston had made no secret of the fact his relationship with the well-spoken young convict had developed on board the *Lady Penrhyn* on the voyage out. Tench was too much of a gentleman to mention that, though, as he didn't wish to cause the young woman to blush even more, so he returned his attention to the tribal men, who had continued talking amongst themselves and pointing to the various women. One of the men then came forward and pointed to the sleeve of Esther's dress and rubbed his thumb and forefinger together while speaking unintelligibly.

'He wants to feel the material of your dress,' said Tench.

'Should I let him?' asked Esther.

'If you don't mind,' replied Tench.

Esther hesitated for a moment before shrugging. 'Why not?'

She handed her baby to one of the other convict women, stepped forward beside Tench and held out her arm. The tribal man took the material of her sleeve and rubbed it between his fingers before turning to his countrymen and encouraging them to do the same.

Esther endured the experience with a smile, while her colleagues passed rather bawdy comments about the anatomy of the tribesmen, which caused Tench and Dawes to look at each other and shake their heads.

The disjointed conversation continued for a few minutes before Tench spoke to the convict women.

'You ladies should be getting back to your duties now,' he directed gently.

'Yes, sir.' They nodded and immediately walked away. It had been a long time since any of them had been called 'ladies'.

Tench tried to get the focus of the tribal men back to their previous topic on the correct name for a kangaroo but without success, as the tribal men remained distracted, obviously discussing their interaction with the women convicts. They then turned to wander away. One of them stopped, and while speaking unintelligibly, he pointed at Dawes and Tench, before pointing to the ground, the visitors' extensive camp and the sun overhead. He then repeated the gestures.

Tench and Dawes looked at each other before Dawes spoke. 'I think he is asking the question that Captain Hunter says they always ask. How long are we staying?'

'I think you're right, so all we can do is indicate we don't understand.'

Tench and Dawes shook their heads and shrugged at the tribesman, who did the same and turned and walked away with the others.

He had only taken a few steps, though, when he looked over his shoulder at Tench and Dawes and pointed to the sheep in the enclosure.

'Kangaroo,' he said, as the hint of a smile creased his face.

*Ref. 22*

# Chapter 27

# Kai'ymay, Gamaragal Land, February 1788

Arabanoo walked back into his camp as the sun cast lengthening shadows across the warm soil. He joined Weereweea as she sat on the ground with her baby daughter lying in her lap. She was preparing some fish, which she and some of the other women had caught from their canoes that afternoon.

After greeting him with a loving embrace, she asked the question that she asked almost every day recently and that they had discussed so much over the past few days.

'What have the Elders decided?'

Arabanoo hesitated momentarily before replying, 'All the traditional nation groups have said it is obvious the Berewalgal want to stay here for a long time. When the Elders ask them how long they are going to stay, they pretend they don't understand.'

Weereweea frowned as he continued, 'They seem to understand most other things we say, but no matter how often the Elders ask them, they just won't answer. The Elders are also concerned that they have no respect for our traditional lore ways. These people don't seem to understand that we belong to these lands and to these waters. We are connected to these lands and waters, not them. When they catch lots and lots of fish in their big nets, they don't want to share any with us. They want to keep it all themselves. They are very rude, ignorant people who don't have any idea about sharing. Then they give us useless little gifts, and seem to think we should be happy with them in exchange for using the land and waters.'

'So, what will our people do?'

'We will stay away from them for now, but we can't let them take all our tucker, so we will watch them closely. Bennelong and some of the others, like Pemulwuy, still want to get all the mobs together and drive the Berewalgal away before any more come here. They say there was just one of their huge canoes many seasons ago, and now look how many there are.'

'Hmmm.' Weereweea nodded.

'They and some of the others are worried that if we don't drive them away now, more will keep coming, and none of us want that.'

Arabanoo looked down into his wife's soft brown eyes and saw the deep worry that had inhabited them since the visitors had first arrived. A feeling of utter helplessness rapidly engulfed him.

# Chapter 28

# Sydney Cove, 27 February 1788

Almost the entire colony had been assembled to watch the executions. Tench and Dawes stood at the back of the crowd. They couldn't count the number of such executions they had witnessed in their lives, but they had never become desensitised to the horror of the fact they were about to watch a person die. The whole process still repulsed them.

They and the entire crowd looked on as James Freeman felt the hangman's rope when it was placed over his head and tightened around his neck. Freeman was surprised that he was even aware of the itch caused by its coarseness, because his whole body was now consumed with terror. The next feeling he became aware of was the wetness in the crotch of his pants. He just wanted to scream about the injustice of the whole situation. Yes, he was guilty of stealing seven pounds of flour from a fellow convict, but only a couple of weeks ago, other convicts had been found guilty of similar crimes, and they hadn't been hanged! They had received sentences like flogging or banishment on bread and water to the newly named Pinchgut, the barren rock outcrop in the middle of the harbour. He didn't think for one moment when he stole the flour that he could hang for it.

The rope began to tighten, and he was ordered to climb the ladder beside him, which had been carefully placed directly under a large tree branch. He slowly, hesitantly placed one foot on the first rung. It was a spectacle that was greeted by a huge range of emotions from those in the audience. The convicts watched with emotions which varied from dread, lest it ever happen to them, to enjoyment at the spectacle of it, because it wasn't them... this time. Most of the sailors, marines and naval officers were so hardened by many years of witnessing such punishments that they felt very little at all. The sadists obviously enjoyed it, while others had never adjusted to the horror of watching a person kick and writhe as they were strangled to death on the end of a rope.

The only group that was all totally intrigued by the whole spectacle was the local tribespeople, who were watching from the shelter of the tree line that surrounded the camp.

The judge advocate, David Collins, who had been standing near Major Robert Ross, quickly stepped forward and spoke to the condemned Freeman.

'Prisoner, I have a proposal for you.'

A shocked Freeman stopped on the first step of the ladder and looked anxiously at Collins, who continued, 'I am prepared to pardon you.'

'Oh, thank you, thank you, sir,' Freeman burst forth.

'Ah, ah, prisoner, let me finish,' Collins continued. 'I am prepared to pardon you on one condition.'

'Oh, yes, sir, yes, anything, sir,' Freeman interjected again.

'The condition is that you become the colony's executioner,' Collins said flatly.

Freeman fell silent and stared at Collins briefly before dropping his eyes to the ground. He knew exactly what that meant, and its full consequences flashed through his mind in an instant. Although his life would be spared, apart from undertaking the executioner's abhorrent tasks, he would inevitably be executing his friends and colleagues. Consequently, he would be universally reviled by them, and he would be completely isolated. His existence would become almost unbearable.

He thought for a moment, raised his eyes to Collins and nodded. 'Yes, sir. I'll do it.'

'Good man.' Collins gave him a half-smile, patted him on the arm and ordered the marine who had been acting as the stand-in executioner to remove the rope from Freeman's neck.

Ross joined Collins and ordered that the next prisoner be brought forward. Thomas Barrett was then led forward to the base of the ladder under the tree.

Ross turned to Freeman and said, 'You start your duties now.'

'Oh, no, sir.'

'Now, prisoner!' barked Ross.

'Oh, no, please, sir,' begged Freeman.

'Take that rope and put it around the prisoner's neck,' demanded Ross, bringing his face to within a few inches of Freeman's.

Freeman hesitated and looked to Collins, whose face revealed nothing.

Ross grabbed Freeman by the front of the shirt and yelled, as spittle splattered Freeman's face, 'Now, prisoner, or I'll have you shot on the spot!'

Freeman again glanced at Collins, who again showed no reaction. He looked back at Ross, who still held the front of his shirt, and nodded. 'Yes, sir.'

Ross released the front of Freeman's shirt. 'Now, get on with it,' he ordered as he took the noose from the marine and thrust it into Freeman's hand.

Freeman stared at Thomas Barrett, who stood next to him at the base of the ladder. Barrett raised his eyes to Freeman, his former colleague and now executioner. Freeman met his gaze with a look that begged for forgiveness. Barrett had just confessed to Reverend Johnson that he was guilty of the crime and admitted that he had long warranted the ignominious death he was about to face. That did not, however, prevent him experiencing exactly the same level of terror that had gripped Freeman only minutes before.

Freeman hesitantly put the noose around Barrett's neck. 'Sorry, Tom,' he whispered as he did so.

Barrett did not respond. He was too consumed by the feeling of the fatal rope around his neck. When commanded, he slowly climbed the ladder, and moments later, he was kicking and writhing as the rope slowly, gasp by gasp, strangled the life out of him. The convicts stared, the sadists smirked, the humanitarians dropped their eyes and, back within the tree line, Arabanoo gasped in shock before turning away, muttering, 'Savages.'

*Ref. 23*

## CHAPTER 29

## SYDNEY COVE, ALBION, MARCH 1788

As soon as Watkin Tench was released from the makeshift lock-up, he strode straight to the tent of his friend, William Dawes, to vent his frustration. He had been arrested by Major Ross, along with four other officers, for their failure to reconsider their decision in a court martial over which they had presided. Marine Privates Hunt and Dempsey had been involved in a dispute over a woman convict, and Hunt had punched Dempsey in the face. Ross had determined that as he was the aggressor, Hunt was to be court-martialled. The court presided over by Tench had given Hunt the option of either asking for a public pardon from Dempsey in front of the whole battalion or receiving one hundred lashes. Ross was not happy with the options.

Dawes was sitting at his small desk, sketching a plan of the town of Albion, which was the name Phillip had given to the new colony on Sydney Cove, when he looked up from his work and immediately saw the immense frustration on his friend's face as Tench burst forth, 'I cannot believe that man... He is just so... so...' The usually articulate Tench was totally dumbstruck.

'Infuriating?' offered Dawes.

'Yes, and...'

'Arrogant?' offered Dawes.

'Yes, and...' Tench still struggled.

'Vexatious, pestiferous, obnoxious?' Dawes suppressed a smile.

'Yes, all of those. Exactly! And don't you dare smile. This could not be more serious. The man is a pig.' Tench had finally thought of an appropriate descriptor. 'We – and that includes you, my friend – are under his command in this isolated colony on the far side of the world.'

'Watkin, I know how serious it is, but it's the first time I've ever seen you stuck for words, so I apologise if it appears I was being flippant. You know I despise Ross, probably every bit as much as you do, but–'

Tench cut him off. 'He hasn't just had you arrested.'

'No, I'm sorry, he hasn't, but... Look, just sit down, calm down and we'll discuss this as rationally as we can.'

Tench hesitated, looked at the chair, looked at Dawes and sat down. As soon as he did so, Dawes poured him a cup of a sweet tea made from a local plant that the visitors had recently discovered was a pleasant substitute for real tea, which was in short supply in the colony. Dawes pushed the cup across the desk to Tench.

'Thank you.' Tench nodded a little reluctantly.

'Alright, now what is the situation, precisely?'

'Well, I'm still under arrest, but he has released us all, obviously because he realises we are needed to fulfil our roles in the operation of the colony.'

'You're still under arrest?' questioned Dawes with some surprise.

'Yes, technically, but despite being a stubborn pig, Ross isn't a fool. So, he has released us to do our duties while we remain under arrest and he attempts to have us court-martialled.'

'What? Really?'

'When you think it through, with us five the subject of the court martial, he doesn't have enough officers to preside over it, because one is on Norfolk Island, one is very ill and two are the subject of Ross's displeasure.'

Dawes smiled broadly. 'Hmmm, a curious situation indeed.'

'Very curious, but the issue is that this new court system here has been established to provide some sort of objectivity in the dispensing of justice in the colony. And if Ross thinks he can behave like an autocrat and arrest those who disagree with how justice is best served... Well, hopefully the governor can straighten him out.'

Tench took a mouthful of his tea before continuing, 'As you well know, he wants to inflict the harshest of punishments on the convicts for the most minor misdemeanours, and he then wants the marines punished even more harshly than the convicts, to maintain discipline, he says. All we are trying to do is bring some balance to the justice system here. These convicts need to be given some incentive to reform and not just punished brutally and repeatedly, especially now there is an increase of scurvy and dysentery amongst them.'

'I couldn't agree more, but I don't like our chances of ever convincing Ross of that.' Dawes paused briefly before adding, 'Just how long does he propose to keep you under arrest?'

'I have no idea.'

The two friends looked at each other and shrugged simultaneously.

'Let's just hope Phillip can get him to see some sense,' Dawes offered.

Tench nodded before looking into his almost empty cup. 'This sweet tea is quite satisfactory, really, isn't it?'

'Indeed it is,' Dawes replied, pouring more tea into Tench's cup before continuing, 'Just changing the subject somewhat, have you heard about the issues with the natives?'

'Well, I heard murmurings that some problems were occurring, but I haven't heard details.'

'It seems the problem arises when our fishermen are hauling the seine. The natives come down to the water's edge and often assist, but they expect a share of the catch. To me, this is perfectly fair and reasonable – after all, we are fishing in their waters and taking huge catches of fish, and they are helping.'

'Surely our fishermen are obliging them in that, aren't they?'

'Yes, but the problem arises when they can't agree on a reasonable share. Just in the last couple of days, while you've been under arrest, there was a clash when, for some reason, our men refused to give them what they regarded as a fair share. They were then attacked with clubs and stones and driven off from the entire catch.'

'Hmmm.'

'And it also seems the natives have attacked a group who were out trying to find some local herbs, fruits or vegetables.'

'What's the governor proposing to do about it?'

'I'm not sure at this stage, but from what I've heard, it appears this may be a result of our people stealing the natives' spears and throwers to sell to the ship crews when they return to England. It's extremely profitable, as you could guess.'

'They'd be much sought after in London,' observed Tench.

'It's understandable, then, that the Indians would react this way. So, the governor is going to need to ensure he takes all means necessary to eliminate that sort of behaviour by our people, convict and free alike.'

Tench nodded. 'Yes, or matters could really escalate.'

# CHAPTER 30

# SYDNEY COVE, MAY 1788

An almost breathless John Hunter hurried up to Arthur Phillip as the governor was about to enter his canvas house.

'Sir, I must speak with you. I have most disturbing news.'

Phillip motioned Hunter through the door. 'Come in, come in. What is it?'

The two naval officers entered as Hunter spoke. 'Sir, we have just discovered the murdered bodies of two of the convicts. They have been killed by the natives in the most shocking manner.'

Phillip shook his head as he slumped into his chair. 'No!' he muttered. 'What happened?'

'Sir, they were down harbour cutting rushes, and it seems they were just attacked and most brutally butchered. Surgeon White is examining the bodies now.'

'Did they do anything to provoke the natives?'

'We are not aware that they did anything, sir. They were down harbour where they were supposed to be, but we're not sure how the whole incident came about.'

'Well, we must do a...' Phillip paused as Major Robert Ross entered. 'Ah, Major Ross, this is a most terrible incident.'

'Aye, it most certainly is, sir. I have just viewed the bodies of the two men, and one of them has the most horrific injuries. He has two spears in him, and the savages have beaten his brains out, and his eyes be out as well. Surgeon White believes this was probably done by the birds, however. He is unclear at this time how exactly they have killed the other man.'

Phillip slumped even lower in his chair before a wave of anger saw him sit forward.

'We have to stop this one way or another, gentlemen.'

'Aye, we most certainly do, sir,' said Ross. 'We must take swift and decisive action and teach these savages a lesson. How many marines would you like me to assemble for a punitive expedition? Twenty, thirty?'

'I think twenty should suffice, Major. What do you think, Captain?'

Hunter hesitated briefly before responding, 'Well, sir, I think you need to consider if, indeed, a punitive expedition is the best course of action in the circumstances, because–'

Ross now cut his fellow Scotsman off gruffly. 'Consider what, Captain? We need to act swiftly and decisively to teach these savages a lesson. It is as simple as that.' He turned to Phillip and continued. 'You must remember, sir, that this isn't the first time they've murdered convicts. It is just the first time we've actually found the bodies.'

'We don't really know that with any certainty,' Phillip replied. 'For all we know, those other convicts may have just run off to try their luck in the bush. Now, please, let the captain finish.'

Ross glared as Hunter continued, 'Well, Excellency, by your own words, you are determined to develop amicable relations with the natives as per your orders.' Phillip nodded. 'So, obviously, taking twenty or thirty marines out to slaughter them is hardly going to do that. Also, sir, as you well know, there are hundreds, probably thousands, of natives out there, which raises two points for consideration. Firstly, how do you decide which of them are responsible for the murder of these men? Or do you just go and slaughter some who may know nought about these murders? That would hardly seem to be just.'

Ross fumed, while Phillip nodded and replied, 'Go on, Captain. Your second point is?'

'Sir, if we provoke the natives to band together and attack us, they be in such numbers that they could either destroy us completely or, at the very least, inflict enormous casualties upon us.'

Ross could be silent no longer, and he burst forth, 'You are completely mistaken in that assertion. Our superior weaponry would destroy them all.'

'I'm sorry, but I have had far more contact with them than you, and I am far more aware of their numbers and the lethal nature of their weapons,' Hunter responded firmly.

Ross was about to reply when Phillip interjected, 'Alright, gentlemen, I understand your differing views. Allow me to properly consider my response, and I will advise you. Major, I must say, though, that I do believe Captain Hunter has a point regarding not wanting to provoke the natives into a full-scale attack on our camp, because, regardless of our superior weaponry, given their large numbers, they could undoubtedly inflict enormous casualties. I also don't believe, from the little I know of the natives, that they are likely to line up in straight military lines, waiting to be shot. They are far more likely to attack us from all directions in the dead of night, and that is not a prospect I relish. Nevertheless, I do agree that we cannot allow this matter to go unpunished.'

'Aye, sir,' Ross responded, 'you make a valid point regarding the way these savages are likely to attack, if they do, but that is all the more reason why we should prioritise the building of proper fortifications for the colony.'

Phillip concluded, 'Yes, I'm well aware of your feelings on the matter of fortifications, but that is a simple matter of priorities. Now, gentlemen, if you would excuse me, I'd like to consider our options quietly.'

\*\*\*

Early the next morning, Watkin Tench waited outside Governor Phillip's house with ten armed marines. It wasn't long before Phillip emerged, dressed ready for an excursion into the bush.

Tench immediately greeted him. 'Good morning, Excellency.'

'Good morning, Captain.'

'Now, sir, I understand you are to lead us today.'

'Yes, I am. This matter is just so important I wish to go out and see for myself what is going on with the natives. I wish to see if we can discover who murdered these men. And if we can determine who it was, we will undertake a most forceful punishment of them.'

Tench nodded a little hesitantly. 'Yes, sir.'

Moments later, Phillip and Tench led the marines eastward to the edge of the camp and onto the roughly beaten path through the thick bush, towards where the convicts' bodies had been found the previous day. It was late autumn, and the rain that had fallen over previous days had ensured the path was a slippery combination of mud and leaf litter from the variety of tall eucalypts that formed the canopy and the grevilleas, lilly pillies and other bushes that sprouted wherever the sun permeated the canopy. It was a strictly single-file path initially, and Tench led the way in front of the governor until they came to a point where it met a broader track that had been worn over thousands of years by the bare feet of the local tribespeople.

At that point, Tench slowed slightly and allowed the governor to join him in the lead.

'Now, Excellency, it won't be long before we arrive at the place where Captain Campbell advised me he found the bodies of these men.'

'Very good. Hopefully, we will be able to find some sort of evidence as to how this tragedy happened and who may have been responsible.'

'Yes, sir.'

'And then we will search for those responsible. Hopefully, we will be able to find them with some of the men's clothes or tools in their possession, because I'm informed both were missing when the bodies were found.'

'They were, sir, but do you really intend to kill them if we do?'

Phillip paused for a moment before replying, 'Captain, I don't see that we have any alternative. It is not as if we can arrest them and bring them back to face trial. How could that possibly work with natives who don't speak English and who would have no idea whatsoever of what is going on?'

'Yes, sir, I see that would be extremely challenging.'

'Challenging? Challenging? Why, it would be completely impossible! I believe we have no option, because we simply must demonstrate to them that they cannot slaughter our people with absolute impunity. We have to show them there will be consequences for their actions.'

At that moment, the group emerged from the thick bush into a lightly wooded area around a cove on the harbour's southern shore. On the edge of the cove were thick rushes that the colonists used for thatch, and it was here that Tench advised Phillip the first of the bodies, the badly beaten one, had been found.

'Captain Campbell advises that the second body was found just in the bush on this side, sir,' Tench said, pointing to the eastern side of the cove.

Over the next half an hour or so, Phillip had the marines search the area thoroughly for anything remotely related to the crime that may point to the identity of the perpetrators. It had been a totally fruitless search, however, by the time Tench called the marines together, and they began walking along the track further eastward.

As the governor and the marine captain walked side by side along the harbour's edge and the morning sun attempted to force its way through the gloomy sky above, it was the governor who spoke first.

'Do you find it curious, Captain, that while we've been walking, we haven't sighted a single native?'

'To be honest, not really, sir. They do have an uncanny ability to vanish into the bush when a group of heavily armed redcoats come trudging along.'

The pair continued in silence as they wound their way along the sodden track. The further they walked, the more frustrated Phillip became at their inability to sight even a single native, let alone one who may be in possession of incriminating evidence regarding the murdered rush cutters. When Phillip finally complained to Tench about their lack of success, Tench responded, 'Sir, perhaps we could head south towards Botany Bay, where there is that village of some significant size.'

'Yes, I had heard mention of that. What do you know of it?'

'Well, sir, it is entirely different to the usual shelters we see the Indians inhabit here around the harbour, where they use caves and simple bark lean-tos. This village has far more permanent structures. There are over a dozen quite substantial huts or houses in which a whole family may live. There would be over sixty people in the village, I believe. That is including men, women and children.'

'Alright, then. Hopefully we will have a little more luck down there. Do you think, though, that the culprits who murdered these convicts could live at that distance from where these murders occurred?'

'I really have no idea, sir, but from the little I know of the Indians, it seems possible that those down towards Botany Bay may be an entirely different tribe to those around the harbour here.'

'Hmmm.' Phillip nodded. 'They may well be, but at least they may be able to give us some idea of the identity and whereabouts of these perpetrators.'

'Yes, sir.'

'Now, lead the way, please, Captain.'

Tench followed the track eastward for a short distance, before it came to another leading south towards Botany Bay, where he then turned, closely followed by Phillip and the marines. It was approaching midday, and Phillip again joined Tench in leading the redcoats as they wound their way along the well-beaten track.

'Sir, would you like to stop soon and allow the men to have some lunch?' inquired Tench.

'Yes, soon, but I just don't want to stop yet when we have nothing to show for our morning's work.'

'Yes, sir.'

'Please understand, I am absolutely determined to find these culprits and teach them a lesson that they just cannot murder our people without suffering the most severe consequences.'

At that moment, Phillip's redcoats walked into a large clearing, in the middle of which was a huge party of local tribespeople less than forty yards in front of them. Phillip's party stopped instantly in their tracks and fell silent.

'My God!' gasped Phillip beneath his breath.

Tench's military training took over, and he immediately surveyed the locals to determine the numbers of warriors and weapons.

'How would you like to handle this, sir?' he murmured out of the side of his mouth as the locals began moving slowly towards them.

'Obviously, very calmly and quietly, Captain, wouldn't you think?'

'Yes, sir, given that I estimate there are around three hundred of them, and over two hundred are men with spears, I think calmly and quietly is our only option,' responded Tench.

'Alright, men, put your muskets down on the ground where you stand,' Phillip ordered.

Phillip and Tench did so themselves and immediately held out their hands, palms upturned towards the slowly approaching warriors. The warriors stopped as Phillip and Tench then moved quietly towards them. Tench could feel his heart beating out of his chest and sensed the governor's doing the same. He'd had many encounters with the locals during his few months in the colony, and they had always been on friendly terms. This, however, was very different, as he had never met such a huge group, and he knew that if matters now did turn sour and the Indians chose to attack them, they would have no chance.

'Friends, friends,' Phillip uttered clearly.

One of the tribesmen replied with something unintelligible to the foreigners, immediately pointed to Tench's waist and then touched his own side.

'I don't think he likes my sword, sir. I'll put it down as well,' Tench whispered as he unhitched his scabbard and slowly lowered it to the ground.

The local tribesmen then put down their spears and approached the foreigners with broad smiles. As they did, Tench felt much of the tension ease from his body. He stood and watched as eight of the mature-aged local Elders began interacting with Phillip, showing him conspicuous respect as they did so.

'They obviously know who you are, sir,' Tench observed quietly.

'Hmmm.' Phillip nodded. 'It would appear so. It is apparent, then, that they know a lot more about us than we do about them.' He paused before adding, 'While they are being so friendly and respectful, I will attempt to prevail upon them to allow us to have a look around their village over there and see if we can find any evidence of these murderers.'

'Excellency, with great respect, may I suggest there is no point in our risking the possibility of infuriating the Indians when we can do nothing even if we find something?'

'I see your point, but we are here now, and they appear very friendly, so let's see if they will allow us to look around their village,' Phillip persisted.

With that, Phillip turned and began speaking slowly and gesticulating to the locals. It wasn't long before it became apparent that they understood his request and motioned him towards the village.

Phillip began to follow their hosts, with Tench and the unarmed marines trailing along behind. Tench turned to his men and said, 'Now, men, you know what you're looking for. Any sign whatsoever of the murdered rush cutters. If you see anything, don't make a fuss about it. Just quietly draw it to the attention of the governor or me, and we will handle the matter.' As he said those words, Tench thought that he should really add, *And that will be by doing absolutely nothing.*

As Tench followed Phillip through the huge mob of locals, the tension returned to his body as he became more sure that they were taking a very unnecessary risk that could see them all killed. A few minutes later, it became apparent that Phillip had finally reached the same conclusion, as he was being escorted by an ever-increasing number of local tribesmen during his brief look around the first few huts. Phillip quite abruptly stopped his search, nodded to the escorting locals and politely took his leave.

'I think we should head back to our camp, don't you, Captain? We've seen enough here. There is absolutely no sign whatsoever of any evidence.'

'Yes, sir.' Tench nodded, suppressing a smile.

Having thanked the locals, the visitors recovered their weapons from the far side of the clearing and began the long walk back to Sydney Cove.

'It is interesting to wonder, Excellency, why such a large group of the Indians were gathered at that village. Quite clearly, there were far more in that group than would actually live there.'

'I have no idea,' was Phillip's reply, 'but what I am interested in is finding out precisely why those rush cutters were attacked and murdered. After that little encounter today, I am more convinced than ever that these natives don't attack us without reason.'

'Yes, sir, it would certainly appear so.'

'So, Captain, when we get back to our camp, I would like you to undertake an investigation, question any convicts that may have been working with the murdered pair and find out if there was anything they did that may have provoked the natives.'

'Yes, sir, certainly.'

*Ref. 24*

\*\*\*

It was late the next morning when Watkin Tench entered the governor's house and, without even a morning greeting or exchange of pleasantries, he said, 'You were right, Excellency.'

'Was I? Well, I'm pleased to hear it, but about what in particular?'

'About the murdered rush cutters, sir,' Tench responded. 'They had stolen a canoe from the Indians.'

'Ahh, so it was just as I'd thought.' Phillip slowly shook his head as he added, 'But why would they be so stupid as to do that and provoke the natives?'

'I have no idea whatsoever, sir, but it appears others of our people have been regularly stealing their weapons and tools.'

Phillip looked quizzically at Tench, so Tench continued, 'They are, of course, very valuable artefacts back in London.'

'Aah, of course.' Phillip nodded. 'And the punishment of death must be considered appropriate in the circumstances, as it also applies here for any significant theft. As it must be.'

'Yes, sir, and it would appear that it is the nature of this "payback" system, which is apparently so much a part of their cultural ways.'

'Hmmm,' responded Phillip. 'Well, we need to get through to our people that they simply cannot do anything to provoke them, or we will be undermining the success of this colony.'

'Yes, sir.'

'I mean, we are having enough problems growing food in this soil and keeping our animals alive and healthy.' Phillip then interrupted his train of thought to add, 'Did you know we've just had two bulls and four cows disappear without a trace?'

'No, I hadn't heard that, sir,' replied Tench.

'It seems they just wandered off in the middle of the night. There's no sign that they were taken by the natives, but that's our breeding stock, so it is most concerning. Anyway, the point I was making was that we have enough problems trying to keep this colony going without the natives killing our people every time we need to go outside the immediate boundaries of our camp.'

Tench nodded again. 'Yes, sir. It is concerning.'

'Yes, most concerning. So, will you ask Major Ross to ensure everyone in this colony is fully aware that they are simply not to interfere with or steal from the natives, or they will suffer the harshest of punishments?'

Tench hesitated. 'Excellency, do you think you may wish to advise Major Ross of that instruction? It will have more authority coming from you... and besides, Major Ross still has me under arrest... technically.'

'Ah, yes, I had forgotten about that. What a ridiculous situation that is. Yes, yes, just ask the major to come and see me as soon as he can.'

'Certainly, sir. Thank you.'

# Chapter 31

# Birrabirragal, Late May 1788

A small group of local warriors stood within the shelter of the tree line, observing events at the visitors' camp. They watched as the visitors continued with one of the main activities they had pursued since they had first set up their camp a few months earlier – clearing the land. When they had arrived, they had focussed on the vegetation in the small cove on the ocean side of Birrabirragal. They had then planted some strange seeds into the Mother Earth while the locals watched on. Now, the strangers continued to clear even more land, including a wide variety of food plants that were so much a part of the locals' diet. One of the few plants they usually left in place was the sweet tea that the locals had seen the visitors picking at various times.

'Do you know why they're pulling out all that good tucker?' Arabanoo asked Colbee, who was standing beside him.

'I have no idea. These are very strange people. They seem to have no respect for the Mother Earth and the tucker she provides.'

The group continued watching while intermittently discussing the strange ways of the visitors before wandering back along the water's edge to where their canoes were hidden.

As they retrieved their canoes from under some bushes, Bennelong muttered, 'These people… we should have just driven them away when they first landed. Now we have to hide our canoes so they don't steal them, like they steal everything else. Our weapons, our tools. Everything they can get their greedy hands on.'

Colbee nodded. 'Yes, it is most strange that they steal our weapons and tools when their own are much better than ours.'

'They are just greedy,' responded Bennelong bitterly.

Arabanoo thought for a moment before asking, 'Colbee, why is it that we can just share everything we need and these strangers steal things that they don't need, things that must be worthless to them?'

Colbee also thought for a moment before responding, 'I don't know, but hopefully, as we have killed those two thieves that stole the canoes, they will now understand how our system of payback works and they will stop stealing things from us. Things that we really need.'

# CHAPTER 32

# SYDNEY COVE, 24 JUNE 1788

It was early evening, and an exhausted Watkin Tench was sitting slumped on the edge of his stretcher bed in his partly completed little house. He'd had to spend a fair amount of his time working on it as a labourer, assisting a couple of the convict artisans, who were providing the building skills. Tench may have been able to speak Latin and quote Shakespeare and Voltaire ad nauseum, but they were not skills that helped build a house. It was a situation in which many of the officers found themselves – providing labour for skilled lower-ranked soldiers or convicts. Consequently, there were several officers who were still living in tents as winter set in. As for the unskilled convicts – they were set the most laborious and demanding of tasks.

Tench heard the voice of his friend William Dawes outside his makeshift canvas door.

'Watkin, are you there?'

'Yes, Will. Come in.'

Dawes entered, and Tench immediately noticed he had a piece of paper in his hand.

'What have you there?'

'It's something quite depressing, I'm sorry to say. Interesting, but depressing,' Dawes replied.

'Oh, depressing! Lovely. Just what we all need. You think this place isn't depressing enough, with the crops failing, cattle wandering off into the bush, never to be found, and dingoes killing sheep? Do you really think we need something else to depress us?'

Tench ranted only half-seriously, though, because despite the never-ending list of problems confronting the colony, it still was not sufficient to completely overwhelm his innate optimism.

'It is just incredible, isn't it?' said Dawes. 'No-one could have dreamt of all the things that have gone wrong with this colony in just six months.'

'I'm sure the authorities in London didn't dream of it, or we wouldn't be here… or they would have at least sent out a supply ship by now,' Tench responded.

'Do you think they care?' Dawes responded, joining his friend's gloom. 'We're on the other side of the world. Does it matter to them if we all starve to death?'

'I certainly hope so, and I hope they send a supply ship soon,' Tench responded, before immediately picking up his overt mood. 'Anyway, enough of that depressing talk. What piece of news do you have to depress us with all over again?'

'Well, you are aware that we have yet another hanging tomorrow morning, aren't you?'

'Of course. The two convicts who, instead of celebrating the King's Birthday with the rest of us, decided it would be a good opportunity to do some thieving from the officers' marquee.'

'Yes, exactly. And what I have here is a letter written by one of those convicts, a chap named Samuel Peyton, to his mother. He is illiterate, so he dictated it to one of the literate convicts, but it is a most sad and tragic correspondence.'

'May I see it?'

Dawes handed the letter to Tench, who read quietly by the flickering light of the two candles in his tent.

*My dear and honoured mother! With what agony of soul do I dedicate the last few moments of my life to bid you an eternal adieu, my doom being irrevocably fixed, and ere this hour tomorrow I shall have quitted this vale of wretchedness to enter an unknown and endless eternity. I will not distress your tender maternal feelings by any long comment on the cause of my present misfortune. Let it therefore suffice to say that impelled by that strong propensity to evil which neither the virtues nor example of the best parents could eradicate, I have at length fallen an unhappy, though just, victim to my own follies.*

*Too late I regret my inattention to your admonitions, and feel myself sensibly affected by the remembrance of the many anxious moments you have passed on my account. For these and all my other transgressions, however great, I supplicate the divine forgiveness; and encouraged by the promises of that Saviour who died for us all, I trust to receive that mercy in the world to come which my offences have deprived me of all hope or expectation of in this. The affliction which this will cost you to bear! Banish from your memory all my former indiscretions, and let the cheering hope of a happy meeting hereafter console you for my loss. Sincerely penitent for my sins, sensible of the justice of my conviction and sentence, and firmly relying on the merits of a Blessed Redeemer, I am at perfect peace with all mankind, and trust I shall yet experience that peace which this world cannot give. Commend my soul to the divine mercy. I bid you an eternal farewell.*

*Your unhappy dying Son,*
*Samuel Peyton.*

Tench let the letter drop into his lap and looked at Dawes, hesitating before he spoke.

'Imagine his poor mother, receiving that letter in several months' time. She will be heartbroken.'

Dawes nodded. 'Yes, it would be enough to shatter any mother.'

'It just shows, though... Well, actually, it provides several revelations. Firstly, it reveals so well the depth of feeling of a person confronted with execution, even when that person is what many would term a lowly convict.'

Dawes cut in, 'Exactly, and many in our society would not believe them capable of such depth of feeling.'

Tench nodded. 'Hmmm, and it also shows the terror of the death sentence that we so readily impose in our society. I mean, how is that poor lad feeling tonight? He must be physically ill with terror knowing the morning will see a rope put around his neck and the life strangled out of him.'

'A terrifying thought.' Dawes nodded. 'And it also shows the benefit of his faith in God. At such a time, the only hope he can cling to is his faith in the Redeemer. What would he have without that faith?'

'Nothing, absolutely nothing. I certainly hope my faith would stand up in such circumstances, as I'm sure yours would, Will.'

'Yes, I certainly believe it would.'

Tench paused and looked down again at the letter on his lap. 'Would you mind leaving this with me for a short time? I would like to copy it, as I think I can certainly find a place for it in my book.'

'Of course, of course. I think your readers will find it of great interest.'

*Ref. 25*

## CHAPTER 33

## SYDNEY COVE, 13 JULY 1788

John Hunter had just arrived on board the *Alexander*, where he was welcomed by Lieutenant John Shortland, who was the naval agent in charge of the fleet's transport ships. Shortland had had a very significant role in preparing the ships for the voyage and had worked closely with Hunter in that capacity. The pair had developed a firm friendship in the time they had known each other.

The *Alexander* was the largest ship in the fleet and was leading the fleet transports *Friendship* and *Prince of Wales* and the store ship *Borrowdale* on the return voyage to England. Hunter was checking all was organised for their departure the next morning, as well as saying his goodbyes to Shortland and his crew. It wasn't long before the two men were locked in conversation over a mug of rum on the serious issues of their voyage, the route to be taken and the health of the crew.

'Now, tell me, have you fixed on your route yet?' inquired Hunter.

'Yes, I have. Now, I know you believe we should go around the Horn, but it's just at this time of year, with the ice and the weather down there, I feel it is a better option to sail north to Batavia, where I'll be able to get fresh food for the crew. As you well know, with their diet being so inadequate here, and some in the colony already showing early signs of the scurvy, I'm very concerned that it won't be long before my crew start showing signs of it.'

'I understand your thinking perfectly, but it's just that I believe you can reach the Cape of Good Hope significantly faster than you can via Batavia, and aye, I understand fully the issues of sailing round the Horn at this time of year.'

'But you believe it is worth the risk?'

'Look, sailing around the Horn is never easy, no matter what time of year. Of course, the ice and gales are worse during this southern winter, but it is so much faster, which is crucial – especially when, as you say, you're concerned about the health of the crew.'

'Surely, though, you can see the benefit of sailing north towards the tropical sun rather than south into the ice.'

'Aye, that is a very natural feeling, and it's your ship and your crew, so it is entirely your decision. I understand the benefits of sailing north and the risks of sailing south.'

'Thank you. I think I'll leave my final decision until we are at sea and I can determine what the prevailing winds are doing.'

Hunter nodded, knowing full well that he had not persuaded Shortland, but his friend was too polite and respectful to say so to his face. He thought, though, that he may still offer one last piece of advice.

'One thing I should stress, though, is if you do decide to sail around the Horn, don't be tempted to sail up the coast to Rio de Janeiro. Use the wind and get across to the Cape of Good Hope. It will be so much faster.'

'Thank you, I will.' Shortland smiled.

Hunter finished his last mouthful of rum and got to his feet, as did Shortland.

'Whichever way you go, I hope all goes well for you.' Hunter looked him in the eye and added, 'Good luck, my friend.'

Shortland smiled as he shook Hunter's hand. 'Thank you, John.'

A few minutes later, as Hunter was rowed away across the moonlit waters of the cove, he and Shortland exchanged informal salutes as they called best wishes to each other. Little could either man dream of the tragic circumstances that would lead to them being reunited some seven months later.

*Ref. 26*

# Chapter 34

# Sydney Cove, 20 July 1788

Watkin Tench and William Dawes again stood on the shore of Sydney Cove with a cold southerly breeze at their backs. They watched in silence as sails cruised down harbour towards the just-risen sun and out towards the open ocean. Most recently, they had watched as the *Alexander* led three other ships to return to England. Tench and Dawes had shared a range of emotions at their departure, including an increasing feeling of isolation, looking at the rapidly emptying cove. It was vastly different now to the bustling little place it had been in the first few months, when all eleven ships of the fleet were anchored there. Now only three remained. Then, the shores had been full of people unloading stores and equipment before preparing the ships for their return voyage. Currently, however, the immediate foreshore was almost deserted, as works were focussed on building the wide variety of infrastructure necessary for the colony, including storehouses, marine barracks, convict huts, roads and the imposing governor's mansion. Building materials were either timber or brick, depending on the importance and security requirements of the respective building.

This morning in the cove, it was the *Supply* that Tench and Dawes watched while the southerly breeze filled its sails. It was on its way to Norfolk Island, which had been charted and named by Captain Cook in 1774, and on which Lieutenant Phillip Gidley King had been ordered by Phillip to establish a small colony.

'I wonder how Lieutenant King and his colony are going?' pondered Tench.

'Hopefully, he's finding the soil more suitable for crops than it is here.'

Tench nodded as he responded, 'The governor mentioned yesterday that he is likely to have to reduce rations again shortly.'

'Not again.' Dawes shook his head. 'I think we gained a somewhat false sense of security about this place when we arrived during summer. The fish were plentiful, and it was wet and warm, so we thought our crops would thrive. Now, though, the fish stocks have dropped dramatically, and the soil is so poor it wouldn't matter how much sun and rain we have.'

'No manure doesn't help either,' added Tench.

'Exactly.' Dawes paused briefly before adding, 'So let's hope these expeditions the governor is planning to Broken Bay and to the west can find some suitable land.'

'Mmmm, indeed. Apparently, the soil in this Rosehill area is more promising, so the sooner we can start farming there, the better. Seriously, though, as we have discussed before, there were some very serious oversights in establishing this colony.'

Dawes nodded as Tench continued, 'How could they propose to establish a farming-based colony when they sent out ploughs, but no bullocks or draft horses to pull them? So, it's not just the lack of fertile soil, it's our inability to till and fertilise it properly that's the problem.'

Tench was about to continue, but Dawes jumped in. 'And some convicts with farming experience would have been of assistance too.'

'Yes, we have plenty of convicts with vast sailing experience, but sadly, they are useless when it comes to farming,' added Tench.

'But whose fault is this mess? The governor's, the Home Office's? I don't really know.'

'Well, I wouldn't blame Phillip too much. At least he ensured we had enough ammunition, which is more than Ross could do! The incompetent bully.'

'Spoken like a man who he still has under arrest,' mocked Dawes.

'Very funny, Will. He's just too stubborn to accept how ridiculous that situation is and allow common sense to apply.' Tench paused before continuing with more elevated spirits, 'Anyway, may we move off the subject of Ross and the incompetence of the organisation of this colony and return to the subject we touched on a moment ago? The matter of exploring the country to the west of Rosehill?'

'Of course.' Dawes nodded.

Tench continued, 'I wanted to mention, I hope we both have the opportunity to go along on those expeditions. I really fancy the idea of going where no white man has been before and perhaps discovering a magnificent river with a vast flood plain.'

'Yes, that would be most exciting, but whoever discovers such a river, if indeed there is one out there, would help save the colony.'

'They most certainly would,' enthused Tench.

The two British marines stood pondering the future for themselves and the colony as they watched the *Supply* disappear from view.

'Doesn't it make you feel just so isolated?' murmured Tench.

'Scarily so, in fact.' Dawes nodded.

As they were about to turn away to continue with their daily duties, Tench hesitated and again looked towards the harbour's entrance.

'What are you looking at, Watkin?' Dawes inquired.

'Just hoping against hope that we might see a supply ship from England.'

'Well, you could waste your whole day doing that,' Dawes responded as he wandered away, towards the beginnings of the humble little High Street, which ran south, away from the western shore of the cove.

*Ref. 27*

# CHAPTER 35

# SYDNEY COVE, 12 AUGUST 1788

A twenty-one-gun salute had marked the start of celebrations of the birthday of His Royal Highness, the Prince of Wales, and just as on the birthday of His Majesty King George two months earlier, the officers were dining with the governor. Fortunately, the torrential rain that had been falling for the past two weeks had finally stopped. It had only added to the woes of the infant colony, as it had not only caused almost all work to cease, but it had also extensively damaged the works that were already complete.

Despite the general shortage of food, which saw some drawing slowly closer to starvation and outbreaks of scurvy due to a lack of fresh fruit and vegetables, there was no lack of food on the table for such a celebration. Although fish stocks were much lower than they had been in summer, there were sufficient to more than adequately feed the thirty men gathered around the governor's table. Fresh kangaroo meat was also provided, courtesy of the governor's greyhounds, which had again run down a mid-sized grey kangaroo early that morning. The meal was another most welcome change from the salt rations that were making up an ever-increasing part of their diet, so much so that they felt they may as well be back onboard ship.

After the celebratory toasts that marked the occasion, it wasn't long before the conversation turned to the parlous state of the colony due to the numerous misfortunes, the damaging rain included, that had befallen it since they had landed. The deaths of many of the sheep from either eating 'rank grass' or from dingo attack had come on top of the disappearance of the several cattle that had strayed into the bush without trace, despite numerous search attempts. Apart from their importance for their own meat and as breeding stock, the livestock were crucial for their manure. There were also the failed attempts to hunt turtles at Lord Howe Island and numerous other food-seeking excursions that had come to nothing. If that all wasn't bad enough, just to completely flatten the spirits of even the most optimistic colonist, the sole surviving cow had had to be shot because it had turned wild and dangerous. The fact that the whole issue was the dominant topic of conversation therefore was no surprise to Tench.

'It is quite apparent, gentlemen,' Phillip began to those seated around him, 'that we are going to have to look at every available option to keep this colony going and ensure its long-term survival.'

Those seated closest to the governor included Major Robert Ross, Lieutenant George Johnston, Hunter, Tench and Dawes. The latter pair normally avoided the company of Ross, but on formal occasions such as this, it was impossible without being conspicuously rude.

Hunter was first to respond. 'Aye, Excellency, and as you have already suggested to me, one of those options may be sending me to Cape Town in the *Sirius* to pick up supplies to at least keep us sustained for the short term.'

'Well, I think it may come to that, but I hope not. There are just so many risks involved. To start with, it will take you many months to make such a trip, and excuse me for saying so, but it is also an extremely hazardous voyage.'

'Aye, Excellency, but I believe I could do the return journey, assuming reasonable winds, in seven or eight months, if I were to sail eastward around Cape Horn.'

'As quickly as that? It took us eight months to sail out here, so that would be remarkable if you could, but Cape Horn? Really? That would only make it even more hazardous.'

The four marines listening to the conversation did not wish to intervene in a discussion about such naval matters, but Ross couldn't help himself.

'I'm sorry, Captain, but with all due respect, I think we need to come up with a better option than you sailing around Cape Horn aboard the *Sirius*, our lifeline to the outside world.'

Hunter was somewhat affronted by Ross's comments, but he remained calm, as always, and he replied, 'Major, I am very aware of how important the *Sirius* is to the colony, but food is also vital. I must confess I'm a wee bit disappointed you have such little faith in my navigational skills. I believe it is an option we need to seriously consider, and the sooner we do, the better.'

Phillip quickly responded to ensure the argumentative Ross did not have a chance to do so. 'And consider it I will, at the appropriate time. But for now, let's focus on trying to find some immediate solutions here. We must get expeditions going to the north to Broken Bay and to the west beyond Rosehill. And we must also get farming established at Rosehill.'

'Yes, definitely, sir,' responded Ross. 'As you know, though, to establish farms out there, we will need to establish a settlement with a detachment of marines, because I imagine the natives be just as treacherous and dangerous out there as they be here.'

A brief silence fell over the group, and Dawes was about to respond before the governor replied, 'Speaking of our friends the natives, they themselves are another very serious problem that we must find a solution to.'

'I've told you my solution several times, sir,' Ross responded. 'We simply have to wipe them out and drive them right away from any area in which we have a settlement.'

'Yes, yes, I know your view, Major, but that would be totally contrary to my orders, and…' Phillip paused for a moment, and so Dawes joined in.

'Excuse me interrupting, Excellency, but it is hardly reasonable, moral behaviour from us as a civilised society.'

'Civilised we may be, Lieutenant,' Ross sneered, 'but they be a bunch of savages, and the sooner we can exterminate them so our colony can grow and further expand our civilisation, the better.'

Dawes was about to respond, but Tench grabbed his arm and stopped him, while Phillip replied, 'Major, apart from my orders and the good Lieutenant's understandable moral concerns, I also have a very practical concern. What about their numbers? We really have no idea how many of them are out there. All we know is that Cook and Banks were completely wrong in their statements that the coast was only sparsely populated. As we have discussed on various occasions previously, we know there are hundreds and hundreds of them, but how many exactly, we have no idea. Nor do we know anything about where they all live. I fear if we started open warfare against them, we might just find they overwhelm us by sheer force of numbers.'

'Aye, sir, but as I have said before, I believe our far superior weaponry and battle tactics would completely decimate them, and as you know, I have been agitating for the construction of some sort of fortification for the colony since we landed. Not only for protection from the natives, but what about the French, if we go to war again with them?'

Tench hated himself for it, but on Ross's final point, he had to agree. He remained silent, though, as Lieutenant Johnston joined in.

'I must say, Excellency, I do have to agree with the major on the matter of fortifications–'

Phillip cut him off. 'Gentlemen, please. I agree with you completely, but it is all a matter of priorities. What is the good of having strong fortifications if we've all starved to death in the process of building them? All our efforts at this time have to be directed to developing a reliable food supply.'

All in the conversation nodded their agreement... except for Ross, who muttered, 'Starve or get speared by the natives.'

'Gentlemen,' Phillip continued, 'I do think it would be very worthwhile for us to try to undertake some sort of census of the natives to attempt to get a better understanding of their numbers.'

'Aye, sir, that sounds like a commendable idea, in theory,' Hunter responded, 'but I think it may prove impossible to put into practice, given the habits of the natives. I mean, we have seen hundreds together at a time on a few occasions, but we don't know how wide an area they come from, or even if they are the same people we keep seeing in different locations.'

'Well, I think it would be certainly worthwhile trying to find out,' added Ross.

Phillip paused for a moment while he fed a morsel of kangaroo to his white greyhound, which sat on the floor beside him. Then he concluded the conversation with, 'Alright, gentlemen, let's discuss it in the morning, but for now, let's relax and enjoy the evening.'

While the conversation turned to more menial topics, Tench allowed his mind to drift as he took in the full beauty of the setting. The officers were all seated at a series of tables that had been placed together to form one extended table outside the governor's canvas house. It was located towards the top of the hill on the eastern side of the cove, adjacent to where the governor's permanent residence was under construction. Warming fires burnt strongly on either side of the table, which had flickering lamps scattered along its length. The location commanded an excellent view over the infant colony surrounding the cove, upon the waters of which frolicked the reflections of the celebratory fires on the western shore.

Tench looked to the north, across the full expanse of the harbour, to see it gently illuminated by the tender light of the full moon as it peered out from behind a small cloud. To add to the atmosphere, above the clamour of the conversation at the table, Tench could clearly hear the sound of Surgeon George Worgan at his piano. As the sublime notes drifted across the water, Tench quietly asked the one man at the table he was sure would know about the tune's composer. After Hunter advised him it was a little-known German composer named

Johann Sebastian Bach and the piece was titled Minuet in G Major, Tench stood up and ambled away from the table to allow himself to hear the music more clearly above the din of the table talk.

A short distance away, he sat down on the earth of the Gadigal and drank in the night. The poet in Tench admired the splendour. The man in Tench longed for a woman with whom to share it.

*Ref. 28*

## Chapter 36

## Sydney Cove, 17 August 1788

John Hunter and Lieutenant George Johnston of the marines sat in the back of one of the four longboats that were dispatched after Phillip had fixed on the idea of undertaking a census of the natives around the shores of Port Jackson. Their orders were not only to count the men, women and children separately but also to count the canoes they saw.

Hunter and Johnston's boat proceeded across the harbour to the northern side, and they began exploring every cove they encountered. Although the rain squalls that had prevailed for the past couple of days had now ceased, the cold southerly wind remained strong, and the longboat rocked as it cut through the choppy surface of the harbour.

As they rounded a headland that protected the enclosed cove from the wind, they were immediately struck by the sight of a large group of canoes gathered about fifty metres off from the sandy head of the cove. As soon as the canoes' occupants saw the British, they picked up their paddles and quickly began heading for the shore.

'They must be women,' Hunter observed to Johnston, straining his eyes to confirm his suspicion.

'Because of the way they are fleeing from us?' replied Johnston.

'Aye, Lieutenant. Their men wouldn't normally be reacting like that.'

Hunter turned his attention to the fleeing canoes and began waving as he called, 'Hello. We mean no harm.'

He immediately directed the oarsmen to follow the canoes towards the shore. As they did so, Hunter continued to make all the signals of friendship that he could think of to the fleeing locals while instructing his men to leave their weapons out of sight on the bottom of the boat.

As they drew closer to the shore, they watched as the occupants of the canoes hurried across the beach, past a large group of their countrymen, and disappeared into the bush beyond. The group of local men on the beach immediately began waving friendly greetings to Hunter and his crew.

'Hello,' Hunter called as he waved back before he instructed the crew to stop the boat a short distance from the shore. The tribal men continued waving and beckoning to the visitors as they wandered closer to the water's edge.

'It seems they want us to come ashore, Captain,' offered Johnston.

'Aye, clearly, but unfortunately, we don't really have time for that. Our instructions are to count them and to complete our survey of our section of the harbour.'

Hunter waved his apologies. 'Sorry, sorry, we can't today.'

At that moment, Hunter noticed one of local tribesmen place his spear in his spear thrower.

'Did you see that?' he asked Johnston.

'See what, sir?'

'The tall one on the left just set to throw his spear,' Hunter replied in a tone that revealed anxiety and confusion.

The words were no sooner out of Hunter's mouth than the local tribesman hurled his spear at them.

'Look out!' Hunter yelled to his crew, and although it was only a couple of seconds, his mind had time to watch the spear in flight as it hurtled towards him. His mind also had time to process a dozen thoughts that included those of his own mortality. The thought that dominated his mind in those moments, though, was one of total confusion as to why the warrior had thrown the spear at them.

His reflex of self-preservation enabled him to duck as the spear sailed over his head. As it did so, he felt a wave of relief flow through his body. It was immediately replaced by the fire of anger as the normally placid Hunter quickly grabbed his gun from the bottom of the boat, aimed above the natives' heads and pulled the trigger as they fled across the beach. The gun misfired, though, and Hunter threw it back to the bottom of the boat in frustration.

Johnston raised his musket to his shoulder and took careful aim as the locals reached the tree line. He pulled the trigger, and the small shot with which it was loaded scattered amongst the trees into which the locals had fled.

'Did I hit any of them, sir?' Johnston asked.

'I don't know, but that small shot won't have done them any real harm from this distance, anyway.' Hunter's calmness was already returning as he added, 'Which is a good thing. We're not here to shoot the natives.'

Hunter instructed the sailors to row away before he turned to Johnston. 'Now, Mr Johnston, can you tell me what that was all about?'

'I have no idea, sir. They seemed as friendly as can be.'

'Aye, for sure, but one thing that's clear is they simply don't want us here. But perhaps, also, they felt they were protecting their women.'

*Ref. 29*

# Chapter 37

# Sydney Cove, 27 August 1788

John Hunter and Major Robert Ross sat in front of Phillip's desk discussing the latest tragedy to befall the young colony, the loss of five lives when a longboat from the *Supply* was overturned by waves while attempting to land on Norfolk Island.

'It is just such a tragedy. Mr Cunningham was a fine man,' Hunter opined.

'Yes, yes, so I understand,' said Phillip. 'The other concern for us, though, is just how dangerous it is trying to land on Norfolk.'

'Aye, Excellency. From all reports, it is extremely dangerous, as there be simply no reasonable harbour there at all.'

'We need the timber and the flax, but most importantly, as you well know, the soil there is proving far more fertile than we have so far discovered here. So, at this time, it is just vital for the survival of our colony.'

Hunter and Ross both nodded as Phillip continued, 'Unfortunately, we simply must take the risk, for the time being at least.'

'Aye, agreed, sir,' said Hunter.

'Now, Captain, I also want to advise you that unless there is some dramatic change in our fortunes here, I do believe that I will shortly be asking you to take that voyage to the Cape of Good Hope for supplies.'

'Aye, sir, I expected as much from our recent discussions. It is just so disappointing that there has been no sign of the store ships from England we were so hoping for.'

'*Disappointing* would be an understatement,' Phillip stated flatly. 'Anyway, we must deal with the situation as it is.'

'Of course, sir.'

'Now, Surgeon White advised me yesterday that the health of many of the convicts is in a parlous state, with malnutrition and scurvy increasing alarmingly,' said Phillip.

'Aye, and even some of the lower ranks of my marines are beginning to suffer,' added Ross.

'So I feared, Major.' Phillip paused and looked at Hunter. 'Captain, I will need you to be prepared at short notice, so you should consider what you can remove from the *Sirius* to lighten it and create as much room as possible for the stores.'

'Aye, sir.' Hunter nodded.

Phillip paused again and sat forward in his chair.

'Now, gentlemen, onto the matter of the natives and how we can best resolve our problems with them and keep our people safe. Firstly, it is clear my little survey last week to count their numbers was a complete waste of time and resources. What were the numbers again, Major?'

Ross didn't need to refer to the papers in front of him. He had memorised the numbers and immediately replied, 'Sixty-seven canoes, ninety-four men, thirty-four women and nine children, sir.'

'Yes, well, we all know that does not reflect their numbers in any way, as we have all seen many more than that together in one place on numerous occasions.'

'Regardless of the numbers, sir, I repeat I believe we need to take action against them to drive them right away from the areas of our settlement,' offered Ross.

'I am well aware of your view, but I don't believe it is that simple,' replied Phillip. 'To start with, as I have advised on numerous occasions, that would be entirely contrary to my orders, and secondly, on a purely practical level, we are now looking at establishing a farming settlement at Rosehill. What do we do? Do we drive them away from there, as well? And from all the country in between, through which we will have to travel back and forth?'

'Aye, sir,' replied Ross. 'We need to do all we can to ensure the safety of our people and the future of this colony, and we cannot do that when we have savages attacking our people at random.'

'Major, we need firstly to try to understand why they do so sometimes, while at other times they are perfectly friendly and peaceful. You know full well my recent experience with the natives with Captain Tench. They could have slaughtered us as easily as can be, had they wished to, and they didn't. So, we must somehow gain an understanding of them and why their behaviour towards us varies so much.'

Ross said nothing, so Hunter responded, 'Sir, it is a sound idea, but how do you propose we do that when they currently avoid our settlement? Only rarely do we have the opportunity to meet them and hold any sort of discussion.'

'I have been giving that some careful consideration. What if we were to capture a couple of the natives and hold them here with us until such time as they learn our language and we learn something of theirs? We can then learn about their customs and why their attitude to us is as it is.'

'Capture, sir?' replied Hunter, somewhat surprised. 'You mean abduct them and hold them prisoner?'

'I wouldn't express it in quite those terms, but yes, that is in effect how it would operate.' Phillip paused for a moment before adding, 'It would only be so that we can help them understand that we mean no harm... so I think it is something we should consider.'

'Sir, do you believe that a native who is being held prisoner will want to cooperate with us and learn English or teach us their language?' queried Hunter.

'I'm sure once they resign themselves to their situation, they will cooperate.'

Ross now rejoined the conversation. 'Sir, I simply do not believe that these savages would have the intellect to learn the English language. Simple as that.'

'Well, if that is the case, Major, we will learn theirs. It should be very basic, don't you think?'

Ross gave one of his usual mirthless smiles before replying, 'Sir, I think it would be far simpler and more effective to just eliminate them or drive them away. If you don't wish to risk all-out warfare with them due to their numbers, we could simply release the smallpox amongst them. They wouldn't know what it was, and they certainly wouldn't know we were responsible.'

'Major, really? We certainly won't be doing that.'

'Why not, sir? We used it against the Americans in their revolution, and these savages would have even less resistance.'

'Major, I have said we will not be doing that. And I shan't discuss it further. Now, if there is nothing else, I'll let you gentlemen get on with your days.'

*Ref. 30*

# CHAPTER 38

# SYDNEY COVE, 30 SEPTEMBER 1788

John Hunter again sat in front of the governor's desk to receive his final orders for his voyage to Cape Town. This time, instead of being accompanied by Major Ross, his right-hand man Lieutenant Bradley sat beside him.

'Captain, is everything in order for your departure tomorrow?' Phillip inquired, with a sense of stress and urgency creeping into his tone.

'Aye, Excellency. It is all done. My only concern is around the absence of the carpenter in recent times. With him being required for duties onshore, the carpentry on the *Sirius* has been a little neglected.'

'Have you been able to undertake the essentials to ensure its safety?'

'Aye, I believe so. I certainly hope so, but it is hardly an ideal situation, sir.'

'Yes, hardly ideal. And what have you been able to dispense with to lighten the vessel?' inquired Phillip.

'We removed eight cannons with their carriages, and the twenty-four pound of shot with each. Also, twenty half-barrels of powder, a spare anchor and various other miscellaneous items, sir.'

'Good, good.' Phillip nodded. 'Now, there is something else I would like you to leave behind.'

Hunter's brow furrowed slightly as he inquired, 'Aye, and what would that be, sir?'

'Well, I need you to leave the ship's longboat,' Phillip advised almost hesitantly.

'Sir, really?' Hunter responded as he glanced at Bradley, who looked quite aghast.

'Yes, Captain... Look, I understand your reaction perfectly. I believe I would feel exactly the same if I were in your position... but we need the longboat here in the colony for so many reasons that I'm sure I don't need to explain to you.'

'Sir, I understand that the colony needs it, but to undertake a voyage of this size and importance without a longboat, especially when we will be taking minimum provisions with us anyway... Not to mention that the crew are not in the best of health.'

'I'm very aware of the poor health not just of your crew, but of everyone in the colony, and I regret enormously that I have to dispatch you on this voyage with your crew in poor health and without a longboat, but unfortunately, that is the position in which we find ourselves. And if we are to avoid the tragic failure of this colony and associated loss of life, I need you to do it.'

Hunter thought for just a moment, but it was long enough for him to realise the difficult position that both he and Phillip were in. Phillip needed the longboat to help catch fish to feed the colony and for numerous other odd tasks, so he decided not to press his case.

'Aye, sir, I understand,' he responded. 'Whatever you believe is best, sir.'

'Thank you,' a relieved Phillip replied. The last thing he wanted was to have the man whose mission it was to save the colony from disaster leaving with a bitter, resentful attitude. Phillip knew Hunter well by now, though, and knew he was too good a naval officer not to embrace the challenge of such a vital voyage.

The three men sat in silence briefly before Phillip spoke first. 'And, Captain, are you still fixed on taking an eastward passage around Cape Horn?'

'Aye, sir. I know you believe sailing west is by far the shortest route and therefore the best, but I believe using the strong westerly winds at the high latitudes will ensure a much faster voyage to the east.'

'I'll leave that entirely up to you. You know my view – sailing west is an unproven route, but it is so much shorter. If you have any fortune at all with the winds, it must get you there in far less time.'

'Aye, sir. I won't make a final decision until we are well at sea and can take account of the prevailing winds.'

Hunter was mindful that this was exactly what his friend John Shortland had said to him prior to his departure for his return voyage to England. He was also sure that when Shortland left the harbour, he would have gone exactly where he always intended to go – to the north. Hunter knew he would also do exactly as he intended and sail east around the Horn.

'Good idea, Captain, and I'm sure you'll make the correct decision. I must say that I really have no idea why I'm giving you any advice at all, particularly after the way you completely outsailed me on the voyage here.'

'I wouldn't say that, sir. I think I just picked up some lucky breezes,' replied Hunter.

'Kind of you to say, but we both know that isn't really true.' Phillip smiled.

'Sir, we would be honoured if you would come on board and dine with us tomorrow evening while we sail to the entrance of Port Jackson, and then we can leave the harbour and begin our voyage first thing the next morning.'

'Thank you, Captain. I'd be delighted to join you.'

*Ref. 31*

# Chapter 39

# Sydney Cove, 1 October 1788

Almost the entire population of just over nine hundred people within the colony were given leave from their duties to gather on the shores of Sydney Cove and watch the *Sirius* weigh anchor. Every one of those watching was fully aware of just how important its voyage was to be for the survival of the colony as a whole and for them as individuals. Their feelings of desperate hope were only exacerbated by the sight of the almost-empty cove in front of them. There were again only three ships at anchor, with the *Supply* having returned from its voyage to Norfolk Island at the end of August. All in the colony were fully aware that with only those ships, even if they wanted to abandon the struggling colony and return to England, they simply couldn't do so. They were stuck.

Tench and Dawes were amongst the gathered crowd and shared similar feelings to the masses.

'What do you think their chances are, Watkin?' asked Dawes, seeking reassurance.

'Well, perhaps I can put it this way: if I had to select someone to sail for my life, it would be Captain Hunter.'

'Agreed, and that is precisely what he's doing. I just hope we are all still alive if or when he returns,' Dawes pondered.

'Hopefully, Phillip will just keep cutting rations to ensure we are.'

'The challenge then will be maintaining discipline in a colony where all are starving, including us officers. I would suggest that will be extremely difficult.'

'Hmmm.' Tench nodded.

Both men stood in silence for a few moments, watching as the *Sirius* slowly disappeared around the point of the cove.

'On a somewhat lighter, more positive note, did you get any more of your manuscript finished?'

'Thanks for asking, Will. I have just sent a brief postscript with Captain Hunter this morning to take to the Cape of Good Hope, but as you know, the bulk of it I sent in July with Lieutenant Shortland on the fleet ships. Hopefully, they are having a safe passage, and it will be well on its way by now.'

'I'm sure they are, and that's wonderful that it's going to be published,' Dawes enthused.

'I'm still continuing on with the rest of it, though, to encompass the remainder of my stay in the colony.' Tench paused before adding, 'I must say that I am finding the whole process most enjoyable and rewarding.'

'Pleased to hear it. We all need something to relieve the tedium in this place. I have the wonders of the night sky, and you have your writing.'

'Yes, well, that doesn't mean I don't miss some of the distractions of London at night, and living the life of a marine means I have spent far too little of my life there.'

'But you've seen the world,' offered Dawes.

'I do enjoy seeing different parts of the world, but I enjoy it far more when people aren't shooting at me and I'm not hungry the whole time.'

'Oh, you're so hard to please,' mocked Dawes.

Tench shook his head with a smile before calling down harbour, 'Good luck, Captain Hunter!'

*Ref. 32*

## Chapter 40

## Off the South Coast of New South Wales, October 1788

The wind and rain that had been plaguing the colony in recent weeks had returned, and the *Sirius* was sailing almost straight into it as she headed south, away from Port Jackson. Hunter and Bradley stood on the quarterdeck, scanning the horizon for any break in the weather, as the *Sirius* ploughed its way through the rapidly increasing swell. They were deep in conversation when they were joined by James Heatherly, one of the ship's carpenters.

'Aye, Mr Heatherly, what is it?' inquired Hunter.

'I beg your pardon, Captain, but I need to acquaint you with the fact that the ship has begun taking water,' Heatherly advised rather hesitantly, holding onto his hat as a sudden squall hit the ship.

'What? Really?' Hunter responded, glancing at Bradley.

'Yes, I regret to say it is, sir.'

'She has always been perfectly watertight in the past. How has this happened?'

'We are not sure yet, sir,' Heatherly replied apologetically. 'We are just working on finding out the precise nature of the problem and working out if we can repair it, but I thought we should let you know straight away.'

'Aye, of course, Mr Heatherly. Now, if you would return below decks and continue your work, but please keep me informed of your progress.'

'Yes, sir,' mumbled Heatherly as he hurried back below deck.

Hunter shook his head. 'Well, that's most concerning, just a day into our voyage.'

'Yes, Captain,' responded Bradley. 'Most concerning, sir. Hardly a promising start. This dirty weather and a leaky ship. I wonder what the cause is?'

'I have no idea, but one thing is certain now – we must sail eastward, around the bottom of New Zealand and around Cape Horn. Despite the governor's preference for a westward route, with a leaky ship, the last course we could consider setting is one to the west, into the wind.'

'I agree completely, but you weren't ever seriously considering the westward course, were you, sir?' inquired Bradley.

'Well, no, not really, but I can now advise the governor that we considered it, but in the circumstances, we had no option but to sail with the wind.'

Bradley smiled through the wind and rain blowing in his face as Hunter continued, 'Now, Mr Bradley, you'll need to get some men onto the pumps immediately while the carpenters try to identify the problem. Given the health of the crew, though, the last thing we need is to have them manning the pumps as well.'

'I agree, sir, but it just has to be done,' replied Bradley, before he quickly left Hunter with the helmsman on the quarterdeck.

\*\*\*

Within a few days, the carpenters had identified the cause of the problem as being the corrosion of one of the butt bolts by the copper just below the surface on the starboard side of the ship. Although it seemed only minor, it was sufficiently serious to allow the ship to take on ten to twelve inches of water every two hours, which the crew were continually required to pump out.

After eight days of sailing parallel to the coast of New South Wales and some two hundred miles out to sea, when it was determined they were parallel with Van Diemen's Land, Hunter steered the *Sirius* to the east and set a course towards the south cape of New Zealand. Bradley stood beside him as the helmsman spun the wheel in the pleasant morning sun.

'Well, personally, Mr Bradley, I found that a little disappointing.'

'How do you mean, sir?' replied Bradley. 'Do you mean the issue with the ship taking water?'

'Aye, but that isn't disappointing, that is most worrying. No, what I found disappointing is the fact that we didn't discover any islands.'

'Oh, yes, sir. Of course.'

'Given that Cook discovered so many islands off the north coast of New Holland, I was certainly hoping we might find some, steering the course that we did to the south.'

'Yes, sir, it would be lovely to add to our knowledge of the southern oceans and perhaps be able to put a name on a new island on the world map,' agreed Bradley.

Hunter didn't answer immediately, but just nodded and smiled at Bradley, because Bradley's comment was exactly what was in his mind. It would really mark him as a great naval explorer if he could discover some new land masses or even a few islands. It would be a crowning glory on his distinguished career.

Finally, he responded, 'Aye, that would be a fine achievement, but we have a far more important purpose on this voyage.'

*Ref. 33*

## Chapter 41

## Southern Pacific Ocean, 22 October 1788

For the first time in the ten days since the *Sirius* had sailed below the southern cape of New Zealand, the light variable winds she had been experiencing finally turned to blow strongly from the west. It was enough to put a smile on the strong, weather-beaten face of the ship's captain as he stood on the quarterdeck with Lieutenant Bradley.

Hunter had set his course between those taken across the Pacific some fifteen years earlier by James Cook on his second voyage of discovery aboard the *Resolution* and by the *Adventure*, captained by Tobias Furneaux. They had taken parallel courses across the Pacific, and now, Hunter was steering a course between the two. Despite the fact he was totally focussed on making the return trip to Cape Town as quickly as possible, Hunter still clung to the hope that he may come across undiscovered islands. And hopefully, they might be ones that provided some fresh fruit. He was in a buoyant mood as he began chatting to Bradley.

'Now that is a good feeling, isn't it, Mr Bradley? The wind at our backs. There is nothing quite like it.'

'It certainly is wonderful, Captain. Especially after the last few weeks we've had.'

The two sailors watched as a variety of sea birds, including albatross, petrels and gulls, began swooping and plunging into the water off the starboard side of the ship.

'It is amazing, isn't it, Mr Bradley, how they travel so far from land,'

Hunter the naturalist enthused. 'We would be over three hundred miles from any known land mass where all these birds must nest, yet here they are, out in the middle of the South Pacific, doing a little fishing.'

'Yes, it is quite remarkable, sir.'

'Aye, and how do they find the land mass they want without getting lost? I certainly wish I could navigate like them, without instruments.'

'Now that would be very impressive, sir,' Bradley replied.

The two sailors continued watching the birds and marvelling at their skills of flight before Bradley said, 'You certainly are in a good mood, Captain. Is there a reason for that?'

Hunter looked at his lieutenant and thought for a few moments before replying, 'That is probably a good question. To be honest with you, all I can think is that perhaps I have been feeling the weight of this mission. And then, with the ship taking water and the dirty weather, I was beginning to fear that we may not make it before many in the colony have perished. So, perhaps the change in the breeze has just given me the hope that we may be able to make it in time. And hope is all we have, Mr Bradley. All we have.'

The two men continued watching the aerial acrobatics show for some time before Hunter finally spoke.

'This is so impressive, Mr Bradley, that I think I'll go to my cabin and get my sketchbook and paints.'

'Good idea, sir.'

A few minutes later, Hunter returned and set himself up to capture the spectacle that nature was providing for their entertainment. It was a perfect afternoon for him. He could relax and enjoy two of his great loves, nature and painting, and he could do so with the wind at his back. Hunter wanted to soak it in, because he knew in his sailor's gut that it simply wouldn't last.

*Ref. 34*

## Chapter 42

## Southern Pacific Ocean, 14 November 1788

The three-masted naval war ship *Sirius* had now reached fifty-six degrees south latitude and was heading further south to sail around Cape Horn. Hunter's buoyant mood of three weeks earlier had been blown away by the persistent gales from the Antarctic. The captain and his lieutenant stood beside the helmsman, peering anxiously through the sleet and snow biting at their eyes and restricting their view to just over two hundred yards. This was despite the fact it was the middle of the long daylight period experienced at that high latitude at that time of year.

Hunter was trying to balance the need for a rushed voyage to Cape Town and return with the need to progress slowly, cautiously, to avoid collision with the islands of ice he was expecting to encounter any day now. Despite his many years at sea, Hunter couldn't help the anxiety tying a knot in his stomach. He was wrestling with the conflict between haste and caution when his thoughts were disturbed by Bradley's voice yelling above the noise of the gale.

'Look, sir! Off the starboard bow.'

Hunter looked, fearing the sight of an ice island emerging from the mist. A wave of relief swept over him as he saw a huge humpback whale breach not far from the bow of the ship. It was followed a moment later by another smaller humpback doing the same but far less effectively. Shortly after, the mother and calf repeated their show even closer to the starboard side of the *Sirius*, while all on board watched with a degree of awe and wonder. Then, off the port bow, several more whales appeared, breaking the surface and spouting.

'No matter how often I see those creatures, I am always amazed at their size and their...' Bradley hesitated, searching for the right word.

'Majesty?' offered Hunter.

'Yes, Captain.' Bradley nodded.

'Aye, they certainly are wonderfully majestic creatures,' responded Hunter. The practical sailor in him, though, couldn't help thinking it was a shame they didn't have a harpoon on board as the pod of whales passed in front of the ship. He returned his attention to enjoying the whales' performance and became aware that the knot of anxiety in his stomach had disappeared. He immediately put his mind back on the task at hand and turned his focus to the restricted limits of his view to continue searching for islands of ice.

As he did so, he felt the knot tighten in his stomach.

*Ref. 35*

## CHAPTER 43

## SYDNEY COVE, 19 NOVEMBER 1788

Tench and Dawes stood amongst the small crowd that had gathered on the western shore of the cove to watch the departure of the last two transport ships on their return voyage to England. On this occasion, though, they were joined by their colleague Lieutenant George Johnston, who had undertaken the survey of the local inhabitants with Captain Hunter back in August. At twenty-four, Johnston was a pleasant-looking, strongly built young man who had joined the marines as a ten-year-old to fight alongside his father in the American Revolutionary War. He had been given his commission as a second lieutenant at just twelve years of age due to his father's connections, and he continued fighting in the American War until he was fourteen. The shared experience of fighting in that war gave him something of a bond with Tench.

The three men stood in rather sombre silence for a short time, watching as the two transports sailed down the harbour, before Johnston spoke. 'This is a rather sad day, isn't it, Watkin?'

'It is indeed. One cannot help feeling the isolation now,' replied Tench rather gloomily, running his thumb along the inside of the white diagonal strap of his uniform.

'Total isolation,' added Dawes.

'Almost total,' responded Tench, looking at the *Supply*.

The other two men simultaneously cast their gazes to the tiny naval tender, which at just seventy feet long and one hundred and seventy tons, was the smallest ship in the fleet. It now sat entirely alone in the cove as the colony's solitary link to the outside world.

'Well, it is total for some of us,' Dawes observed. 'There are over nine hundred here, and only a tiny proportion of those would be able to fit on the *Supply* if the decision was made that we had to abandon the settlement.'

Tench nodded. 'Yes, you're right, of course.'

'I wonder how the governor would make the decision about who stayed and who went, if it ever came to that,' pondered Johnston.

'Hmmm, interesting question,' said Tench, 'but I'm not sure which I would want to do. Stay or go.'

'Well, I'd want to go, surely,' responded Johnston, somewhat surprised at Tench's comment.

'Maybe, but look at it this way – by the time the decision was made to go,' Tench explained, 'we would have even less food than we do now, and scurvy is continuing to be an issue, even here on land. You can imagine, then, how bad it will be after a couple of months at sea.'

Dawes joined in. 'Alternatively, we could take our chances here. Hopefully, the new settlement at Rosehill will be producing some worthwhile crops in the near future.'

'Yes,' Tench said, 'but the decision to stay or go will have to be made well before we know whether the crops at Rosehill are successful or not.'

'Mmmm, yes, that is going to be the challenge,' responded Dawes.

The three men returned their gazes to the departing transports as they continued to sail down harbour.

'By the way, George, how are things going between you and your very attractive young convict helper, Esther?' inquired Tench.

Johnston hesitated briefly before answering, 'Well. Very well, really. She is most helpful around the place and milks the goat and tends the garden.'

'From the few conversations I have had with her, she certainly seems both well-spoken and intelligent,' said Tench.

'Ahh, yes, far more so than most of the convicts, but as you know, they are quite a varied lot and include all types.' Johnston paused before adding offhandedly, 'But you'd expect her to be well-spoken. After all, she is the daughter of a marine officer.'

'She's what?' blurted Tench and Dawes in unison.

'Her father is a major in the marines,' said Johnston rather casually.

'Really? That's amazing,' Tench replied, still stunned. 'How did she end up here as a convict?'

The three men had been standing side by side, looking out at the harbour, but now Tench and Dawes moved to stand in front of Johnston so as not to miss a syllable.

'That's rather a long story, but the short version is that her mother died and her father obviously couldn't look after her, so he sent her away to live with another family. She ended up falling in love with the son of the family and they were married in secret. That is how she came to have her baby, Rosanna.'

'Right, go on,' urged Tench.

'So, when the mother of the family discovered they had married, she accused Esther of seducing her son and turned her out of the house, onto the street.'

'Oh, the poor young thing,' responded Dawes sympathetically.

'Then she was accused of stealing some material, which she says she didn't do,' continued Johnston.

'And do you believe her?' inquired Tench.

'Yes, Watkin, as a matter of fact, I do. She is a fine young woman.'

'And the point is, one couldn't really blame her if she did, in those circumstances,' replied Dawes.

Tench nodded. 'Yes, I have to agree with you there. I suppose that is a worthwhile point, though, isn't it? We don't really know what has brought these convicts here and how many of them are here due purely to unfortunate circumstances prevailing upon their lives.'

'No doubt that's true,' added Dawes.

'Having said that, some of them are just out-and-out villains and deserve to be here,' responded Tench. 'Tell us more about Esther, though.'

Johnston was comfortable enough with Tench that he didn't mind the questioning, but he wasn't going to be too specific.

'Well, she is my housekeeper,' Johnston replied as he looked directly at Tench, 'and I've acknowledged to you before our relationship does go beyond that, but how much further it will end up going, I don't really know yet.'

Tench smiled. 'Was that a twinkle I just detected in your eye, George? Will you marry the girl?'

'Watkin, leave the poor man alone, will you?' intervened Dawes.

'Alright, just to please you, but I must admit I can't help feeling a sliver of jealousy, George,' Tench added before falling silent.

The three marines returned their gazes to the two transports as they continued to sail down harbour before quite suddenly disappearing beyond the headland that projected from its north shore. Just as quickly, the three marines' levity disappeared, to be replaced by their previous feelings of gloom and isolation.

'I wonder how Hunter is going?' murmured Tench, to which Dawes replied, 'Let's hope he's safe.'

*Ref. 36*

\*\*\*

Standing on that same headland behind which the transports had just disappeared was a group of local warriors and Elders. They watched the ships sail past and head towards the harbour's entrance in the same sombre silence as the marines and the rest of the crowd on the southern shore. The reasons for their feelings were, however, entirely disparate to those of the visitors. They knew exactly what the departure of the last two transports meant.

'They're not leaving. They're staying!' murmured Colbee.

'I said we should have driven them away as soon as they arrived,' replied Bennelong angrily.

'What will we do now?' pondered Arabanoo.

'The Elders will decide what is best,' Colbee replied firmly. 'I will talk with them.'

\*\*\*

Later that same day, Arabanoo and the other tribal men were returning to their camp when they met up with some of the women from the mob, who were walking back after collecting various edible berries and root vegetables. Weereweea was amongst them, and she and Arabanoo greeted each other with their usual mutual affection, before Arabanoo kissed their baby, who she was carrying in a possum skin on her back. As they strolled together along the track to their camp, Weereweea knew immediately that her husband had something worrying him.

'What's wrong, Boo?' she asked gently.

Arabanoo paused before replying, 'Two more of their giant canoes left today, so there is only one remaining.'

Concern lined Weereweea's face.

'They have left almost all the strangers behind,' Arabanoo continued. 'There are hundreds of them. It simply means they must be staying for a very long time. They can't leave now.'

'What will we do?' Weereweea asked.

'At this stage, the different clans can't all agree. Pemulwuy and the Bideegal people want to attack them whenever they can to drive them away, but our Elders want to try to live in harmony with them as long as they respect our ways and don't take too much of our tucker.'

Weereweea walked beside him in silence, listening while Arabanoo continued, 'Bennelong says that they don't respect our ways, take too much of our tucker and don't think about the future. He said he saw a group of them go to a duck's nest and take some eggs out of it. When they left, Bennelong went to check the nest, and instead of taking just a couple of eggs, so there are ducks for the future, they had taken all of the eggs. He says that sort of stupidity shows they have no idea of how to live in harmony with Mother Earth on our land. They have no respect for our tucker and bush medicines. They will completely destroy all our traditional ways and how we survive off our land, if they stay.'

'What do you think we should do?' Weereweea asked, looking intently at Arabanoo.

'I don't really know. I will trust the Elders and lore holders to guide us, but I don't think we should attack them like Pemulwuy wants to. I would rather try to be friendly to them. Somehow, we need to teach them something of our cultural ways and how to live in harmony with the land, so they don't destroy it.'

At that point, they arrived at the camp, where their young son rushed across to greet them both. Arabanoo picked him up and threw him into the air, causing the child to giggle as his father caught him an instant later. Although they didn't verbalise it, both Arabanoo and Weereweea shared exactly the same thought – what a lovely distraction from the worries of their situation their children were. Sadly, though, that thought was immediately shoved aside in both their minds by the worry of what would happen to those beautiful children if the strangers continue to stay.

# CHAPTER 44

# APPROACHING CAPE HORN, 24 NOVEMBER 1788

After several days of fine weather with the westerly wind filling the sails of the *Sirius*, the weather had turned again. Sleet and snow gnawed at the faces of Hunter and Bradley as they continued to scan both sides of the ship for the dreaded islands of ice that they had still not encountered, despite the fact they were now approaching Cape Horn.

No sooner was Hunter starting to think they might just be lucky than he heard the scream of the seaman in the crow's nest above.

'Ice! Ice off the starboard bow!'

Hunter immediately spotted a huge iceberg emerging through the mist, rapidly approaching the starboard bow of his ship, but before he could say anything, Bradley was spinning the wheel to port.

Several of the crew raced to the bow as the mountain of ice loomed in front of the ship. For a moment, even Hunter thought they were all doomed, but slowly, the *Sirius* turned and began sliding past the white mountain. It dwarfed the *Sirius*, which at one hundred and ten feet long and five hundred and forty tons, was almost microscopic in comparison.

The danger wasn't over, though, as Hunter looked at the enormous length of the ice island and realised it was going to take them considerable time to pass it. At the moment, the wind was blowing from the south, and the *Sirius* was sheltered by the shadow of the gigantic iceberg. Although the calm water was a blessing, the fact they were sheltered from the southerly breeze meant it was impossible for them to put any distance between the *Sirius* and the treacherous ice.

'Just maintain this course, Mr Bradley, and hope this wind doesn't change direction before we clear the ice,' Hunter ordered, knowing full well that any change in the wind would be catastrophic for his ship and crew.

*Ref. 37*

## CHAPTER 45

## SYDNEY COVE, LATE NOVEMBER 1788

Another large crowd had gathered to attend yet another hanging in the fledgling colony. Tench and Dawes stood amongst them, in their usual position towards the back. This time, the victim was James Daly, who had been found guilty of burglary. It was not the first offence of the somewhat notorious Daly. A few months earlier, he had faked the discovery of gold on the shores of the harbour by breaking up an old pair of buckles and mixing them with dirt. The ruse was quickly discovered, however, and he was sentenced to one hundred lashes and to wearing a canvas frock with the letter 'R' sewn into it to indicate he was a rogue.

As Daly was led over to meet his destiny at the hands of the still-reluctant executioner, his convict colleague, James Freeman, Tench spoke quietly to Dawes.

'Now, if our friend Johnston's helper, Esther, is at the top end of the convicts in regard to their breeding and behaviour, this chap is surely at the bottom. A scoundrel and a villain if ever there was one.'

'Yes, I have to agree with you there. A rather fertile imagination, though!'

'You mean his bogus gold discovery?'

'Exactly,' responded Dawes.

'Well, as we both know, plenty of them have vivid imaginations, so Daly isn't alone in that regard.'

Dawes knew Tench was referring to the fact that since they had landed, various convicts had claimed to have discovered large rivers, valuable ores and quarries of limestone and marble, so he replied, 'Indeed he isn't.'

At that point, he looked up to see Freeman place the noose around Daly's neck. He added, 'Come on, Watkin. Let's go. I don't need to watch this.'

'I agree,' replied Tench. He turned and strode away with Dawes while Freeman sent Daly plunging into eternity against the backdrop of a stunning sunny morning in the pretty little cove.

The two friends walked together in silence for a few moments as they crossed the recently completed bridge across the stream that ran down into the cove.

'Watkin, I need to go and see how some new works are progressing further upstream. Will you join me?'

'Certainly,' responded Tench, and they turned to walk along the edge of the stream.

Again, the two friends made their way in silence for a short while before Dawes spoke. 'How do you think the governor is going to resolve these ongoing problems with the natives?'

'I must admit I don't really know, but they are just getting worse,' Tench responded. 'Apparently, there is no sign whatsoever of the soldier and the convicts who disappeared two days ago.'

'Yes, so I heard. And that follows so closely the death and wounding of the others last week.'

'Mmmm.' Tench nodded. 'One thing is clear – it is the tribe down around Botany Bay that is so dangerous and unpredictable.'

'You know my view on that. They are only dangerous and unpredictable when our people provoke them.'

'I largely agree with you, but the Botany Bay tribe, led by this Pemulwuy chap, seem to need almost no provocation whatsoever,' suggested Tench.

'The point is, we don't know exactly what our people are doing out there in the bush that may provoke them,' replied Dawes.

'Phillip could not be any clearer in his instructions that we are simply not to interfere with the Indians.'

'Yes, but our people are hardly going to come back here and admit they've been interfering with them anyway.'

'Hmmm, I imagine you're correct there,' Tench admitted. 'One thing that I have heard the governor mention as a possible option to help resolve the situation is to capture a couple of them and hold them here with us.'

'What!' responded a stunned Dawes. 'What purpose could that possible serve? He can't think that would do anything other than provoke them.'

'Well, I didn't say he was going to do it. He's just thinking about it, and his reasoning is that he's very frustrated by our inability to communicate effectively with them.'

'So, we just go and kidnap a couple of them, drag them away from their people and their families and hold them prisoner? They're human beings, and the governor is so arrogant that he thinks it's alright to abduct them!'

'Will, it's not me saying this, I'm just telling you what the governor is thinking. He wants them to learn our language, and he wants to learn something of theirs, so we can communicate effectively and tell them we mean no harm.'

'No harm? What about the fact we're taking over their land?' responded Dawes, totally exasperated. 'And is he really suggesting we would show the natives we mean no harm by actually doing them harm and holding them prisoner? Surely even a fool can see how flawed the logic is in that idea.'

Tench had no response. He just stopped and looked at his friend, who continued.

'Look, I was discussing this whole issue with David Collins just last week, and he was saying we have absolutely no legal right under international law to be here claiming this land as our own. This whole colony is based on a lie, according to Collins. Yet what do we do? We come out here and try to take over the whole place, with no respect whatsoever for any of the natives' rights to their own land, and with no attempt to make a treaty with them, or...'

Dawes paused to draw breath. Tench jumped in. 'Hmmm, perhaps there is a certain degree of justice, then, in the fact we are struggling so much to survive here and keep the colony going, but I would like to hear Collins's take on the whole issue, as I'm quite intrigued.'

'That's easy to organise. I'd like to hear some more detail on the matter myself, so why don't you come up to my hut tomorrow evening? I'll ask Collins to join us if he's free. I'll let you know if he's otherwise engaged.'

'Please do, because that should be interesting,' responded Tench.

At that point, the two marines arrived at where some roadworks were continuing in High Street, but only the supervisors were present, as the convict workers were all at the hanging. As the colony's engineer, it was Dawes's responsibility to design the works and ensure they were correctly constructed. After undertaking his inspection and discussing various issues with the supervisor, he and Tench began their return walk.

'Look, Watkin, you're the one with the good relationship with the governor,' said Dawes, immediately returning to their earlier subject. 'Please do all you can to dissuade him from such a course of action.'

'I'll certainly do what I can, but if Phillip makes up his mind, it will be well beyond my powers of persuasion to convince him otherwise.'

*Ref. 38*

# Chapter 46

# Dawes's Hut, Late November 1788

Tench and Dawes met with Lieutenant David Collins, who, at just thirty-two years old, was the colony's judge advocate and most senior legal officer. He was another veteran of the American Revolutionary War, which may have caused the premature greying of his full head of curly hair. When the group had finished exchanging pleasantries and catching up on the latest news in the colony, they turned their attention to the issue that had brought them together for the evening.

'David, please, as you've explained to me, would you outline your views on the legality of this colony?'

'Certainly, but I must start by explaining these are not just my views, but the views of many very learned legal professionals at home and in Europe.'

'Yes, sorry, you had mentioned that to me, but please go on, because Watkin is a little dubious about the issue.'

'I wouldn't say I'm dubious,' replied Tench, sipping on his tea before replacing his cup on Dawes's rough-hewn little table, around which the three officers sat. 'It's just that, unlike you, I haven't had the benefit of hearing David's view on the matter. So, David, please continue.'

'Most certainly. Let's start with the most basic principles of international law when it comes to the issue of exploration, discovery and claiming land for one's country. The first principle is that simply to see a land mass for the first time – or, should I say, to be the first European to see it for the first time – does not give you, or your country, the right of ownership over it.'

'Well, that's understandable.' Tench nodded.

'I should also explain that this whole issue of dominion and sovereignty over lands has been discussed and debated by great legal minds in Europe for over a hundred years.'

'Really?' responded a somewhat surprised Tench.

'Yes, we Europeans have been conquering and colonising foreign lands for centuries now, as you well know. It is understandable, then, that it is a subject that has caused much discussion by minds far greater than mine regarding its ethics and legality. In his book *A Methodical System of International Law*, J. G. Heineccius states a nation who only seized a thing with its eyes, but does not take hold of it, cannot be said to occupy. That is why this massive land mass does not belong to the Dutch or French. As you well know, Abel Tasman claimed Van Diemen's Land for the Dutch as long ago as 1642, but do they own it?'

'No,' replied Tench.

'Of course they don't, because they have never occupied it,' said Collins, before continuing, 'And what of the French's annexation of the west coast of this huge continent?'

'Obviously, I knew about Tasman, but I certainly didn't know the French had annexed the west coast.'

'Well, they did, my friend, as recently as 1772.'

'Really?' Tench was rather stunned.

'Yes, despite the fact the Dutch had discovered the west coast well over a century before, they had never claimed it,' explained Collins. 'It was Louis de Saint-Alouarn on the ship *Gros Ventre* who annexed it for the French after landing at Shark Bay in 1772.'

Dawes immediately interjected to ask Tench with a smirk, 'So, my friend, do you believe the French own the west coast of this continent?'

'Certainly not,' was Tench's quick reply. 'How can you possibly own something just by sailing past it and claiming it as yours?'

'Exactly!' responded Collins before continuing, 'Alright, now here is where it starts to get interesting. Given that fact, what right did our esteemed navigator Captain James Cook have to claim the entire east coast of the continent when he did so on Possession Island in 1770?'

'Hmmm.' Tench nodded. 'I see your point, but–'

Dawes jumped in. 'But nothing, Watkin. Let David continue.'

Collins smiled at Dawes as he continued, 'Our French friend Monsieur de Saint-Alouarn performed exactly the same sort of ceremony as Cook, raising the flag, firing guns, reading a proclamation, but we both agree with international law that that means nothing–'

Tench interjected, 'But we have established a colony here now.'

'Exactly, but we will come to that. Firstly, let us agree that in August 1770, Cook's little ceremony on Possession Island gave us British no more rights over the east coast than de Saint Alouarn's ceremony gave the French over the west coast... Agreed?'

'Yes, well, I suppose so,' Tench said reluctantly.

Dawes smiled. '*Yes* is the correct answer, Watkin, not *I suppose so*.'

Again, Collins continued, 'Now, you may understand that Cook's claim is even less valid when you find out what his specific instructions included.'

'And what was that?' Tench asked, happy to play his friend's game.

'They stated that he was to take possession of convenient locations *with the consent of the natives*,' Collins explained.

'Really?' responded Tench.

Collins nodded. 'So, Cook didn't have the right to claim it in the first place, and his little ceremony at Possession Island was as meaningless as our French friends' on the west coast, and it was even made more invalid by the fact that he had made no attempt to obtain the consent of the natives.'

'Alright, so now we come to our little colony here. What do you say about its validity?' probed Tench.

'To answer that, I'll make two points. Firstly, another great mind on the subject of international law, Emmerich de Vattel, wrote in the 1750s that "every nation that governed itself under whatever form, and which does not depend on any other nation, is a sovereign state".'

'I can see where this is headed, but were the Indians governing themselves?' queried Tench.

'De Vattel says *in whatever form*, and certainly, they may not be as sophisticated as we in Europe, but it would appear they have been here for thousands of years, and they have certainly been independent of any other nation.'

'Pretty difficult to argue, then, that they don't have sovereignty over this land.'

'Watkin, I tend to think the term should be *impossible*, not *pretty difficult*,' interjected Dawes.

'Hmmm, I think I have to agree,' responded Tench, leaning back in his wooden chair, causing the legs to dig into the dirt floor of Dawes's hut.

'My second point is,' stressed Collins, 'given the issues of legality under international law, why did the British government choose to establish a colony here? Well, this is where it gets really interesting.' Collins continued, answering his own question. 'As recently as 1785, when the British government were looking to establish a new colony on the west coast of Africa, the House of Commons committee investigating it reported it was highly likely that the local natives would, without resistance, give up as much of their land as necessary for a stipulated rent. They believed this would be the case as all the Dutch and Portuguese possessions on the west coast of Africa had been acquired in that way.'

'Yes, I did have a vague understanding that that was normally the case,' said Tench.

'Exactly. But in the orders that were given to Phillip, there is absolutely no mention whatsoever of paying the natives for their land or making any sort of treaty with them, as is usually the case. The only mention of the natives is that we are to live in "amity" with them, which, of course, is rather difficult when you are in the process of stealing their land.'

'But if the normal procedure for the Dutch, Portuguese and us is to negotiate some sort of treaty or payment, why wasn't Phillip instructed to do so?' asked Tench.

'It seems that was because in 1785, when Sir Joseph Banks and James Matra put their proposal to our government for the establishment of a colony at Botany Bay, they said the natives were so nomadic that they had no concept of ownership of the land and no form of government. It would therefore be impossible to pay them for the land or make a treaty. Probably most importantly, though, Banks and Matra said the place was so thinly populated they wouldn't put up any resistance anyway.'

'Well, we know none of that is true,' responded Tench.

'Yes, but the government thought it was,' responded Dawes.

'No wonder Botany Bay appeared to be such an attractive option for them, then – no resistance, no payment and no tricky treaties.'

'Exactly,' responded Collins.

'Given all that, it's not entirely surprising we have ended up in rather a mess... but how do we resolve it?' pondered Tench.

'You will understand that we can hardly expect it to go smoothly when it is illegal and based on a lie,' responded Dawes.

'So, I repeat, how do we resolve it?'

'I don't really know,' replied Collins, 'but I think a good starting point would be to have some meaningful dialogue with the natives regarding a treaty and some compensation.'

'And meaningful dialogue cannot start with abducting them and holding them prisoner,' Dawes added, his face reddening slightly.

*Ref. 39*

## CHAPTER 47

## FIFTY-SIX DEGREES SOUTH, CAPE HORN, 26 NOVEMBER 1788

The *Sirius* had now been three days amongst the ice islands near Cape Horn and had repeatedly needed to change course quickly to avoid disastrous collisions. Hunter was in his cabin, studying his charts of Cape Horn and Terra Del Fuego and trying to identify the exact location of Diego Ramirez Island. He wanted to sail past it to ensure he was well clear of the Cape so a change of wind direction would not prove disastrous. He was in the middle of comparing the charts with his and Bradley's own observations when there was a knock on his door.

Although his first inclination was to say, *Go away, I'm busy,* he responded with, 'Come in.'

The ship's surgeon, George Worgan, entered. 'Good morning, Captain.'

Worgan and Hunter had an excellent relationship, since Worgan owned the only piano in the colony, which had been transported there on Hunter's *Sirius*. The pair's mutual love of music meant they had spent numerous nights gathered around it with other likeminded souls, singing songs from Worgan's extensive and varied repertoire. Hunter had found Worgan to be not only an excellent pianist, even better than himself, but also wonderful company and a dedicated surgeon.

'Aye, good morning, George. How are the crew?'

'Not well, I regret to say. Signs of the scurvy are starting to show with a few of the men, and I'm most concerned that it will not be long before more fall to it.'

Hunter paused before replying, 'The extract of malt is not proving effective, then.'

'It is no doubt slowing it, but as you know, it is no substitute for fresh fruit and vegetables.'

Both men were well aware that the crew had not had any significant amount of fresh fruit or vegetables since they left Cape Town on the outward voyage, some fifteen months ago, so it was virtually inevitable that scurvy would strike at some point.

'Captain, I did want to ask if you have any estimate of when we are likely to reach Cape Town.'

'I am sorry, but my attention for the moment is focussed on navigating our way safely around Cape Horn and avoiding the islands of ice amongst which we have found ourselves, but please be assured that as soon as we have done that safely, I will be in a position to more accurately determine our likely arrival time in Cape Town.'

'Yes, Captain, I'm sorry. My concern is that if the crew succumb to the scurvy, we won't have sufficient crew to sail across the South Atlantic.'

'Aye, I understand, but all you can do is keep them as healthy as you can, and we will try to struggle through.'

Worgan turned to leave, but feeling he had been a little abrupt with his good friend, Hunter added, 'George, please be assured, as soon as I believe I can give you an accurate estimate of our arrival in the Cape, I will do so.'

'Thank you, Captain.' Worgan nodded as he walked out the door.

Hunter followed soon after, with his charts under his arm, and rejoined Bradley on the quarterdeck. The rain and clouds had cleared, and the sun was smiling from a brilliant sky. It was nearing the peak of summer in the high latitudes, when the days were extremely long, and even when the sun finally descended from view, it continued to cast an eerie glow throughout the few brief hours of night. The westerly wind had also eased a little, and the *Sirius* was cruising gently between the ice islands on either side.

'Mr Bradley, is there any sign of this Diego Ramirez Island?'

'No, Captain, none whatsoever,' replied Bradley.

'And you have checked your observations?'

'Yes, sir. They agree precisely with yours.'

'Well, if that is the case, we should have seen it by now,' responded Hunter with a clear note of frustration in his voice as he looked at his charts again.

'Perhaps it doesn't exist, sir,' ventured Bradley hesitantly.

Hunter looked at him for a moment and smiled before replying, 'I don't think previous mariners could be that mistaken, Mr Bradley. I don't think they were seeing things. I tend to believe it is out here somewhere, but just not where they have shown it on the charts. They may not have had the opportunity to take the accurate observations we have.'

'Mmmm.' Bradley nodded. 'You're probably right, sir.'

'And I'm sure Mr Diego Ramirez would hope his island hasn't disappeared.'

'Now, wouldn't that be something, sir? Having an island named after you?'

'I suppose it would, but I don't think that is ever going to happen to either of us.'

'Well, it wouldn't have to be an island, sir. It could be a mountain or a river or a strait.'

'Like the Straits of Magellan, perhaps.'

'Exactly, sir, and have your name on the map for all time!' enthused Bradley. 'Even a headland would satisfy me.'

'I haven't really thought about it.' Hunter was an honest man, but that was a lie. He continued, 'I think one would need to be a far greater man than you or I, Mr Bradley. After all, in my opinion, Magellan was probably the greatest mariner of all time. The first to circumnavigate the world, and he did it over two hundred and sixty years ago. Tragically, of course, he died on the way, but his crew completed the voyage.'

'Amazing feat, and the first to round the Horn, too, wasn't he, sir?'

'Ahh, good question. Yes and no, because he didn't actually round the Horn – he sailed through the Straits of Magellan to reach the Pacific, hence the name. You see, at that time, they thought Terra Del Fuego was part of a great southern land mass that couldn't be sailed around. That's why he had to navigate through the straits.'

'Interesting, sir,' said Bradley. 'I wasn't aware of all that... Do you think there is one?'

'What? You mean a great southern land mass?'

'Yes, sir.'

'Well, one of them has already been discovered, and that's New Holland. But is there another one further south of here?' Hunter paused and peered at the southern horizon, and Bradley followed his gaze. 'I don't really know, but these ice islands have to come from somewhere. Many of them that have rolled over show signs of earth on their base, so perhaps they have broken off from some bleak, inhospitable land mass down there somewhere.'

The two men stood in silence, staring at the southern horizon.

At that point, out of the corner of his eye, Hunter saw an albatross plunge into the sea in pursuit of a fish. It made him look up and now, having resolved his immediate navigational question, he allowed the artist in himself to take in the beauty of his surroundings. It was a playground of nature, he thought, as he watched multiple types of birds soaring and diving from the heavens while seals swam alongside the *Sirius* and yet another pod of whales crossed behind the stern. And all this was happening against the backdrop of the gigantic ice islands, which, if it were not for the dread they engendered, would actually be simply spectacular. They were an almost translucent turquoise where they rose out of the water, before ascending towards the sapphire-blue sky, covered in the softest of white, white snow.

Hunter looked at Bradley, who he realised had been watching his reaction to their surroundings.

'Ah, nature.' Hunter smiled. 'If you're not admiring its beauty, you're cursing its fury.'

It wouldn't be long before they would both again be doing the latter.

*Ref. 40*

## CHAPTER 48

## FIFTY-SIX DEGREES SOUTH, CAPE HORN, 27 NOVEMBER 1788

Captain John Hunter was sound asleep in his cabin. He was sleeping as only a veteran sailor can on a ship that is rolling and swaying in the swell. After fourteen hours straight on the quarterdeck battling a rising swell driven by an erratic breeze, he was exhausted. He was so sound asleep that, at first, he mistook the sailor shaking him as just the motion of the ship.

'Captain. Captain, sir, wake up. Lieutenant Bradley needs you urgently on deck.'

In the fog of his deep sleep, Hunter's mind momentarily returned to the coast of Norway, where his father had woken him from a similarly deep sleep. He feared for a moment that the *Sirius* was to suffer a similar fate, and this time, he knew there would be no Norwegian fishermen on a nearby beach to save them.

Hunter pushed those nightmarish thoughts from his mind and immediately swung his feet to the floor and pulled on his boots. Moments later, he was pulling on his coat as he joined an anxious-looking Lieutenant Bradley on the quarterdeck. Before Bradley could speak, though, Hunter immediately saw what the urgency was – they were almost entirely surrounded by icebergs, and the ferocity of Cape Horn was returning rapidly.

'Islands of ice everywhere, sir!' Bradley yelled above the roar of the tempest. 'I have been trying not to wake you, but this ice field just keeps increasing.'

'Aye, you've done the right thing, Mr Bradley. My place is here, not asleep in my cabin.'

'Thank you, sir. And there looks to be an absolutely massive one coming up off the starboard bow.'

Hunter immediately raised his telescope in the direction Bradley was pointing as deep lines of worry and fear creased his brow. They were in an almost identical position to that which they had encountered just a few days before. A mountain of ice on their starboard side, and them hoping and praying the wind wouldn't change direction. What made the situation so much worse this time, though, was the smaller icebergs scattered off their port side.

'We're going to have to get as far away from that as possible. If it's that big above the waterline, it will be enormous below it, so we're going to have to take her closer to the smaller ones on our port side.'

Bradley said, 'Yes, sir,' as he swung the wheel to port.

'Let's just hope this gale doesn't change direction while we're trying to pass this monster,' said Hunter.

'Our luck held last time, sir, so let's pray it does again. It's been from the south-west for the past hour or so, but prior to that, it was very changeable before it started picking up.'

They both watched as the *Sirius* drew parallel to the mountainous iceberg, which provided a little shelter from the increasing gale.

'That must be three hundred and fifty feet high, Captain,' muttered an awe-struck Bradley.

'Aye, at least, and look – you can't even see the end of it. It's miles long.'

The two men briefly watched the seals, penguins and birds that used it as a refuge and resting place, before again focussing on the massive iceberg, trying to determine its full length. So focussed on attempting to determine the extent of the giant ice island, the two mariners didn't notice a much smaller one emerging from the mist off their port side, rapidly drifting ever closer. Finally, Hunter spotted it.

'Look out, Lieutenant!' he yelled.

Bradley instinctively swung the wheel back to starboard as Hunter rushed to the side of the ship and peered over the rail into the depths of the deep dark sea. Many of the panic-stricken crew quickly followed. They watched breathlessly as the iceberg disappeared below the waterline and the hull of the *Sirius* passed within feet of it. Hunter looked up at the wall of ice beside him. It was so close he felt he could almost reach out and touch it. He had no time for such moments of fantasy, though, and hurried back to Bradley's side as the *Sirius* gradually pulled away from the iceberg.

'Now, as soon as we get past this wee one, head back to port and right away from that monster,' Hunter ordered as he motioned to the mountain of ice on their starboard side.

Bradley managed to maintain the *Sirius* along a steady course between the two icebergs, and it wasn't long before they were clear of the small one on their port side and able to steer away from the looming monster to their starboard.

Although safely away from the imminent danger of the ice, they were now fully exposed to the gale, which had reached its peak. The hull of the *Sirius* rose on each wave and crashed into the troughs between as the sodden wind slapped the faces of the crew.

Despite the perilous situation, Hunter was now quite calm, in spite of the fact he had to yell his assurance to Bradley above the roar of the tempest.

'Hopefully, we'll be alright now, Mr Bradley. We're well south of any charted land, and if there are no more icefields, this wonderful little ship should get us through.'

'Hope you're right, Captain. But won't it depend where exactly Diego Ramirez Island is? After all, we wouldn't want to come across it in this gale.'

'I'm sure the various chart-makers could not be that far out in their observations. We must have passed it by now.'

Hunter was right, but he didn't know that the location of Diego Ramirez Island was the least of their concerns.

*Ref. 41*

## CHAPTER 49

## AROUND CAPE HORN, 12 DECEMBER 1788

The cold, the biting, ravenous cold, gnawed at the weather-beaten face of John Hunter as he stood on the foredeck peering at the white icebergs on the horizon. Despite his countless voyages to all parts of the globe, Hunter had never been this far south, and the intensity of the cold here was something he had never experienced before. The chill wind blowing from the south felt like it was hurling icicles through the freezing sky, like leaves on a winter wind. *It must be blowing straight off a huge mass of pure ice*, he thought as he turned and rejoined Bradley and the helmsman on the quarterdeck.

'Finally around the Horn, sir.' Bradley attempted to smile in the face of the biting wind.

'Aye, Mr Bradley. So let's take her north for a wee while and try to get away from the worst of this cold and weather. Set a course nor-nor east.'

'Yes, sir,' Bradley responded as he watched the helmsman swing the wheel.

\*\*\*

John Hunter had always expected the scurvy to affect his crew. After all, George Worgan had warned him it was beginning to show its ugly presence, but neither man had expected it to hit as hard and as quickly as it did. The symptoms of the disease – ugly, blood-filled sores on the skin, corkscrew hairs, gum disease, loss of teeth, pain in the bones and shortness of breath – were unmistakable and were rapidly affecting one crew member after another.

Hunter was on deck with Bradley when the ship's surgeon approached him.

'Captain, I regret to say I have some sorrowful news,' Worgan said hesitantly.

'What is it, Mr Worgan? The scurvy?'

'Yes, sir. It has just claimed its first victim, Henry Fitzgerald.'

'Oh, no! I am sorry to hear that,' Hunter responded with genuine regret. 'The poor chap looked to be very poorly when I spoke to him just a few days ago.'

'Yes, sir, and he was a good seaman, but my bigger concern is just how quickly it is beginning to affect more and more of the crew. Just this morning, three more men have collapsed into their bunks, unable to continue their duties.'

'Aye, that is most concerning. I am hoping now, though, that as we are finally around the Horn, we are steering a course northward for a wee while in the hope that the warmth of the summer sun will have a beneficial effect on the crew's health.'

'I hope so, Captain, but as you know, nothing will restore it like fresh fruit and vegetables.'

'Aye, and I know I promised to advise you when we can expect to reach Cape Town.'

'Yes, you did indeed.' Worgan smiled.

'Well, now we are around the Horn and clear of the worst of the ice, given reasonable winds, I would expect to arrive by the end of the month.'

'Thank you, Captain.'

Hunter was about to allow Worgan to go about his duties when he stopped the surgeon.

'Mr Worgan, somehow or other, we need to ensure there is a remedy for the scurvy carried on all long voyages. As we have discussed, some elixir of various vegetable acids should provide a solution if carried in sufficient quantities.'

'I certainly believe that would be of great assistance, sir.'

Worgan immediately returned below decks to care for the ailing crew members to try and ensure enough of them stayed sufficiently healthy to sail the *Sirius* across the South Atlantic. A task that would be increasingly difficult, due to the need to constantly have part of the crew manning the pumps of the leaking vessel.

*Ref. 42*

## Chapter 50

## Sydney Cove, 18 December 1788

It was early on a cloudy summer morning, and Watkin Tench was preparing for his trip to the new farming settlement at Rosehill when a rather anxious William Dawes hurried up to him.

'Watkin, have you heard?'

'Heard what?' Tench responded, confused.

'A huge number of natives have just assembled up at the brick kilns and appear very threatening.'

'Really? How many?'

'I've been told by one of the convicts that it is over a thousand.'

'I find that number hard to believe, but however many there are, let's hope they don't attack the men there. We'd better head up immediately.' Tench slipped his sword into its scabbard and picked up his musket.

'I'm told Johnston has already taken a detachment up there, but yes, let's see if we can assist. I'd hate the situation to get out of hand.'

Tench and Dawes hurried along the path south towards the brick kilns in a gait that was part brisk walk and part jog. The kilns were located near the top of the hill about a mile south of Sydney Cove, and Tench and Dawes were nearly halfway there when they saw Johnston and several marines heading back towards them along the track.

As they approached each other, Tench called out, 'What happened, Lieutenant?'

'The natives have taken off back into the bush, Captain,' came Johnston's reply.

'Thank heavens,' responded Dawes as the two parties met.

'Yes, the convicts at the kilns were trying to scare them off by pointing spades and shovels at them in the manner of guns, and then my detachment arrived and they took off into the bush.'

'Well, that's a relief!' said Dawes. 'How many were there? We were told over a thousand.'

'That was the number I was originally given, but when I arrived, there were less than one hundred. It was certainly a large group, and the men at the kilns understandably were fearful for their lives.'

'I wonder what they were doing there,' said Tench.

'I have no idea, because there were enough of them to kill all the men at the kilns, if they had attacked before we arrived,' said Johnston, 'but they didn't, so who knows what they were doing? Anyway, I've left half of my detachment there to protect the men for now, so I don't expect they will come back.'

'Alright, I don't believe there is anything to be gained by us going up to have a look. We may as well return with you, as I'm just about to go out to Rosehill.'

Tench and Dawes then walked back down the hill with Johnston and his men and continued the conversation as they did.

'My concern,' said Dawes, 'is that this incident might encourage Phillip to pursue this ill-conceived plan of his to abduct some of the natives and hold them captive while we study them!'

'That may well be his solution, and it may be reasonable,' responded Johnston. 'He will no doubt want a report from me on this incident.'

'Well, it's hardly reasonable, as they didn't do anything wrong,' replied Dawes. 'They didn't attack anyone. Surely they have to be able to wander around their own land as they like.'

'Yes, one would certainly think so, but we will see what the governor makes of the whole situation,' said Tench, attempting to defuse his friend's increasing frustration.

*Ref. 43*

## Chapter 51

## South Atlantic, 30 December 1788

John Hunter entered the crew's quarters below the deck of the forecastle, which were almost totally occupied by the scurvy-riddled ill, who now numbered forty, leaving Hunter with the bare minimum needed to sail the ship and man the pumps. He was immediately slapped in the face by the sound of the painful moans of the dying and the stench of excrement in the cramped space, where even the shortest amongst the crew had to stoop to move around. To make matters worse, the only ones that seemed to be enjoying the additional stench and filth were the ship's rats, which appeared to have multiplied even more rapidly than normal and scurried around the place with total disregard for the human beings. The only humans in the quarters well enough to move around, though, were the dedicated George Worgan and his equally dedicated assistant Tom Jamison.

Hunter made his way over to Worgan and crouched beside the ailing sailor he was caring for. Hunter was about to speak, but Worgan spoke first. 'You know John Shine, don't you, Captain?'

Hunter knew John Shine very well, but he didn't for a moment recognise the decaying mess of humanity lying in front of him as the once heavily muscled, always laughing, able seaman. The face of the scurvy-riddled person lying here now was covered in blood-filled sores, surrounding a mouth that was almost entirely toothless and swollen with gum disease.

'Aye, of course,' responded Hunter. 'How are you, John?' The moment the words were out of his mouth, he wished he could take them back. He felt like a fool asking a man in that state such a question.

Amazingly, though, Shine responded with a barely audible mumble. 'I'm alright, sir.'

Hunter smiled at him. 'You always were a tough bastard, John.'

Worgan cut the conversation short. 'And just on the other side of you, sir, is Joe Caldwell.'

'Aye, Joe, the two of you would be the best darn topmen in the British Navy.' Hunter smiled as he patted the hand of the equally unrecognisable seaman.

'They are indeed, sir,' agreed Worgan.

Hunter then raised his voice a little to address all the men in the tiny infirmary.

'Men, the reason I came down here is to let you know that we are now less than two days from Cape Town, so think of your loved ones and do all you can to hang on until we can get you fresh provisions the moment we arrive.'

The announcement was met with a muffled cheer from the few of them well enough to do so.

'Thank you, Captain,' murmured Caldwell.

Hunter stayed and spoke to those of the ailing crew who had the strength to respond, but he felt a sense of both relief and great sadness as he returned to the fresh salt air of the deck above.

\*\*\*

'Land ho!'

It was the call from the crow's nest that the entire crew had waited three long months to hear, and it came as the morning mist cleared from the ocean's eastern horizon. It was the call that had Hunter clambering up the ladder to the deck faster than he had in his entire naval career. He even managed to beat the much younger Lieutenant Bradley to the quarterdeck. Once there, he immediately raised his telescope to his eye, and there, through the morning mist, he saw it – that unmistakable outline. It was Table Mountain.

'Are we there, sir?' called an almost breathless Bradley as he rushed up to join his skipper.

'Aye, indeed we are.' Hunter beamed, handing his telescope to Bradley and pointing into the distance. 'Table Mountain!'

Bradley looked through the telescope, saw the famous mountain and immediately held out his hand to shake his captain's.

'Congratulations, sir.'

'Mr Bradley, as always, thank you for your tireless efforts,' responded Hunter, patting Bradley on the shoulder. This was as much emotion as the reserved naval officers would allow themselves, but further down the ship's deck, the few crew who were well enough to be on deck were cheering and hugging each other as an enormous wave of relief swept over the *Sirius*. Undoubtedly the most emotional and demonstrative were those who were already showing the early signs of scurvy.

As the celebrations continued, George Worgan made his way up to the quarterdeck to join Hunter and Bradley. Hunter greeted him with a smile and pointed to the horizon.

'Table Mountain, Mr Worgan.'

Worgan glanced over his shoulder as he murmured his response. 'That is such a shame.'

'Why would you say that? We're here,' responded Bradley.

Worgan looked at Hunter as he spoke. 'John Shine died just a moment ago, sir.'

'Oh, I am so sorry to hear that... when we are so close,' responded Hunter sombrely.

'So am I, so sorry,' added Bradley.

'He was such a good sailor,' said Hunter.

'And a good man,' replied Worgan. 'He really was keeping his mate Joe going, and I'm rather worried now that Joe won't last the day without him.'

Worgan was right, and that afternoon, by the time the *Sirius* drew alongside Robin's Island, heading towards Table Bay, Joseph Caldwell had joined his best mate John Shine in being buried at sea.

\*\*\*

Hunter and Bradley stood looking up at the sails of the *Sirius* with lines of concern marking both their faces.

'Mr Bradley, given the direction of the wind and the few healthy crew we have, I'm not going to attempt to sail around that reef at this time of day. Let's just take her into Robin's Island so we are moored before nightfall.'

'Yes, sir. A sensible decision,' responded Bradley.

'Aye, and I believe just having her at anchor in port will have a very positive effect on the spirits of the men laid low with the scurvy. We should be able to get some fresh food for them immediately.'

Shortly afterwards, the *Sirius* dropped anchor in nine fathoms of water right off the flagstaff and landing place of Robin's Island. Hunter sent Bradley ashore to speak with the Dutch officer in charge of the island, find out any news from Europe and collect whatever fresh food was available.

A couple of hours later, Bradley returned with fresh food, which was immediately delivered to the scurvy-riddled crew below decks. Bradley then knocked at the captain's cabin, which he entered at Hunter's invitation.

'Now, Mr Bradley, how did you go?'

'Very well, sir. I was given a considerable amount of fresh fruit from the commander's garden, and the men have just been delighted to receive it. I honestly think some of the ill below decks didn't believe we were really in port until we returned with the fruit.'

'Hopefully, they will all recover now and regain full health before we start the homeward voyage. And tell me, what news of Europe did you acquire?'

'It was quite difficult, sir, given that I don't speak any Dutch and they spoke no English, but the good news is that the English and the Dutch are very good friends again… or at least that's what I think he said.'

Hunter smiled and shook his head. 'Let's jolly well hope that's what he said, or it could make our visit to Cape Town a little more difficult than I hoped.'

'Sir, put it this way – they could not have been more friendly and hospitable.'

'Aye, that is pleasing to hear.'

'And, sir, I have the cook preparing us some of the fresh vegetables, so they'll be ready soon.'

'Thank you, Mr Bradley. I'm certainly tired of salt rations, but only if there has been sufficient for the scurvy-affected crew. After all, we can wait the extra day if we need to.'

'Very well, sir. We'll wait the extra day, then,' replied Bradley, rather disappointed.

*Ref. 44*

## Chapter 52

## Gamaragal Land, 31 December 1788

The Grandfather Sun had just risen out of the ocean and begun to warm the earth of the Gamaragal as Father Sky breathed soft whispers of white cloud across the horizon. Arabanoo gathered up his spears and woomera before waving goodbye to Weereweea and his two children. He was about to set off down to the cove with some of the other warriors, but he hesitated momentarily as something inside him urged him to go back. He walked back to his family, who were standing in the shade of the trees on the eastern side of the camp. He gave his children a hug before he held Weereweea to him, looked into her deep brown eyes and whispered, 'I love you.'

She smiled up at him. 'And I love you too.'

Arabanoo turned and followed the other warriors out of the camp, but as he left his family amongst the morning shadows, neither he nor Weereweea had any idea it was to be their final parting.

\*\*\*

Shortly afterwards, Arabanoo and a few of the other warriors were walking along the beach of the cove when they saw two of the visitors' smaller canoes rowing towards them with six men in each one. They stood and watched as the canoes drew closer.

'I wonder what they want?' asked one of Arabanoo's colleagues, standing behind him.

'They always want something,' replied another.

They continued watching as the two canoes came in towards the beach.

'Hello,' called the smiling visitors, waving happily.

All of the locals knew by now that that was the visitors' greeting, so some of them, including Arabanoo, called 'Hello' as they waved back.

The visitors stopped close to the shore and made a show of laying their strange firesticks in the bottom of the boats. The Gamaragal knew this procedure well and immediately placed their spears on the edge of the sand and ambled cautiously across the beach. The strangers began beckoning the locals to come closer. Arabanoo saw them hold up some pretty coloured ornaments and those things that looked like your reflection in a very still pool of water. The warriors all stopped at the water's edge. Arabanoo looked at his colleagues.

'What do you think?' he asked.

'Well, we know how treacherous they are. We can't trust them,' came the reply.

Arabanoo thought for a moment before responding, 'But these ones in the red or blue cloaks have never hurt any of us when they have offered us presents.'

'But they are the same old presents and others hurt us. The ones they call "convicts" have attacked the Gadigal on the other side of the water, and they are all the same. They are all treacherous.'

'But these ones aren't convicts. These are all the leaders in the red or blue cloaks.'

Arabanoo was not a foolhardy or rash character. He tended to be far more thoughtful and cautious. He did, however, believe that Weereweea would love one of the presents, and he could just see the look of joy on her face when he gave it to her. He was also a person of integrity, who was trustworthy himself, and therefore tended to see it in those around him... even though sometimes, it may have been absent.

Arabanoo took a couple of steps, hesitant steps, into the water towards the visitors' boats.

'Don't get too close to them, Arabanoo,' one of his colleagues called.

'It's alright, I'll just get a present for Weereweea,' Arabanoo replied as he walked into the shallow water.

He waded over to the side of the canoe, where a visitor in a red coat sat in the back of the boat, holding out the ornaments to him. Arabanoo reached out, took them, immediately turned around to his colleagues and held them up.

'See, Weereweea will love these,' he said as one of his colleagues joined him in the water.

'Be careful. Don't trust them,' called a tribesman on the beach.

'It's alright,' Arabanoo called back. 'Look.' He again held up the ornaments.

Arabanoo turned and had just started walking away to join his approaching colleague when he heard a splash behind him. Suddenly, he felt something coarse thrown over his head and down around his body. As his eyes looked down and his brain registered it was a rope, he was pulled backwards, and he plunged under the water before he could snatch a full breath.

Arabanoo struggled to the surface as he was dragged towards the boat. He glanced over his shoulder to call for help, only to see his nearest colleague battling to free himself from another rope. Before he knew it, he was again yanked off his feet and set upon by two of the strangers in red coats. They held him under the water to subdue him for what seemed to him to be an age as he again struggled for breath. Paradoxically, he somehow managed to marvel at the beauty of the morning sun sparkling on the surface of the water above him as the little oxygen in his lungs drained away.

Finally, they let him up, and he gasped for breath before screaming to his colleagues, 'Help, help. Help me!'

His colleagues ran the short distance back towards where they had left their weapons on the edge of the beach as Arabanoo was dragged into the large canoe, where he immediately felt another rope being wrapped around him, pinning his arms to his sides. The redcoats who had captured him pushed the boat into the deeper water and jumped back into it.

Arabanoo looked back to his nearest colleague, who had freed himself from his rope and was fleeing towards the others, who had now recovered their spears. They came running down the beach and began launching their spears at the canoes as the visitors rowed away.

'Help me! Help. Pleeease!' Arabanoo pleaded, before turning his attention to the kidnappers, who were quickly tying the rope around his legs as he struggled frantically.

'Let me go! Let me go. Please, oh please, let me go! Don't kill me, I have a family!'

Arabanoo let out the forlorn wail of someone who knows they are about to die as the visitors started firing their firesticks at the warriors on the shore. His colleagues desperately threw their spears and throwing sticks at the retreating canoes in a frenzied attempt to save their countryman.

The visitors continued firing towards Arabanoo's colleagues until they were well out of range of the spears and other weapons. By this time, Arabanoo was completely bound, his arms by his sides and his feet tied together, with the rope attached to the side of the boat. There was no escape. His wailing now subsided to more of a low moan. One of the strangers with more ornaments on his coat than the others and what Arabanoo saw as a small, ugly mouth and dark eyes leant forward, patted him on the shoulder and spoke unintelligibly in a quiet voice.

'Just let me go, please don't kill me,' begged a terrified Arabanoo.

The man with the small mouth continued to pat him on the shoulder and speak unintelligibly to him as the other strangers rowed further and further up the harbour. Arabanoo looked away, back towards his cove, where his countrymen now stood near the tree line.

'Weereweea,' he murmured softly.

*Ref. 45*

# CHAPTER 53

# SYDNEY COVE, 31 DECEMBER 1788

Watkin Tench stood at the front of the small crowd that had quickly gathered as word spread of the capture of one of the natives. There was a buzz of excitement as the two longboats pulled into the small beach at the head of the cove. The ropes around the native's legs had now been released, and he was assisted from the boat by the marine private to whom he was tied.

Tench noted that the naked captive was about thirty years of age and showed no sign of struggling, appearing to be resigned to his fate despite the fact he was obviously very agitated and frightened. He was of medium height and robustly made, with a countenance that Tench believed in happier circumstances would display manliness and sensibility. Like all his countrymen, he had a beard, but his was more towards the thin and wispy rather than heavy and thick. Also like most of his countrymen, he had a front tooth missing. Unlike many of his countrymen, though, he did not have a bone through the septum of his nose.

Standing near Tench was the young convict woman Esther Abrahams, who was now openly Lieutenant George Johnston's partner, and she and her nearly two-year-old daughter, Rosanna, lived with him in his small officer's cottage. Tench nodded a friendly greeting to her and then approached George Johnston as he stepped onto the shore beside the captive.

'So, you managed to capture one, Mr Johnston,' Tench observed.

'Yes, Captain, we had another one briefly, but he managed to escape,'

Johnston replied as he smiled at Esther, who would not approach him while he was on duty, but whose face nevertheless showed her relief at his safe return.

'Well, I'm sure the governor will be content with that.'

'I hope so, because it was extremely dangerous. His tribe mates pelted us with spears, rocks and throwing sticks as we made our escape. We had to fire over their heads repeatedly to warn them off.'

'Are all your men alright?' asked Tench as they began to follow the marine who was tied to the captive.

'Yes, fortunately, but I wouldn't want to do it again. I'd hate to see one of our men lose his life trying to capture a native for the governor's entertainment.'

'Mr Johnston, you know that is not how the governor sees it, but we can discuss that later. How is your captive?'

'Well, sir, he is physically uninjured, but he was certainly distraught initially. He wailed in the most distressed manner.'

'That is perfectly understandable, I would think. The poor chap,' responded Tench as he thought how grateful he was that his friend Dawes was busy elsewhere and not there to see the unfortunate native.

'Certainly,' said Johnston. 'Actually, I felt rather treacherous myself. Befriending them and bidding them to come close only so we could capture him.'

'I can understand that. Are you taking him straight to see the governor now?' inquired Tench.

'My orders are to bathe and shave him and then put some clothes on him before presenting him to the governor.'

Tench said, 'Perhaps the governor might prefer to see him in his natural state first, and you can clean him up later. And he certainly appears to have calmed right down.'

'Yes, he has calmed down quite remarkably, and if you think we should take him straight to the governor, Captain, that sounds fine to me,' responded Johnston.

The growing crowd, made up largely of convicts and sailors,

encircled the group as they began the walk up the hill towards the large double-storey brick house that was the governor's new premises. Although not quite complete, it was vastly superior to the canvas house he had been living in previously. On the way, the captive hesitated a little and appeared concerned by the increasing crowd.

'Stand back. Give us some space,' ordered Johnston.

While the marines pushed the crowd back, Tench took the opportunity to try to reassure the captive and walked over to him, speaking calmly and soothingly.

'It's alright,' Tench said, patting him on the upper arm. 'We are not going to hurt you.'

The native looked straight into Tench's eyes without speaking.

'I'm Captain Tench,' he continued, tapping himself on the chest. 'Captain, Captain.'

The captive looked at the epaulettes on the shoulders of Tench's coat and reached out and touched them. 'Bengadee,' he said. Tench was surprised and delighted that the captive was now sufficiently calm to engage with him.

'Epaulette,' replied Tench as he touched them himself and then repeated, 'Epaulette.'

The captive repeated, 'Bengadee.'

'Perhaps we should start him on something a little easier, Captain,' suggested Johnston.

'Yes, indeed. Excellent idea.' Tench smiled.

He looked into the crowd, spotted Esther and bade her to come forward, which she did, with young Rosanna holding tightly to her hand. Tench then pointed to Esther and said, slowly and deliberately, 'Wo-man... Wo-man.'

The captive looked at Tench and back at Esther, smiling at her and repeating, 'Wo-man.'

Tench beamed. 'Yes, well done.'

The captive gave Tench a half-grin in return, while Esther smiled modestly and glanced at Johnston, who nodded approvingly to her.

Tench pointed to young Rosanna, who clung to her mother's hand rather nervously.

'Girl... girl,' he repeated.

The native looked at Tench rather quizzically before mumbling, 'Garl,' as he crouched down in front of Rosanna and smiled at her.

Rosanna maintained her tight grip on her mother's hand but managed a brief smile back. The Gamaragal warrior gently touched the sleeve of her dress and spoke quietly to her in the local language. Tench and Johnston looked at each other and shrugged as the captive stood up, pointed happily at Rosanna and attempted to tell them something about her.

'Alright, let's go and see the governor,' Johnston responded and instructed the marine to whom the captive was tied to move on.

'That was rather incredible, wasn't it, Mr Johnston?' Tench observed. 'I imagine he found a woman and child far less fearful than us marines.'

'Sounds logical, sir.'

As they moved up the hill towards the governor's house, Tench watched the captive closely and noted that he seemed to be increasingly accepting of his situation. He was having a curious look at the various features of the new colony that he had not seen close up before. When the group arrived at Phillip's front garden, Johnston told the crowd to disperse and get on with their duties, which they quickly did with a little encouragement from the marines. The group that remained with the captive was now reduced to just Tench, Johnston, Lieutenant Ball and two marine guards. As they entered the garden, Tench observed the captive's reaction to the tame chooks scratching around, which hardly moved as the group walked past. The captive stared at them and pointed while saying something unintelligible to Tench.

The almost-completed Government House, which served as both the governor's residence and office, was Georgian in design and consisted of a large lower storey with a verandah running across the front. The lower storey included the governor's office and a large dining room. A second storey covered only half the lower storey and contained the bedrooms. In the yard at the back of the building were various outbuildings, including the kitchen, bakehouse, stables, offices and work shed.

As the captive's group approached the building, one of the governor's convict servants leaned out of the second-floor window. The captive's reaction was one of total surprise as he looked up and saw her. He immediately stopped, pointed at her and began talking in a highly animated fashion.

'Do you have any idea what he is saying?' Tench asked Johnston.

'No idea at all, sir,' was Johnston's honest reply.

'Well, given his animated tone, he is obviously quite surprised by her. Do you think he might believe she is really that tall?'

'Surely not,' replied Johnston.

'Whatever it is, he is obviously most surprised by her, and I can't work out what else it could be. Anyway, let's show him what a two-storey building looks like inside.'

At that point, Johnston rang the small brass bell that hung beside the door. The captive, who wasn't watching him, was quite startled by the strange sound and jumped backwards as much as his restraints would allow.

Tench put his hand on the captive's shoulder and said soothingly, 'It's alright, it's alright, it's just a bell. Look,' and rang the bell himself.

The captive was again a little startled but far less than the first time.

'It's just a bell,' Tench said, pointing at it.

The captive reached out and rang it himself, which caused him to burst out laughing. He rang the bell again, and this time his laughter was joined by his captors'.

'Well, there's nothing like enjoying the simple things in life, is there?' Tench asked Johnston.

'No, certainly not,' was Johnston's reply as one of Phillip's servants opened the front door.

As the group began to enter, the captive stopped and again rang the doorbell, causing him further mirth.

After the group entered, they were joined by William Dawes, who had heard about the capture of the native and had immediately hurried to the governor's house. They were shown into Phillip's office, where Phillip sat behind his desk, talking to Major Ross. They both got to their feet as the naked captive was led in.

'Aah, Lieutenant, I see you caught one. Are there any others?' asked Phillip.

'No, sir. We briefly had another, but he was able to escape,' Johnston replied.

'Well, you shouldn't have let him,' Ross cut in.

'I'm sorry, sir, but it was extremely dangerous. We were attacked with spears and were lucky to escape without someone being killed or injured.'

'Yes, yes, I'm very pleased you were able to capture one, so well done.'

'Thank you, sir.' Johnston nodded.

'Now, let's hope he can learn English and we can learn something of his people's customs, so we can come to some sort of understanding of their behaviour towards us,' said Phillip.

'We're on their land,' Dawes murmured quietly to Tench, but it was a comment that Phillip either didn't hear or chose to ignore.

'Now, how does he seem to you, Lieutenant?' Phillip asked, looking intently at the captive standing before him.

'Well, he was most distressed and inconsolable at first, Excellency, but he has settled down now and seems quite accepting of his situation.'

'Ah, that's good.'

'Captain Tench was actually trying to teach him some words of the English language on the way here, sir.'

'Oh, already? And how did he go, Captain?'

'Quite well, sir. I think he should pick it up reasonably quickly, or I hope he does.'

'Good, good,' responded Phillip.

'Actually, sir, if you would indulge us for a moment, I'd like to see if he has understood the meaning of the first word we tried to teach him,' offered Tench.

'Certainly. Please go ahead.'

'If I may, sir,' said Tench, taking a painting of Her Royal Highness the Duchess of Cumberland off the wall. He showed it to the captive and pointed at it.

The captive looked at Tench and then down at the painting.

'Wo-man,' he said, and Tench smiled and nodded as the others laughed happily.

'Well done, well done. Woman.'

'Excellent, Captain.' Phillip nodded. 'Excellent start.'

'Let's hope it is all as easy as that,' Tench responded, feeling rather pleased with himself and the performance of his new project.

'Now, gentlemen, do we happen to know his name?' Phillip inquired.

'No idea yet, Excellency,' replied Johnston.

'Until we can work out what it is, let's call him Manly, after the cove where he was captured and the manly warriors of his tribe,' Phillip said.

'Sounds like a most appropriate name, sir,' Tench agreed as the others nodded.

'Alright, now, let's show we mean the poor chap no harm and give him some food,' Phillip suggested before directing his assistant to organise for the kitchen to prepare something.

The next twenty minutes or so were taken up with Phillip and Tench trying to communicate with Manly on everything from their names and titles to his name and the names of the various objects in Phillip's office. Particular attention was paid to showing him a series of plates with images of a wide variety of animals, including elephants, rhinoceros and tigers. Manly appeared to be both intrigued and confused by the images.

As they finished the session and were about to take Manly into the dining room, two of Phillip's greyhounds walked out from behind the desk, where they had been sleeping. Manly immediately stopped and stared at them, revealing to Tench what appeared to be a mixture of curiosity and fear. Phillip also noticed Manly's reaction and told the dogs to sit, which they did. He patted them on the head, which immediately appeared to relieve Manly's hesitation, and he moved forward and patted them as well. He made a comment to Phillip that caused Tench to observe to Dawes what a soft, melodious voice he had. Dawes nodded his agreement.

Manly was then led into the dining room and sat at a small table beside the long one where Phillip and the senior officers sat on special occasions. Manly was served a large plate containing both fish and duck, which he began eating with great relish, using his fingers. All in the room, including the governor, looked on wistfully, as it had been a long time since any of them had enjoyed a meal of that size.

'I don't really believe it is necessary to feed him quite so much, sir,' commented Ross.

'Major, we want the natives to think food is plentiful for us. The last thing we want them to know is the truth about how desperate we are.'

'I realise that, sir, but we are all on starvation rations, and you're feeding this savage—'

Phillip cut him off. 'Major, I'm not going to argue with you about it. The man can eat as much as he likes as long as he is here. Hopefully, he will be a key to our survival.'

'I beg to differ, sir,' argued Ross. 'The key to our survival is Captain Hunter returning with supplies.'

'Well, I agree with you there, but I shall not be arguing with you about how much the man eats.'

'I'll take my leave, sir. I have other duties to attend to,' Ross said bitterly as he turned on his heel and walked out the door.

'Thank heavens he's gone,' Dawes commented quietly to Tench.

As Manly continued to demolish his meal with unbridled enthusiasm, he was offered a glass of red wine. He looked at it, smelt it and pushed it away.

'It's very good,' urged Phillip, taking a mouthful and offering it again to Manly, but he shook his head and pushed it away.

Manly was then offered water, which he drank happily. When he had finished the duck and fish, he was offered bread and salt beef. He smelt both but refused to eat either. He was then offered another piece of fish, which he ate happily, and when his meal was completed, he wiped his hands on the side of his chair.

'No, no,' said Phillip, shaking his head, as the others in the room chuckled. Phillip smiled and handed Manly a small serviette-style towel, which Manly used quite fastidiously to wipe his hands and face.

'Good, excellent,' said Phillip. 'Hopefully, he now understands we mean him no harm. Now, gentlemen, if you could take Manly out and give him a bath, haircut and shave... oh, and also, for heaven's sake, put some clothes on him.'

'Certainly, Excellency,' responded Tench.

Tench, Dawes and Johnston, along with the two marine guards, took Manly around the back of Phillip's house, where they sat him down on a tree stump. One of the colony's barbers, who had been waiting outside, produced a comb and scissors and was about to start to cut Manly's hair when he pulled away, nervously shaking his head.

'It's alright. He won't hurt you,' Tench assured him.

Again, the barber tried to approach Manly with the scissors, but again, he pulled away.

'It's alright, it's alright,' Tench repeated before directing one of the marines to swap places with Manly. The barber then set to work on the marine, while Manly watched on intently, becoming more relaxed as he did so.

'See, he is not going to hurt you,' Tench assured Manly. 'Now, shave him, please,' he continued to the barber.

Watching the haircut was one thing, but watching a shave was entirely another for Manly, who lived in a community where all the men had beards. In Tench's eyes, he clearly found the whole process quite fascinating.

When the barber had completely shaved the marine, Manly was quite happy to resume his seat on the tree stump and sit still while the barber cut his hair. It was quite long and curly, and as it fell into his lap, Manly gleefully picked up the pieces and began plucking out the vermin in it. When he put one in his mouth, Tench and Dawes expressed their disgust and shook their heads. Manly looked at them both and quizzically shook his head.

'No, yuk, no!' said Tench, again shaking his head.

Manly shrugged his shoulders and discarded the vermin he held between his fingertips. Tench and Dawes nodded approvingly and smiled at him.

When the haircutting and shaving process was completed, Manly was placed into a tub of warm, soapy water. It was something he quite relished as his hair was washed and the fine layer of dirt and mud that covered his skin was gradually scrubbed away.

'I certainly look forward to the day we can communicate with the poor chap well enough to ask him about his people and their culture,' mused Dawes.

'Why do you say "poor chap", Mr Dawes?' Johnston asked. 'We are looking after him very well, and he's certainly had more to eat today than I've had in a week.'

'We've just abducted him from his people, from his family, and we're holding him captive in chains,' replied Dawes. 'I would think "poor chap" is a very appropriate term.'

Johnston nodded. 'Yes, perhaps you're right. I hadn't thought about it quite like that. I must say, then, that I somewhat regret my part in it, but let's hope some good comes of it for the colony.'

'You were only acting under orders, so you can't be responsible–' Tench replied, but Dawes cut in.

'And let's hope some good comes of it for his people… as well as for the colony.'

'Certainly,' agreed Johnston.

At this point, Manly was told to get out of the bath, despite the fact he seemed content to sit there all afternoon. The marine helped Manly dry himself off before Johnston gave him a pair of trousers, a shirt and a hat. The three marine officers explained how to put the clothes on and helped Manly do so. When fully dressed, Manly studied his arms and legs. He appeared quite pleased with how he looked. The marine then put a handcuff on his left wrist, and his reaction was to hold it up and admire it as he smiled broadly. Tench was struck by the whiteness of his teeth against his freshly washed dark skin.

'Bengadee, bengadee,' Manly said, happily showing the handcuff to those around him.

'Bengadee?' Tench said. 'I'm sure that's the word he used to describe my epaulettes.'

'Really?' replied Dawes.

'Yes, I think so,' Tench responded, as he pointed to his epaulettes. 'Bengadee,' he repeated.

Manly nodded. 'Bengadee.' He pointed to the epaulette and to the handcuff.

Dawes looked at Tench. 'What can an epaulette and a handcuff possibly have in common that they use the same word for them both?'

'Perhaps he thinks the handcuff is a bracelet,' Tench replied.

'And if he does, he could think they are both decorations or… perhaps ornaments,' suggested Dawes.

'That sounds like a possibility. We'll find out soon enough, I suppose, but I must say, it is going to be a very interesting challenge trying to learn their language in this way.'

'Most definitely,' agreed Dawes.

At that moment, the marine guard began tying the rope that was attached to the handcuff around his own waist, causing Manly to yell in horror and try to push the handcuff off his wrist.

'I think he realises it is not a bracelet,' commented Dawes. 'The poor chap.'

He and Tench then tried to calm the horrified captive, but to no avail, as Manly was quite inconsolable while the marine guard kept a tight hold on the rope. As Manly's horror and anger gradually turned to sadness, he sat on the nearby tree stump, put his head in his hands and sobbed gently. Tench and Dawes looked at each other with expressions of regret and understanding.

'Captain,' said Johnston, 'now that we have completed the feeding, bathing and grooming process that the governor required, I'd like to relieve my marines of guard duty. Do you think we could have a trusted convict allocated to the task of guarding him?'

'I'd like to have a marine guard him for the first few days, until we can determine his behaviour and if the natives make any attempt to come and rescue him,' Tench replied. 'But go and speak to the governor and see what he wants. After all, this is his project.'

*\*\**

That evening, Tench and Dawes returned to the governor's premises to check on how Manly was settling into his new environment. Johnston had organised to have his marine relieved of the duty of being tied to Manly, and a convict had been substituted. The convict selected was a young man named Joseph Wright, who was both trustworthy and very large – the two criteria that Phillip had insisted on. A marine had nevertheless been tasked with the role of guarding the pair for the short term.

The two marine officers arrived just in time to watch Manly prepare his own supper. He had been provided with some fresh fish, which he threw onto the fire in front of him with no preparation whatsoever. When the fish were warm, he pulled them out, scaled them and pulled the skin off with his teeth. He gutted them, threw them back onto the fire and cooked them through before eating them.

*Ref. 46*

## Chapter 54

## Sydney Cove, 1 January 1789

The silvery light of the morning sun edged the scattered clouds on the horizon as Tench and Dawes walked up the hill to Government House to check how Manly had endured his first night in captivity.

Choosing not to impose on the governor, they proceeded around the back of the house to the small outbuilding where Manly had spent the night tied to his convict companion with manacles around his ankles. Various marines had taken their turn to stand guard. They arrived to find him sitting on the ground, looking rather sullen and depressed.

'Good morning, Joe. How is our captive this morning?' Tench asked, addressing the convict to whom Manly was attached.

Joe stood up to reply, and Tench thought what an imposing figure of a young man he was, being well over six feet with broad, muscular shoulders and arms.

'Pretty good, Captain. He's not very 'appy, but I s'pose that's understandable, sir. In 'is situation and all.'

'Yes, indeed it is,' Tench replied.

'Has he had his breakfast yet?' asked Dawes.

''As 'e 'ad his breakfast, sir? My oaf he has. 'E's 'ad enough for five men, sir. He may be a bit sullen, but there's nuffin wrong wif 'is appetite, sir.'

Tench and Dawes chuckled quietly as Tench replied, 'Yes, we found that yesterday. He certainly has a very healthy appetite. Anyway, that should be good for you, Joe. He may come to share some with you.'

'I must admit, Captain, he did this mornin'. He was very 'appy to share wif me. He were very kind, sir.'

'Well, that's good for you, then,' Dawes replied.

'My oaf it is, sir. Much better than the starvation rations the guvna has us on.'

'Please remember, Joe, we are all on the same rations as you convicts, and that includes the governor,' Tench advised.

'So I'm told, Captain, so I'm told,' Joe replied, sounding rather unconvinced. 'I should also tell ya, sir, that 'e 'ad a little accident after he finished his breakfast.'

'Really? What happened?'

'He was sitting wif 'is back to the fire, sir, and 'e got too close, and the tail of his shirt caught fire. I put it out straight away, so no 'arm done. He didn't want to put on anuver one, but I prevailed on 'im.'

'Good, good for you. He wasn't burnt, though, was he?'

'No, no, sir. He's fine.'

Tench smiled at Dawes and shook his head before turning back to Joe.

'Now, what about last night? How did he sleep?'

'We started with the lamp on, sir, and 'e was very unsettled, but when I turned it off, 'e settled down and slept well.'

'That's good.' Tench paused as he looked the convict up and down, and then changed the subject completely. 'Joe, you seem like a fine young chap, and I'm told you're very trustworthy – that's why you have this job. So, tell me, how did you end up being transported out here?'

'I was a wheelwright, sir, and workin' 'ard, but lost me job through no fault of me own, and ended up fallin' on hard times, like so many of us 'ere, sir. I needed to eat, and I ended up stealin' some lead from a roof. I were only sixteen at the time, sir, and I got caught, and 'ere I am.'

'I'm sorry to hear that,' replied Tench. 'Just sixteen... that's so unfortunate, but hopefully you can make something of yourself here.'

'That's what I plan to do, sir. Just behave meself. See out me time and make something of me life 'ere. The guvna says there'll be opportunities for us if we behave. I just wish we 'ad more to eat. Big chap like me, sir, needs more than the little chaps.'

'Hopefully, if Manly keeps sharing his meals with you, you'll get sufficient food.'

'Yes, sir. I 'ope so.'

'Now, Lieutenant Dawes and I are just going in to see the governor and ask about taking Manly here for a walk around the colony, up to Lieutenant Dawes's observatory on the hill. So, if you wait here, we'll be back shortly.'

\*\*\*

A short time later, Tench, Dawes, Manly, Joe and the marine guard commenced their walk down the hill and into the heart of the tiny colony, which consisted of just two parallel streets running south away from the shore of the cove. Those two streets were lined on either side by very basic, quite miserable huts with glassless windows. The only glass in the colony had been installed in the governor's far more comfortable house. As a substitute, the windows had narrow pieces of flexible, green branches woven together like lattices. They served the purpose of providing some protection against the elements and curious, hungry possums, while at the same time allowing airflow and light into the small huts.

The captive native and his entourage immediately began to attract a crowd. Those with children seemed particularly eager to show them the strange man. Tench and Dawes were keen to stop and continue Manly's English lessons.

Deciding to ensure yesterday's lesson was well learnt, Tench immediately pointed to one of the woman convicts. 'Woman,' he said.

'Woman,' Manly repeated.

'Good, good,' Tench replied before turning to Dawes. 'He certainly seems to know that one.'

Tench spotted Esther Abrahams in the small crowd and bade her to come forward, which she immediately did, with young Rosanna holding her hand.

'Good morning, Esther.' Tench smiled.

'Good morning, Captain,' Esther replied modestly.

Manly crouched down and greeted young Rosanna in the local language as he held out his hand to her.

Esther looked at Tench, who nodded. 'Yes, she'll be fine.'

Esther stepped forward to the black man, who looked so different to yesterday – his hair was cut, he was shaven, he was clean and he was wearing clothes. The total effect was to make him look far less scary and intimidating.

The prisoner smiled at Rosanna, who returned his smile and slowly reached out her hand to his. He took it gently with his handcuffed hand and patted her hair with his free hand as he chatted away soothingly to her.

'Rosanna, say hello to the man,' Esther urged her gently.

'Hello,' the tiny child responded.

Seeing that it was safe to do so, a few other parents brought their children forward to meet the 'wild' black man, who was safely restrained, but who seemed as gentle as a puppy dog anyway.

Tench watched intently as the captive greeted each of the children. Although what he was saying was completely incomprehensible, Tench noted how gently he touched the children's hands and heads. He also noted it seemed to entirely change Manly's mood, which to this point had been quiet and sullen but was now happy and chatty. Tench took the opportunity to name as many things as he could, like 'girl', 'boy', 'shoes', 'dress', but Manly was quite selective about those he tried to pronounce.

When the lesson was over, the prisoner's escorts continued the tour on the way to Dawes's observatory, with both Tench and Dawes naming as many things as they could along the way. Once again, Manly was selective about what he attempted to pronounce and what he didn't, and his melancholia gradually returned after his interaction with the children.

Shortly after, they arrived at Dawes's place on the western side of Sydney Cove. It was the highest point in the colony and enjoyed spectacular views in all directions. They showed Manly Dawes's little hut before Tench dismissed his marine guard and Joe, assuring them they would guard Manly and with the manacles on his ankles, it would be easy to ensure he didn't escape.

'Hopefully, it will be easier to work on his language skills without the distraction of those two,' Tench said.

'Yes, hopefully, or…'

'Or what?' asked Tench.

'Or we could just let him go.'

'Will, we are not letting him go, so don't even suggest such a thing,' Tench replied sharply.

'Alright, alright, I shan't mention it again,' Dawes replied quickly, knowing his friend well enough to know when not to push him.

'Good. Now, show our friend your telescope. I'll be interested to see what he makes of that.'

Dawes showed Manly the large telescope with which he had been provided to study the stars of the southern sky. After a short time winning Manly's confidence in using it, he was quite stunned when Dawes aimed it down the harbour for him. He quickly pulled it away from his eye and looked at the other end as if there was an image attached to it. He turned it around, held it up to his eye and again quickly checked the other end, much to the amusement of Tench and Dawes. He then held up the other end to his eye and looked even more confused. Slowly, though, as Dawes pointed out various landmarks, Manly obviously became aware of what the telescope was doing. He uttered some words of wonderment and continued to use it to take in the view from every direction, particularly to the north-east – to his own country.

There, on the headland where he had stood with his clan almost a year earlier and watched the eleven giant canoes sail into their harbour, he could see a column of smoke gently wafting into the clear morning sky.

'Gweeun,' he murmured, and he sighed deeply.

Tench and Dawes looked to the distant headland, and they too could discern the smoke.

'The poor chap knows that is from his countrymen,' Dawes observed.

'Mmmm, but what was the word he used? Was it "gweeun"?' replied Tench.

'Yes, I think so, but what does it mean? Does it mean "my people" or "fire" or...?'

'Or "smoke",' Tench offered as Dawes began taking notes. 'Yes, it could be any of several things.'

Fortunately, there were the remains of an open fire near where they were standing, so Tench and Dawes took Manly over to it and continued working on learning as many words as they could. They soon came to the conclusion that 'gweeun' meant fire.

They found that although Manly remained quite sullen, particularly since seeing the smoke from his tribesmen, he was being helpful and cooperative in telling his captors the names of the various things they pointed out to him and in learning the English words as well.

When Tench pointed to a harbour island a short distance to the west, Manly immediately said, 'Me-mel.'

'Me-mel,' both Tench and Dawes repeated.

It was the island on which Phillip had left three goats to forage to ensure they couldn't wander off into the bush surrounding the colony due to the lack of fencing. The island quickly became known to the British as Goat Island.

Despite his complete cooperation in naming such landmarks, the one thing their captive didn't want to reveal was his own name.

'Isn't that strange?' Dawes observed. 'He is prepared to tell us the names of everything except himself.'

'Hmmm.' Tench nodded. 'It is quite apparent that he just doesn't trust us.'

'Understandably so.'

Tench and Dawes decided to focus on teaching Manly their names, deciding Tench would be called 'Captain' and Dawes would be called 'Will', believing 'Lieutenant' would be too difficult for their student to pronounce at this stage. The two marines were well satisfied with their student's progress when they finished the morning's lesson and began the walk back through the township to the governor's house, where they had been invited for lunch to celebrate New Year's Day.

Lunch at the governor's house was always a splendid affair but was looked forward to even more than usual in these times of near starvation rations for all, including the senior officers. It was also the time of year when fish were plentiful, and the governor allowed the officers to share his rapidly dwindling supply of wine.

Tench and Dawes entered with Manly. Joe had been reattached for the walk across town but was now made to wait outside during the lunch, along with the marine guard. Manly was seated on a chest near an open window while the officers sat at the governor's long table. Although all enjoyed the food and wine, there were none as well fed as Manly, who ate fish after fish and then a kangaroo rat the size of a rabbit.

'Do we really have to feed that savage quite so much, sir?' questioned Ross.

'Major, I have already explained that young Manly can eat as much as he likes,' Phillip replied impatiently.

'But he eats enough for four men, and my marines are desperate for food.' Ross paused momentarily before adding, 'And he has absolutely no manners whatsoever.'

Ross's comment made all at the table turn their attention to the captive for a moment. As if to demonstrate Ross's final point, Manly picked up his empty dinner plate and was about to throw it out the window when the convict servant standing next to him grabbed it from his hand.

'Did you see that?' yelled a horrified Ross.

All at the table immediately burst into laughter. The confused captive looked at them and, not wanting to be left out of the joke, joined in himself.

As the laughter eased, Tench joked, 'Perhaps he has some Greek heritage,' thereby causing another wave of mirth around the table.

The only one at the table not laughing was Ross, but even he was not prepared to ruin the levity of the situation, so instead gave one of his customary mirthless smiles.

Having eaten his fill, Manly sat on the chest and, using his hat as a pillow, lay down for an afternoon nap, which caused further chuckles from the table. Phillip commented to Tench, 'I think you're wrong, Captain. He's not Greek, he's Spanish.'

To the amazement of all watching, Manly was asleep within a few minutes.

'Gentlemen,' commented Phillip, 'I do think it would be a good idea if we were to take Manly back down harbour where he was captured to show his people that we have done him no harm and he is safe with us.'

'Sounds like an excellent idea, sir,' responded Tench. 'Could I have the responsibility of doing that?'

'You can most certainly come along, but I will be taking him myself. I want the natives to be aware of my involvement in his capture and to demonstrate I will ensure no harm will come to him.'

'Certainly, sir.'

\*\*\*

Shortly after lunch was completed, Manly woke from his afternoon slumber. He was reattached to his convict escort and taken in a longboat back towards Manly Cove, where he had been captured just the previous day.

Phillip and Tench continued his English lessons, pointing out various features of the boat and their surroundings as they were rowed down the harbour. Although Manly was very selective in repeating only some of the names they attempted to teach him, he did respond by pointing out various features of the landscape, and his teachers quickly realised he was telling them the local names for various coves, headlands, islands and other landmarks.

As they approached Manly Cove, the locals who had been on the beach quickly disappeared back beyond the tree line.

'Well, that's understandable, isn't it, sir,' commented Tench.

'Yes, perfectly understandable,' responded Phillip. 'Let's hope we can encourage them to come out again.'

Phillip directed the crew to stand off a short distance from the shore in the hope that the locals would emerge from hiding.

'They probably don't even recognise Manly, sir. Being shaven and wearing clothes and a hat, he would be totally unrecognisable to them.'

'Good point, Captain.'

Phillip removed the captive's hat and helped him remove his shirt, which he cooperated with fully. Phillip then had him stand in the boat so he was clearly visible to his countrymen hiding beyond the tree line. It wasn't long before they emerged and walked cautiously down towards the beach.

As soon as they were within easy earshot, they began calling to their captive colleague. It quickly became apparent to Phillip and Tench that the situation was making Manly very emotional as tears began to appear on his cheeks. When he sighed deeply and raised his leg to reveal the chain on his ankle, it was obvious to Tench that his countrymen had asked him why he simply did not escape. Tench also noticed him repeat the word 'Weerong' several times and interpreted that to be the local name for Sydney Cove, where he was being held. Tench couldn't help but wonder if he might be asking them to come and rescue him. The whole exchange appeared only to further exacerbate Manly's emotional state, so

Phillip ordered the crew to pull away from shore and head back to the colony.

As they made their way back up harbour, Tench asked Phillip, 'How do you think that went, sir?'

'Not as well as I would have liked. I really didn't wish to further upset poor Manly, but at least his countrymen have now seen that we have done him no harm.'

Tench nodded in agreement, but once again, he was pleased Dawes wasn't with them, because Tench was sure he would not have been able to resist responding to Phillip with some sarcastic comment about Manly being held in chains. Tench himself was also beginning to have serious doubts about how keeping one of them in chains could possibly have a positive effect on relations with the local natives. Despite those doubts, though, he was determined to do all he could to see the experiment succeed. If it didn't, he could only envisage dire consequences for either or both the British and the locals.

*Ref. 47*

# Chapter 55

# Sydney Cove, 2 January 1789

It was a surprise to no-one when Manly presented with a rather severe case of diarrhoea the next day. When Tench and Dawes went to visit him in the afternoon, hoping to continue their mutual education, his ailment prohibited it.

'Surgeon Callam tried to give 'im some medications, but he refused 'em all, sir,' Joe explained.

'Well, that's not surprising, really,' responded Dawes.

'It's most unpleasant, sir. It's bad enough when I've 'ad dysentery meself, but it's much worse being chained to 'im.'

'Yes, I can imagine it would be,' replied Tench, suppressing a smirk. 'But at least being tied to him does give you some benefits, like extra food.'

'That it does, sir, that it does – and what a lovely little benefit that is, eh?' acknowledged Joe.

As the three continued their conversation about Manly's condition, he joined them. He motioned to his stomach, his buttocks and his mouth before pointing towards the woods on the eastern side of the colony.

'What do you think he is saying, Mr Dawes?' Tench asked.

'I'm not sure, Captain, but he is obviously quite desperate to tell us something.'

Manly repeated the gestures and began trying to walk towards the woods as he pulled on the chain that fettered him to Joe.

'Obviously, he wants to go somewhere,' said Dawes.

'Joe, let him go where he wants to, and we will come along with you,' Tench advised.

Manly walked out of the backyard of the governor's property and began heading towards the uncleared bush, which was about one hundred yards away to the east. As they approached it, Tench's mind began ticking over as to why Manly had been so desperate to take them to the woods in such a hurry, so he raised the issue quietly with Dawes while they followed along a few paces behind Manly and Joe.

'Will, do you think there could be any connection between our trip back to Manly Cove yesterday, Manly's conversation with his fellow tribesmen and his urgent hurry to come into the woods now?'

'I'm not sure what you are thinking there, Watkin.'

'Well, if you recall, he kept yelling the word "Weerong" to them, and we thought it must be their name for Sydney Cove. Could he have been asking them to come and rescue him? Perhaps he was asking them to just wait in the woods and he would come out?'

Dawes looked at Tench with an expression that was part surprise and part worry.

'I certainly hadn't thought of that, but I suppose it is a possibility,' Dawes acknowledged.

'Joe, just hold on for a moment, would you?' Tench instructed. 'The lieutenant and I need to discuss something.'

Joe stopped and pulled on the chain connecting the prisoner to him. Manly halted but looked at Tench and Dawes rather quizzically as they continued their discussion quietly and out of earshot of the other two. The fact that Manly was at that moment struck by another bout of diarrhoea gave Tench and Dawes the excuse to move further away to avoid the stench that wafted on the breeze.

'Will, I'm just aware of the circumstances here. Not only do we have the combination of circumstances I have just outlined, but we also don't have our guns, and as we know, if there is anything the Indians here are afraid of, it's our guns. Our swords don't seem to concern them.'

'And understandably so, when they have spears. Anyway, I understand your point, and although Manly just doesn't seem the treacherous type, there is no point in being plain foolish about it. Remember, though, it was us who acted treacherously in capturing him in the first place.'

'Mmmm.' Tench turned to look into the bush that began about forty paces from where they stood. 'Well, are they in the woods or not?'

Dawes peered into the bush. Although it was a bright, sunny day, the tall gum trees cast dark shadows across the thick undergrowth, making it difficult for him to see beyond the first few yards of bush.

'How would we ever know? They could easily hide amongst all those trees and undergrowth,' Dawes observed.

Tench nodded. 'Well, let's go and ask Manly again and see if we can get a better understanding of why he wants to go in there.'

He and Dawes walked the few paces to where Joe and the captive stood. Before Tench could question the prisoner, Joe, who had overheard small parts of the officers' conversation, asked nervously, 'Do you think there might be blacks in there waiting to attack us, Captain?'

'We don't know, to be perfectly honest,' Tench replied.

'Captain, I don't think it's a good idea to go in there, if the blacks is waitin' to attack.'

'I can understand that, but just let us see if we can get an understanding from Manly of why he wants to go in there before we decide what we do,' Tench replied calmly before turning to the prisoner and asking, with accompanying hand signals, 'Why do you want to go in there?'

Manly looked at him blankly, so Tench repeated the question slightly louder, making the age-old error of believing when it came to a foreign language, it was a matter of not hearing rather than not understanding.

Dawes saw the futility of the questioning and cut in. 'Look, Captain, he simply cannot understand a question like that, so I think we have to trust him.'

'You may be right, but given we just don't know, I don't think we can ask Joe to remain tied to him while we find out what he wants in there.'

'Thank you, Captain, thank you,' a relieved Joe responded.

'Alright, he can be fettered to me,' offered Dawes.

'I was going to suggest the very same thing.' Tench smiled.

When the fetter had been transferred and Joe had set off to wait for them back in the governor's yard, Tench and Dawes stood in silence for a moment and peered into the thick bush. Tench couldn't help thinking it was strangely quiet in there. The usual cacophony of bird noises seemed to be completely absent. A wave of anxiety swept over him, and his stomach churned, but he made himself turn to Dawes.

'Will, are we ready?'

'I hope so.' Dawes smiled nervously.

The two battle-hardened marine officers, led by the Gamaragal warrior, set off to cover the short distance to the thick bush. As soon as they entered the shadows, Tench and Dawes could see there were no warriors lying in wait for them – not that they could see in the immediate area, anyway. Knowing how well the locals could hide themselves, though, the knots of tension in both their stomachs were only partly relieved. They both noticed that their prisoner immediately began looking around at the ground as they walked, and it wasn't long before Tench stated the obvious.

'It is quite apparent that he is looking for something. If we knew what, we could help him.'

'Well, at a guess, Watkin, can I suggest he may be looking for a plant to cure his condition?'

Manly continued to lead the marine officers this way and that before he stopped near the base of a large gum. He immediately knelt down and began digging at the roots of a native fern plant growing there. Within a few moments, he had extracted it and began brushing the dirt away from the roots before pointing at the water canteen that Dawes had slung over his shoulder. Dawes immediately handed it to

Manly, who poured some of its contents onto the roots to wash away the remaining soil. As soon as he had done that, he began chewing on the roots.

After a minute or so, he stood up and handed Dawes back his canteen as he said in the strongest local accent imaginable, 'Tank you, Will.'

He then turned to Tench and said, 'Tank you, Captain.'

Tench and Dawes looked at each other, totally stunned.

'Did he just say what I think he said?' asked Tench.

'I think he did,' Dawes responded.

Tench turned back to the prisoner and nodded. 'Thank you, Manly.'

The prisoner shook his head, and with the fingertips of his right hand tapping firmly on the middle of his chest, he replied, 'Arabanoo.'

*Ref. 48*

## CHAPTER 56

## CAPE TOWN, 2 JANUARY 1789

By 10 a.m., the *Sirius* had made the short trip across from Robin's Island under an easy sail and anchored in Table Bay some ninety-one days since leaving Port Jackson. Once again, Hunter immediately sent Bradley ashore to inform the governor of their business in the port and their need for supplies.

After updating his journal, Hunter went up on deck to check on the health of the crew who were well enough to be there, enjoying the healing powers of the summer sunshine. He and George Worgan then stood at the starboard rail of the ship, discussing the crew's health while they watched the activities on the shore of the bustling port town, which was a hive of activity due to its crucially important location for ships sailing between Europe, India and the East Indies. Of its population of fourteen thousand, many were slaves occupied in a wide variety of tasks from the farms to the docks.

It was the dock workers who attracted the attention of George Worgan, who, out of the blue, asked Hunter, 'Do you think we will ever abolish slavery, Captain?'

Hunter turned to Worgan. 'That is an interesting question, Mr Worgan, and to be honest with you, it is actually one I have discussed at length with some of our colleagues at Port Jackson. Despite all our discussions, though, we really haven't arrived at an answer. There are those such as Lieutenant Dawes, who strongly believe we have a moral imperative to abolish it as soon as possible. After all, the concept of one human being owning another is quite abhorrent. The other belief, though, is that abolition is just not practical or financially viable, as the slave owners would need to be compensated for the loss of their property from government funds.'

'Do you really think that would be necessary? That is compensating them for the fact they "owned" another human being.'

'Aye, I see your point, but one has to remember that slave owners of the British Empire include some of the wealthiest and most powerful people in our society, so trying to abolish it without paying compensation to the owners may be quite impossible.'

'That would be an enormous financial obstacle, one would think.'

'Aye, definitely, but it would depend on just how much compensation was payable, and I fear, given the wealth and power of the slave owners, it may be set at a level that would almost cripple the nation's economy,' explained Hunter.

'Hmmm. Somehow, though, I believe we must find a solution sooner rather than later.'

'I agree, but it shan't be easy.'

The two men returned their attention to the dock, where they observed Lieutenant Bradley getting into the small rowing boat to be returned to the *Sirius*. A few minutes later, he was back on board and full of news from his visit to the governor of the Dutch colony.

'It went exceedingly well, I'm delighted to say, sir,' enthused Bradley. 'Governor van der Graff was extremely helpful. He remembered us well, sir, and when I advised him of our need for stores, he said there is an abundance of all that we require. We are to provide a list to him, and he will organise it to be delivered to our ship.'

'That is most pleasing, isn't it, Mr Worgan?' Hunter responded.

'It certainly is, sir. The crew and those back at Port Jackson will be enormously relieved.'

'And, Captain, the governor also advised he is sending a ship to Amsterdam in a few days, and if we have any dispatches to forward, he will instruct they be delivered to the British Ambassador in The Hague.'

'Excellent. And what of sick quarters for our crew?'

'Yes, sir, that is also being organised, so as soon as you wish to land them, they can be taken there.'

Worgan immediately responded, 'I'll go and organise that, if I may, Captain.'

'Aye, most certainly.'

Worgan departed, leaving Hunter and Bradley alone.

'Tell me, did you receive any other news?'

'Well, sir, the one piece of concerning advice the governor had was that there has been no sign yet of the fleet transport ships arriving here.'

'What?' Hunter was stunned. 'But they left in July. The fourteenth, wasn't it?'

'I believe so, sir.' Bradley nodded.

'That's nearly six months ago. Lieutenant Shortland was planning to sail north to Batavia… unless he decided to take my advice and sail around Cape Horn, but whichever way they went, they should have been here well over a month ago at the very latest.'

Hunter paused as lines of deep concern creased his face.

'What could possibly have happened to them?' he pondered as he turned and gazed towards the empty horizon.

*Ref. 49*

## Chapter 57

## Sydney Cove, 3 January 1789

Tench and Dawes wanted to be the first into the governor's office the next morning to tell him the news. Phillip had been away at Rosehill the previous afternoon, so they had not been able to tell him of their breakthrough.

As soon as they were admitted to his office, they immediately burst forth simultaneously, 'It's Arabanoo, sir.'

Dawes paused and gave way to his senior officer, who continued, 'Excellency, his name isn't Manly, its Arabanoo.'

'Really?' replied a pleasantly surprised Phillip. 'How do you know?'

'He told us, sir, and not only that, he used our names as well and said thank you to us.'

Phillip beamed, believing this was the sort of progress he really needed so he could start communicating with the local tribes. He motioned to his two visitors to sit down.

'That is just wonderful news, gentlemen. Congratulations.'

Dawes chimed in, 'Another very interesting point, sir, is that he appears to have cured his own diarrhoea.'

'Really? How?'

'Well, he asked us to take him into the bush yesterday when his diarrhoea was most severe, and he dug up some fern roots,' Tench explained, aware that he and Dawes were sounding a little like enthusiastic schoolboys. 'He ate them, and according to Joe, he has been totally cured.'

'I'm quite sure poor Joe is pleased about that.' Phillip smiled.

'Most definitely, sir.'

'Are we sure it wasn't just a coincidence that he ate these fern roots at a time when he was over his ailment anyway?' suggested Phillip.

'If that was the case, sir, it was certainly a most happy coincidence,' replied Tench.

'That is most interesting, though, isn't it?' Phillip conceded. 'He just refused any of our medications, but his own bush remedy seems to have cured him.'

'Yes, sir,' responded Dawes, before adding, 'What it does show, though, Excellency, is that these people know so much about this country and its plants, so we have a lot to learn from them about living here.'

Phillip sat back in his chair. 'Mr Dawes, as you know, apart from wanting to stop this petty warfare with the natives, one of the key reasons I had this man captured… What did you say his name was, again?'

'Arabanoo, sir.'

'Yes, Arabanoo, thank you. One of the key reasons I've had him captured was so we can find out more about them and teach them the benefits of British civilisation, because I'm sure they would be most grateful and this petty warfare would cease.'

'Excellency, I understand that, but I believe we could learn from them also, for the benefit of the colony.'

'Perhaps you're right, Mr Dawes, but don't let Major Ross hear you say that. What? Learning from the natives? Preposterous.'

'Yes, Excellency, as you know, we are all well aware of Major Ross's narrow-minded views.'

Phillip nodded. 'Hmmm, but a little respect, please, Mr Dawes. After all, he is your commanding officer.'

'Sorry, Excellency,' was Dawes's chastened reply.

'Right. Now, gentlemen, I would like you to take Arabanoo back down to Manly Cove again this afternoon so his people can see that he is perfectly safe with us. I think it is important to help win their confidence. The last thing I want is an increase in their attacks on us because they believe we have killed or injured one of theirs. I know last time it distressed him somewhat, but I believe it's important they see we are not harming him.'

'Excellency, we'd be most happy to do that,' Tench responded.

\*\*\*

The north-easterly breeze that blew up on most afternoons to help cool the colony in the middle of summer had just arrived as the longboat carrying Arabanoo and his captors made its way down the harbour. On the way, they put into the harbour's easternmost island and shot several water birds before continuing their journey to Manly Cove.

When they arrived at their destination, there was no sign of any of Arabanoo's countrymen on the beach. As the longboat was dragged up onto the sand, Arabanoo began calling out to them, but none emerged from the bush. Tench and Joe helped the fettered Arabanoo out of the boat and onto the sand. They stood there looking along the beach and into the tree line.

Once again, Tench was a little uneasy as he turned to Dawes.

'What do you think, Lieutenant? Should we wait a few minutes, or are we just leaving ourselves in a vulnerable position in case they decide to attack us?'

'Well, Captain, it may be best to stand off the shore in the boat, so if we need to, we can make a quick escape, but let's wait a few moments and see if anyone comes to talk to Arabanoo.'

'Yes, that sounds reasonable,' Tench responded before addressing the marines. 'Keep your muskets at the ready. If we are attacked, don't fire until I say so, and then only fire above their heads.'

A few minutes passed, and there was no sign of Arabanoo's countrymen, so Tench ordered everyone to get back into the boat.

As they began to, Arabanoo leant into the boat and took out three of the water birds that had just been shot. Joe looked at Tench, and the captain nodded.

'Yes, just let him do as he wants to.'

Arabanoo walked a few metres across the beach to where there was a basket made of bark, and into it he placed the three birds before carefully covering them over and returning to the boat.

Dawes looked at Tench and said quietly, 'That was kind of him.'

Tench nodded. 'Mmmm, a present for his friends.'

After they all clambered back into the boat, it was rowed a short distance from shore, where they stood and waited for almost half an hour. There was no sign of Arabanoo's countrymen appearing on the beach, so Tench ordered them to return to Sydney Cove.

When they arrived, Tench, Dawes and a marine guard began escorting Arabanoo and Joe back to the governor's premises. As they did so, though, they met Esther and little Rosanna walking back down the hill. Tench and Dawes stopped and greeted her.

Tench couldn't help thinking how much Esther herself had grown in confidence since he had first met her. Her relationship with Lieutenant George Johnston was now well established and accepted within the colony, as were various other similar relationships with the convict women.

'Rosie, say hello to Captain Tench,' Esther urged her daughter.

'Hello,' said Rosanna confidently.

At that point, Arabanoo stepped forward and crouched down to the child. He reached out his hand and touched her sleeve, smiled and uttered a few words in the local language.

'Say hello to the nice man,' Esther urged again.

'Hello.' Rosanna smiled.

'Hello,' Arabanoo replied, much to Rosie's pleasant surprise.

'Esther, you'll be interested to know we finally found out his name. It's Arabanoo,' Tench advised.

'Hello, Arabanoo,' Esther said.

Arabanoo smiled at the mention of his name.

'Hello,' he replied, patting Rosie on her head, before Tench and Dawes took their leave of Esther and led Arabanoo away, as once again, a crowd was beginning to grow around them.

*Ref. 50*

## Chapter 58

## Cape Town, 5 January 1789

The question that Hunter had been pondering for the past few days – the possible whereabouts of the fleet ships – was answered when Bradley arrived just before midday while Hunter was in his cabin writing up his journal.

'Sir, I have some news of the fleet ships.'

'Aye, and what is it?'

'A Dutch East India ship that has recently arrived advised that they saw both the *Prince of Wales* and the *Borrowdale* in Rio de Janeiro, and the crews were in a terrible state with the scurvy. Many had died during the voyage, and those still alive were so ill that neither ship was able to sail into the harbour without the assistance of additional crew from the shore.'

'That is most disturbing,' Hunter responded before pausing and adding, 'But why would they try to sail up the coast of South America when it is far quicker to just use the prevailing westerly winds and sail across here to Cape Town?'

'Sir, I'm advised that after they sailed around the Horn, they had a very slow voyage up the coast, and the scurvy just ravaged the crew during that part of the journey. While we are on that subject, though, I should mention that all the officers I have spoken to while we have been in port here have been most effusive in their praise of your seamanship to sail from Port Jackson to here in just ninety-one days without a single port along the way.'

'Well, thank you, Lieutenant. Although the praise is pleasing to hear, the scurvy tragically ravaged the crew, so it was not such a wonderful achievement from that perspective.'

'Perhaps not, sir, but we must remember so many of the crew were in poor health when they started the voyage.'

'Aye, but anyway, I am now far more concerned about the fate of those fleet ships and their crews… You know neither of those ships had a surgeon on board. One only has to consider how we would have fared on our voyage if we didn't have Mr Worgan and his assistant. That is just reckless and negligent on the part of those ship owners, and it is such false economy.'

Bradley said nothing but nodded and let his normally placid, controlled captain continue.

'It is simply wrong of the British Government to retain these ships on contracts that don't require them to have surgeons on board… And what of the other ships under Lieutenant Shortland? What news of them?'

'It seems, sir, that they chose a different course not long after leaving Port Jackson. The *Prince of Wales* and the *Borrowdale* turned south-east and sailed around Cape Horn, while the *Alexander* and the *Friendship* continued northwards to Batavia. At this point, it seems no-one here knows their fate.'

*Ref. 51*

## CHAPTER 59

## SYDNEY COVE, JANUARY 1789

Arthur Phillip was perfectly happy for Tench and Dawes to spend much of their time, when they were not occupied by other duties, with Arabanoo, trying to teach him English, while at the same time learning his language and customs. Phillip himself liked to spend any spare time he had working with them on his pet project. Arabanoo had quickly become a source of entertainment for so many in the colony. During the day, children would come and visit to talk to the strange black man who was always so gentle with them.

One humid summer morning, while Tench and Dawes were working on Arabanoo's language skills, Esther brought Rosie and another child she was caring for along to visit Arabanoo. Rosie's friend, Sadie, was obviously the child of convicts and dressed accordingly in clothes that were grubby and worn, which contrasted conspicuously with Rosie's neat little dress. After the adults exchanged greetings, Arabanoo walked over to Rosie and crouched down to say hello.

'Hello, Boo.' Rosie smiled shyly.

'Hello, Rosie.' Arabanoo smiled as he took her tiny white hand in his large black hand.

Arabanoo loved spending time with the children, particularly Rosie, but it made his heart ache for his own, who he longed to be reunited with. He missed them as much as he missed Weereweea.

'How are Arabanoo's English lessons going, Captain?' asked Esther.

'Fairly slowly, but we are getting there,' responded Tench.

'Yes, he's just a bit better at learning English than we are at learning his language, and we're really trying,' added Dawes.

'I imagine that it would be very difficult to learn such a strange language.'

'Well, it should be no more difficult for us than English is for him, but we feel it is important that this is a two-way learning experience,' commented Dawes.

'Esther, you are right, though. His language is very difficult,' added Tench.

'And you can speak Latin.' Dawes smirked.

'Yes, but I read it much better than I speak it, and unfortunately, we obviously don't have anything of Arabanoo's language in writing.'

While the conversation continued, Arabanoo's lunch was brought to him by one of the governor's kitchen staff. He immediately sat on the ground and motioned for the children to sit with him. His meal consisted of half a duck and a large piece of freshly baked bread. He looked at Rosie and uttered something unintelligible before breaking off a piece of duck breast and offering it to her. Rosie took it gratefully and was about to start eating, but she paused and pointed to her little friend.

'Boo, Sadie hungry too.'

Arabanoo smiled as he broke off another piece of breast and gave it to Sadie, who grasped it thankfully in her grubby little hands. Both children ate ravenously as Arabanoo settled in to devour the remainder of the duck with the bread.

'I wish I was that well fed,' commented Esther.

'Don't we all,' agreed Tench.

When the language lessons were over, Tench and Dawes visited Phillip. After updating the governor on Arabanoo's progress, Tench commented, 'I don't know if you've noticed, Excellency, but Arabanoo always gives the tastiest parts of his food to the children when they visit him.'

'I must say I really hadn't watched that closely, but in many ways, I wish he wouldn't do that, as there is little enough to feed him without him giving it away. As for the children, though, I wonder if the poor little blighters are more interested in the food he gives them than in the novelty of talking to him.'

'Hopefully, though, sir, it is a little easier to fill him up now he has acquired a taste for bread.'

'Yes, well, that's something, I suppose,' Phillip replied. 'Interesting that he has also developed a taste for tea but still refuses wine or any alcohol.'

\*\*\*

Arabanoo was also an enormous amusement to the officers whenever they gathered for a meal with Phillip. The after-dinner entertainment always consisted of asking Arabanoo the names for various things they showed him and then laughing at each other's usually feeble attempts to pronounce the local Dharug language. Arabanoo laughed along with them, sometimes because the British attempts at Dharug were highly amusing, but at other times, he laughed merely because he didn't want to be left out of the joke.

Arabanoo's relationship with Phillip was also developing, and Tench believed that he had quickly realised Phillip was the one who ultimately determined his future and if he was ever going to be allowed to return to his family. Tench was totally correct in that belief, as every day, Arabanoo longed to returned to Weereweea and his children. He just hoped that if he cooperated with his captors, one day he may be allowed to do so.

*Ref. 52*

## CHAPTER 60

## TABLE BAY, CAPE TOWN, 19 JANUARY 1789

The *Sirius* had now been in Table Bay for over two weeks. The ill amongst the crew were gradually regaining their health, courtesy of the fresh food provided, while most of the healthy members were able to enjoy port life while the ship was heeled over, having its leak repaired. On close inspection of the hull, though, Hunter was convinced that the ship did need more extensive repairs to address the corrosion of its iron bolts. Unfortunately, there was neither the time nor the resources to carry out the complete repairs the diligent captain felt were necessary.

Hunter was at dockside, standing in the summer sun, discussing the health of the crew with George Worgan, when a concerned-looking Bradley hurried up to them.

'Captain, I have some further news on the fleet ships.'

'Aye, by the look on your face, it isn't good,' responded Hunter.

'No, sir, it isn't. You know the Dutch frigate we saw enter the bay this morning?' Hunter nodded while Bradley continued, 'Well, they have just returned from Batavia. There, they had to assist Lieutenant Shortland to dock the *Alexander*, as it had lost so many crew to the scurvy that there were only four of them well enough to stand on the deck.'

'That's terrible,' groaned Hunter.

'That isn't the worst part, sir. They'd already had to scuttle the *Friendship* because there weren't sufficient crew to sail two ships.

They combined the crews onto the *Alexander* after most of both were buried at sea.'

Hunter looked at Worgan, but both men were lost for words.

'If only they'd followed your advice, Captain, and sailed around Cape Horn,' added Bradley.

'Aye, but there was the risk with the ice and gales at that time of year. As I've said before, those ships should all have surgeons on board,' replied Hunter, totally exasperated. 'They had Mr Balmain for the outward voyage, but with him staying in the colony, they have no-one for the return.'

'As you've said, Captain, it is just false economy.'

'Exactly!' responded Hunter. 'And now all those good men have lost their lives, and they've had to scuttle the ship rather than pay one surgeon. Tell me how those numbers work out.'

The three men paused for a moment while they processed the tragic news.

'Mr Bradley, where are Lieutenant Shortland and the *Alexander* now?'

'The crew that survived were recovering in Batavia before continuing their voyage back to London via here, sir.'

'So Lieutenant Shortland is alright, then?'

'I believe so, sir. I understand he was one of the few still able to stand on the deck when they reached Batavia.'

'Good. That's something. Let's just hope they arrive before we have to depart. I wouldn't like to have to tell Phillip that terrible news without at least being able to advise that the *Alexander* had arrived here safely.'

'Definitely, sir, and especially given the respect Phillip has for Lieutenant Shortland,' agreed Worgan.

'Aye, as we all do. He is a very good man and, as you know, a friend of mine as well, so I am very anxious to see him arrive safe and well. The whole thing is just such a tragedy… such a tragedy.'

*Ref. 53*

## Chapter 61

## Sydney Cove, 17 February 1789

Late on yet another hot, humid morning, Captain Henry Ball was about to set sail on the *Supply* for another trip to Norfolk Island. Shortly before he departed, Phillip joined him on board to wish him a safe voyage. Phillip, like all in the colony, was excessively aware that the *Supply* was their last connection to the outside world. He was also very aware that any voyage to Norfolk Island was a hazardous one, due to the lack of any suitable harbour there, which meant any landing involved significant risk. It was a risk they had to take, though, in the hope that the crops planted at Norfolk had been a success and were able to provide the colony with some desperately needed food, particularly fresh vegetables.

Accompanying Phillip on this occasion were Tench and a special guest, Arabanoo, who Phillip felt may enjoy a tour of the *Supply* and the experience of sailing down harbour in her. Arabanoo had been freed from his fetters for the occasion, as there was nowhere he could escape to.

Ball greeted his three guests warmly as they climbed from the longboat onto the deck of the ship.

'Good morning, Excellency. Welcome aboard!' He smiled as he saluted.

'Thank you, Captain. Are you all ready to depart?'

'Yes, sir, whenever you and your guests have finished your little tour.' Ball turned to Phillip's guests. 'Good morning, Captain. Hello, Arabanoo.'

'Hello, Captain,' Arabanoo replied in his thick Dharug accent.

'Well, he's certainly learning, sir,' Ball acknowledged.

'He is, but we were hoping for faster progress in some areas,' Phillip replied. 'Anyway, we'll take him and show him around the ship.'

The tour began on the quarterdeck and then followed the starboard side of the ship to the bow. At regular intervals, Arabanoo stopped and looked up at the masts, which at this point were devoid of sails – the sails that he and his countrymen had been so struck by when they had sailed into the harbour just over a year ago. He also stopped and inspected the masses of rope that would soon be used to haul the sails up the masts before he looked over the rails to the water below.

'He seems to be enjoying himself, Excellency,' Ball commented.

'As you know, Captain, he has always been quite a curious chap about the new things we have shown him.'

'He is most inquisitive,' Tench added.

Having completed the tour of the deck, Arabanoo was taken below, but both Tench and Phillip observed him to seem quite uncomfortable in the tight confines there, so they quickly returned to the deck.

'Alright, Captain, let's get underway and show Arabanoo what it's like to sail on a ship like the *Supply*,' Phillip said.

Ball immediately gave the orders, and the anchor was raised as the crew set the foresail. In a few minutes, they were underway and sailing down the harbour. Tench looked at Arabanoo to study his reaction. Instead of joy, however, Tench could see an expression of sheer terror rapidly spreading across his face. Arabanoo looked at Phillip and then at Tench.

'No, Guvna. No, Captain,' he said, shaking his head furiously. 'Arabanoo baragat.'

'It's alright, Arabanoo,' Tench assured him, but as he reached out to give Arabanoo a reassuring pat on the shoulder, Arabanoo leapt over the rail of the boat and into the water below.

Phillip and Tench looked over the rail to see Arabanoo surface and begin swimming frantically away.

'The poor chap, he must have thought we were taking him away on the ship,' said Phillip.

'Yes, it would seem so, sir. Something certainly terrified him.'

Captain Ball and several of the crew came to the rail as Arabanoo continued to swim away. The next moment, he began trying to dive beneath the surface, but the buoyancy of his clothes made it impossible for him to do so effectively. His attempts looked rather comical from the deck of the *Supply* and caused widespread laughter amongst the crew.

Tench couldn't help feeling that his friend was being unfairly mocked. 'Gentlemen, I'll have you know he is an expert diver when he doesn't have the encumbrance of our European clothing.'

'He obviously believes we're going to shoot at him,' Phillip observed and then turned to Ball. 'Captain, please have your men pick him up in the longboat.'

'Certainly, sir.'

'I'll go along too,' said Tench, not wanting the already terrified Arabanoo to be picked up by a boatful of strangers.

In a few minutes, the longboat caught up to the fleeing Arabanoo. The sailors immediately began trying to haul him on board, but he struggled quite furiously. Tench moved from the back of the boat to the side where the sailors were attempting to haul him on board and spoke in soothing tones to the struggling swimmer. Although Arabanoo continued to resist, it was a lot less furiously, and finally, he allowed Tench to help pull him on board. When they returned to the deck of the *Supply,* though, Arabanoo was quite melancholy and withdrew from the group, sitting on a crate in front of the quarterdeck where the others stood.

It was the first time in just over a year that Phillip had been sailing on one of the fleet ships, and to Tench's eye, he seemed to be enjoying it enormously as he looked up to see the breeze filling the sails and felt the invigorating salt air on his face.

'Nothing quite like it, is there, sir?'

'No indeed, Captain,' Phillip replied. 'It is a wonderful feeling. And sailing down this magnificent harbour just adds to the pleasure.'

It was not long, though, before they rounded the headland that projected from the north shore almost halfway across the harbour and which Phillip had begun to call Bradley's Point after Hunter's dedicated lieutenant. It was time for Phillip and his party to leave the ship, as it would soon be picking up speed as it sailed north-east along the broadening harbour before taking a starboard tack out into the open ocean.

Phillip's party walked past the disconsolate Arabanoo and began to descend the rope ladder to the longboat. Phillip and Tench were the last to descend, and before they did, they looked at Arabanoo and at each other. They couldn't help smiling as Phillip called, 'Arabanoo, come on.'

Arabanoo immediately jumped to his feet and hurried across the deck, his white teeth beaming against his black skin. Phillip put his arm around him as he was about to climb onto the ladder and said, 'We wouldn't leave you behind, old friend.'

By the time they were in the longboat and rowing away from the side of the *Supply*, Arabanoo was obviously so relieved he was far more garrulous than usual and began pointing out the various landmarks around them, the first of which was the adjacent Bradley's Point.

'Booraghee,' he said.

*Ref. 54*

## Chapter 62

## Table Bay, Cape Town, 18 February 1789

John Hunter looked out across Table Bay towards its entrance to see the afternoon sun shining on the water wherever it was visible between the numerous ships anchored in the harbour. He, Bradley and Worgan were on the dock, overseeing the loading of stores onto the *Sirius* before its departure the next day. They had been delivered by the slaves of the Dutch East India Company, and the ship's crew were cramming them into every spare inch of the *Sirius*, including the officer's quarters.

'Well, that's it, sir. That's the last load,' announced a somewhat relieved Bradley.

'Oh, very good,' responded a rather distracted Hunter.

Bradley paused as he watched Hunter staring out towards the entrance of the bay.

'Looking for the *Alexander*, sir?'

Hunter nodded. 'Hmmm, I certainly am.'

'It is most concerning, sir,' replied Worgan.

'Aye, it certainly is. I was hoping she would be here before we left, but we really have to depart at first light tomorrow.'

'I know, sir. We have a whole colony depending on us,' added Bradley.

'Aye, exactly, and if we wait any longer, we could be waiting for a ship that's on the bottom of the ocean somewhere,' admitted Hunter, a tinge of dread in his voice.

A short time later, Hunter, Bradley and Worgan climbed into the longboat to be rowed back to the *Sirius*. As soon as he was seated in the back of the boat next to Bradley, Hunter again looked towards the entrance of Table Bay. This time, he stopped and stared, for there, sailing around Green Point and into the bay, was a ship. It was heading directly towards them and was too far away for him to identify, but an immense feeling of hope immediately welled inside him. His eyes couldn't confirm it, but his mariner's gut knew immediately… it was the *Alexander*.

He tapped Bradley on the shoulder and pointed. Bradley peered into the distance.

'Do you really think it could be, sir?' Bradley asked.

Hunter momentarily ignored the question as he instructed the oarsmen to row not to the *Sirius,* but towards the ship entering the bay. Worgan, who had his back to the bay's entrance, immediately swung around to see what the other two were staring at before looking back at Hunter and Bradley and asking the same question that Bradley had just asked.

'Could it be, sir?'

Hunter still didn't answer, so intent was he on peering into the distance, but at that moment, the entering ship tacked to clear the reef, enabling Hunter to have a much better view of it.

Hunter beamed as he replied, 'It's a large three-masted bark, gentlemen. It's her!'

The *Alexander* may have carried a boy's name, but to sailors such as Hunter, all ships were 'her', and for a lifelong bachelor like Hunter, it was like watching the return of a long-lost lover – one he'd never had. He was a man who belonged to the oceans of the world and never to any person, so he couldn't fully understand the relief and pure joy now coursing through his body.

As they rowed towards the *Alexander*, though, he realised that he did recognise the emotion. He had felt it just once before in his life – at just nine years of age, when shipwrecked off the coast of Norway, his father had put a strong arm around him and, pointing to the approaching fishing boats, said, 'It'll be alright, son. They'll save you.'

Although the *Alexander* was not about to save his life, its arrival meant his friend John Shortland and his crew were alive and should now be assured of making the return voyage to London safely. And it also meant he could return to the colony with some good news about one of the fleet transports after the tragic fates of three of the others.

The *Alexander* was well inside the sheltered waters of Table Bay as Hunter's longboat approached. The ship's crew, including Shortland, were looking over the rail to see who was approaching. The moment they recognised who it was, the entire crew, led by Shortland, erupted into wild cheering. Hunter, Bradley and Worgan beamed as they waved back, feeling like British monarchs.

Hunter turned to Bradley and Worgan and said, 'It sounds like they be as pleased to see us as we are to see them.'

'They certainly do, sir,' responded Bradley, as Worgan nodded and continued to wave to the cheering crew.

A few minutes later, Hunter was the first of them to climb the ship's rope ladder and land on the deck, where he was immediately greeted by Shortland, who had to push his way through the jubilant crew.

'Welcome aboard, Captain. It's just wonderful to see you.' Shortland smiled.

'Aye, and wonderful to see you, Mr Shortland.' At that moment, Hunter's relief and joy were such that he wanted to throw his arms around Shortland and hug him, but he rarely acted on his feelings and instead merely patted Shortland on the shoulder. It was an action, however, that spoke perfectly clearly to Shortland. His restrained, undemonstrative friend was very, very pleased to see him.

'How are you and yer crew?' Hunter inquired as the two men walked away to the quarterdeck, while the remainder of the crew greeted Worgan and Bradley, who now climbed on board.

'Remarkably well now, sir, especially compared to the first leg of our voyage, which was just a nightmare.'

'Aye.' Hunter nodded. 'I've been told, but I want to hear the full story from you.'

'But what are you doing here?' asked Shortland, quite amazed.

'The colony needs supplies urgently, because the crops continued to fail and we have received nothing from England, so we're here collecting some,' replied Hunter.

'Still nothing from England?' queried Shortland.

'Not a thing,' replied Hunter, quite disgusted.

'That's terrible. And I assume, then, that you came around Cape Horn, for you to be here so quickly.'

'Aye, we did.'

'Well, that just proves it. You were right, Captain. We should have sailed via Cape Horn as you said.'

'Aye, but I get no satisfaction from that when all those men have lost their lives.'

'Yes, sir, and I can only blame myself,' confessed Shortland. Tears began running down his cheeks as guilt for the deaths of so many of his crew collided with the relief of his own survival.

'I wouldn't think that way,' Hunter assured him, feeling totally uncomfortable when confronted with the tears of a fellow navy man, despite the fact he was experiencing one of the most emotional moments of his own life. 'The fact is the ships' owners should have ensured there was a surgeon on board each vessel. Also, we found the ice islands and weather around the Horn a real problem, even at this time of year, so as you feared, it would have been very difficult in winter.'

He quickly changed the subject to allow Shortland to compose himself. 'Do you have any rum left in your cabin?'

'Yes, sir, just the last of it.'

'Good. Well, let's go and have a wee dram... or two.'

At that point, Bradley and Worgan joined them on the quarterdeck. After exchanging the warmest of greetings, Shortland asked Worgan if he would mind checking on the health of the handful of crew who were ill in their quarters before joining them in his cabin. The conscientious Worgan was on his way before Shortland finished his request.

After organising to advise the local governor of their arrival, Shortland led Hunter and Bradley to his cabin.

'Now, Captain,' started Shortland, 'how long did it take you to get here via the Horn?'

'Ninety-one days,' replied Hunter.

'Ninety-one days! But that is eight thousand nautical miles, and it took us a hundred and thirty-seven days just to sail the four thousand nautical miles to Batavia.'

'Hmmm.' Hunter nodded. 'It must have been a dreadful voyage.'

'It was,' acknowledged Shortland, before providing Hunter and Bradley with full details of the tragedy. He concluded by asking Hunter, 'And how was your voyage here, sir?'

'Ours was not easy either, Mr Shortland,' replied Hunter with typical understatement. 'The scurvy hit our crew as well. We lost three men, and we had forty more confined to their bunks, some on death's door, when we arrived here. We barely had enough crew to sail her as well as man the pumps on our leaking ship.'

'And we had some very narrow scrapes amongst the ice near the Horn,' added Bradley.

'Aye, we certainly did,' agreed Hunter. 'So, there certainly be no easy passage from Port Jackson, especially when you start your voyage with a crew that is in poor health.'

The three men continued their conversation for well over an hour before Hunter realised that time was getting on and rose to his feet, saying, 'Now we must go and prepare to sail at first light in the morning.'

'Yes, sir,' replied Shortland.

'Governor Phillip will be pleased to hear that you have arrived here safely after the tragedies that have beset the returning fleet.'

'Thank you, sir. And could you assure him I still have his dispatches to the colonial office?'

'Ah, he'll be delighted to hear that, as they are very important to ensure the colony receives the support from London that it needs to survive,' advised Hunter.

'Yes, sir. The governor stressed their importance to me,' replied Shortland.

'Good.'

'And, sir, on a small side issue, you might also mention to Captain Tench that I still have his manuscript for his publishers.'

'Well, after the perils of your voyage, Mr Shortland, I'm sure he will be pleased to hear that, but more importantly, that you're alive.'

*Ref. 55*

## CHAPTER 63

## SOUTHERN INDIAN OCEAN, 20 FEBRUARY 1789

The *Sirius* was on her way. She sailed out around the Cape of Good Hope and into the Indian Ocean. After nearly seven weeks in Cape Town, the crew were as healthy as they were going to be, and every corner of the ship was stuffed full of supplies for the colony, including six months' supply of flour and countless other commodities, as well as the various items on the private shopping lists of many of the officers in the colony.

Despite the fact that there were some rumblings amongst the crew suggesting they should just forget about the failing colony and head back to the safety of Mother England while they had the chance, such rumblings were quickly squashed by the captain. Consequently, Hunter and Bradley were both in buoyant moods as they stood chatting on the quarterdeck beside the helmsman, who was at the wheel. Seeing Shortland and his crew on the *Alexander* arrive safely in Cape Town had filled them with optimism. On top of that, they had overcome the hazards of the outward voyage – the ice, the gales, the scurvy, a leaking ship and the challenges of rounding Cape Horn, something that neither of them had ever done before.

Now they were starting off afresh with a healthy crew and full bellies, on a course that they had both sailed before, where they knew the westerly winds of the 'roaring forties' would be consistently behind them, pushing them quickly and safely across the southern Indian Ocean to Port Jackson.

That was their hope and expectation, anyway, but only a day after they left the Cape of Good Hope, they were hit with strong gales from the south accompanied by squalls, which dramatically slowed their progress. Both Hunter and Bradley expected them to ease after a day or two, but they didn't. They persisted and persisted for over three weeks.

It was the first sign that this voyage would not go as planned and they were going to have to sail for their lives.

*Ref. 56*

## Chapter 64

## Sydney Cove, Early March 1789

Watkin Tench was sitting in Phillip's office with Major Robert Ross when they were interrupted by Lieutenant David Collins.

'I have just received some very disturbing news, sir,' Collins began.

'What's happened?' Phillip inquired as concern furrowed his brow.

'Some of the convicts who were working at the brick kilns have been attacked by the natives, sir,' Collins advised.

'What? Were they attacked at the kilns?' Phillip asked.

'No, sir. They say they were in the bush picking sweet tea, and it seems some have been killed or injured.'

'Bloody savages,' barked Ross.

'That's most concerning,' Phillip responded, ignoring Ross's comment.

'Lieutenant Johnston has taken a party of marines to try to rescue those who haven't yet returned and to pursue the natives,' Collins advised.

'Excellency, Major, if I may, I'd like to go and see if I can be of any assistance,' requested Tench.

'Yes, yes, by all means, go,' Phillip urged before adding, 'Unless, of course, you have a problem with that, Major.'

'No, sir, that's fine,' Ross replied.

Tench jumped to his feet and hurried out the door with Collins.

'And what further details do you have, Mr Collins?' Tench inquired.

'Very few, sir. I only know that a group of the men came rushing back to the brick kilns saying they had been attacked in the bush. It seems only about half the party had returned safely when Lieutenant Johnston left with the marines to look for the others.'

'How many were in the party that were attacked?' Tench asked as they rushed up the hill towards the brick kilns to the south.

'It seems about fifteen or sixteen, but I'm not exactly sure, sir.'

'What, fifteen or sixteen out picking sweet tea, and they were attacked? There is something very strange there, Mr Collins.'

'Exactly what I thought.'

'To start with, you don't need fifteen or sixteen men to pick sweet tea, and the Indians have never attacked so large a group of us.'

'Yes, one is inclined to think they must have done something to provoke the natives,' Collins suggested.

'Exactly. Anyway, the first thing to do is ensure they're all safe, and then we can try to get to the bottom of the whole matter.'

By the time Tench and Collins arrived at the brick kilns, several of the convicts had returned, and some of them had suffered wounds of varying degrees. Surgeon White and his assistant were there treating them, while marine guards secured the area.

Tench and Collins immediately approached the nearest convict who was uninjured and began questioning him. He was a typically rough-looking character, on the smallish side and, like his colleagues, quite gaunt and clearly undernourished. He scratched his unshaven face, which was creased by anxiety, as the marine officers approached.

'What happened, exactly?' Tench asked.

'We was just out pickin' some sweet tea, Captain, and the blacks just attacked us out of nowhere. We didn't do nothin' to 'em, sir.'

'How many of you were there?' Collins joined in.

'About sixteen of us, sir,' mumbled the convict.

'Sixteen?' replied Tench in mock shock. 'You needed sixteen of you to pick sweet tea? You must have been planning to pick all the sweet tea in the entire colony.'

'There was that many of us 'cause we're scared to go into the bush with only a few of us for fear of the blacks, Captain.'

'Hmmm, and how did that work out for you?' Tench asked sarcastically.

'Where were you when you were attacked?' probed Collins.

'In the bush, sir,' replied the recalcitrant convict.

Collins continued the inquisition. 'Where in the bush? Just close by here, or where?'

'Down near Botany Bay, sir,' the convict admitted.

Tench and Collins looked at each other incredulously.

'Towards Botany Bay?' blurted Tench. 'There is plenty of sweet tea in the bush in the immediate area around the colony. Why would you go all the way down there?'

The convict shrugged his shoulders. 'Dunno, sir.'

'Well, I think we should go and ask some of your colleagues,' said Tench.

Tench and Collins moved on and began questioning the other uninjured convicts, but as they did so, Lieutenant Johnston returned with his party of marines, along with two gravely injured convicts and the body of another, who had a broken spear protruding from his chest.

Tench looked at Collins and shook his head. 'This is serious.'

***

The next morning, Tench and Collins entered Phillip's office to report to Phillip and Ross the details of the previous day's tragic events.

'Well, gentlemen, what have you been able to find out?' Phillip asked as his visitors took their seats in front of his desk. 'Sorry, before you answer, firstly I must ask – what is the situation with the wounded?'

'Apart from the one who was fatally injured, there were a total of seven wounded,' advised Tench, 'two of them quite seriously so, but Surgeon White believes they should both survive. In answer to your first question, though, sir, in simple terms, it is quite clear our men were entirely at fault.'

'What,' scoffed Ross.

'Really?' Phillip inquired. 'Not again! I'm not quite sure if I consider that good news or bad. It is pleasing that the natives haven't just wantonly attacked them, but most disturbing and frustrating that after all I've said about not provoking the natives, they are still doing it. What exactly happened?'

Tench was about to reply when Phillip cut him off. 'How many warnings have I given them all?'

'Very many, sir,' Collins replied.

'I'm sorry, gentlemen. Please continue.'

'As we explained to you yesterday afternoon, sir, they initially insisted they were just out picking sweet tea when they were attacked without provocation,' responded Tench. 'It didn't make any sense. To start with, why would they go all the way to Botany Bay to pick sweet tea when there is plenty of it close by, and why would there be so many of them?'

'Yes, it seems quite a preposterous explanation,' replied Phillip.

'Well, in questioning them last evening, they have admitted they had gone out with the intention of attacking the Botany Bay tribe and stealing their weapons, fishing tackle and other artefacts. They were armed with their tools from the brick kiln as well as several large clubs.'

Phillip lowered his head and shook it before looking up again at Tench. 'Go on.'

'Sir, it seems the Indians had anticipated their intention from previous experience with our people and duly set upon them before they were set upon themselves.' Tench paused before adding sarcastically, 'And our heroes were quickly routed and fled in all directions.'

'Heroes indeed!' mumbled a disgusted Phillip. 'Well, there is only one way we are ever going to get the message through to these people to leave the natives alone. After all, that is why I have Arabanoo here with us – so we can build good relationships with them – and what do these fools do? Go out and attack them!'

'Sir, I don't think you can blame our men entirely,' said Ross. 'After all, if the blacks didn't leave their weapons and fishing gear lying around everywhere, our men wouldn't be tempted to go out and steal them, especially when they are so valuable. The blacks brought this whole situation on themselves.'

'What?' Phillip responded incredulously. 'You've just heard Captain Tench say they have admitted that they went out there to attack the blacks, and as a matter of interest, Arabanoo has recently explained why exactly they do leave their things around the place. Captain, would you like to advise the major what Arabanoo explained to you?'

Tench hesitated for a moment. The last thing he really wanted to do was laud it over his despised commanding officer, because he knew full well that Ross would ensure his life was hell if he did so. He stopped and thought again, though. The fact of the matter was that Ross could hardly make life any worse for him – after all, he was still technically under arrest – so he turned to Ross and looked him in the eye.

'Sir, from what Arabanoo has tried to explain to us, the reason they leave their things around the place is because it would appear there is simply no stealing amongst their people. If they leave something on the ground somewhere, they know with absolute certainty that it will still be there whenever they return for it. It seems they don't have the same view of personal possessions as we do. Everything is shared in their community.'

'Interesting concept, isn't it, Major?' added Phillip.

Ross muttered under his breath as he just managed to suppress his rage.

Phillip continued, 'Gentlemen, I think we must make an example of these men. They must be flogged.'

\*\*\*

Arabanoo and his convict companion, Joe, stood with Tench and Dawes late the next morning when the eight convicts who were well enough to face the lash were led out in front of their assembled colleagues. As the first of them had his shirt removed and was tied to the timber triangular frame, Tench began trying to explain to Arabanoo what was happening and why.

'These men attack your people so Governor angry with them,' Tench explained while making as many appropriate gestures as he could think of. 'Guvna gulah. They are to be flogged so that our people know. Mudjin know not to attack your people.'

'I think we are going to struggle to explain this whole thing to him,' Dawes opined. 'To start with, I doubt there is any word in their language for whip or flog.'

'Probably not, but he will soon see for himself what it means, even if he doesn't have a word for it,' Tench replied.

At that moment, the first stroke of the cat-o-nine tails lashed the convict's back, leaving red welt marks across his naked white skin. Within five more strokes, his flesh was split, and a few strokes later, strips of bloodied skin peeled off his back and were flung across the crowd as the whip was brought back for another stroke.

As per the convicts' code, the victim did not utter a sound for the first dozen strokes, but then the pain became unbearable, and each lash was followed by muffled screams and groans. The seven convicts waiting their turn looked on, trying not to flinch, but with dread etched across their faces.

Tench glanced at Arabanoo, and his feelings of horror and disgust were clearly evident on his face. Dawes, who had been watching Arabanoo the whole time, now looked at Tench.

'He clearly thinks it is totally barbaric, doesn't he?' Dawes observed.

'Mmmm, yes, that is very apparent,' Tench replied.

Tench looked back at the flogging to see huge wounds penetrating the victim's back. At that point, Arabanoo turned away and mumbled something to himself and then began to pull Joe away. Joe looked at Tench for approval.

'Yes, Joe, that's fine. He shouldn't have to watch it if he doesn't wish to.'

Arabanoo and Joe walked away, back up the hill towards Government House, while the flogging of the second convict commenced in the background. Dawes and Tench looked at each other, at the flogging and then back at each other.

'I'm with Arabanoo. We don't need to watch this,' Dawes said quietly.

Tench nodded and they turned and followed their captive and his chum up the hill.

*Ref. 57*

# Chapter 65

# Sydney Cove, Mid-March 1789

'Good morning, Captain. Hello, Arabanoo,' said Esther warmly as she approached Watkin Tench, who was standing on the eastern shore of the cove with Arabanoo, who, although still fettered around his ankles and wrists, was free of his permanent attachment to Joe.

'Good morning, Esther,' Tench responded before addressing the child who held tightly to her hand. 'Good morning, Rosie. How are you today?'

'I good,' replied the little girl before adding with a smile, 'Hello, Boo.'

Arabanoo crouched down in front of the child as he always did and stroked the sleeve of her dress. 'Hello, Rosie.'

Rosie then handed the doll she was carrying to the Gamaragal warrior.

'Tank you,' he responded as he rocked the doll in his arms, causing Rosie to smile broadly.

Although it made her smile, it only served to deepen Arabanoo's longing for his own children. He loved playing with Rosie and her friends, but he wanted to play with his family on the land to which they all belonged.

Oblivious to Arabanoo's feelings, Tench looked at Esther and smiled. 'Rosie seems to like him.'

'She certainly does, very much,' responded Esther. 'I'm surprised at how gentle he is with all the children. I wouldn't have thought the natives would be like that.'

'He is a gentle soul, but I really don't know if they are characteristics shared by other tribesmen.'

Esther nodded. 'Yes, I wonder if they are.'

'Actually, the governor is rather unwell at the moment, and Arabanoo has been visiting him each day, which he has found quite touching.'

'I'd heard that he was ill. Do they know what's wrong with him?'

'No, Surgeon White is yet to determine the exact nature of the malady, but he is confined to bed for the time being.'

The pair fell silent for a moment as they watched Arabanoo and Rosie playing with the doll, before Arabanoo handed it back to Rosie and began his kangaroo impression. Despite his fetters, hopping was quite simple for the athletic warrior, and as always, it caused Rosie to start giggling merrily.

'Kangawoo.' She smiled, pointing at Arabanoo.

Arabanoo smiled back as he whispered quietly, 'Patagorang, Rosie.'

'What did he say?' Esther asked Tench.

'He said "patagorang". There has been some misunderstanding about the natives' name for that particular animal. We called them kangaroos because Cook and Banks advised that was the natives' traditional word for them, but Arabanoo has explained to us that their word for any large animal is "kangaroo". Their word for what we call kangaroos is "patagorang".'

'Really?' responded Esther.

'Yes, but Rosie should probably just keep calling them kangaroos, because everyone else does. And that's obviously why Arabanoo just whispered it. He didn't wish to correct her.' Tench looked down at Rosie. 'Rosie, that's right. Kangaroo.'

Arabanoo immediately caught on and began hopping around again as he looked over his shoulder at the chuckling child.

'Kangaroo, Rosie.'

*Ref. 58*

## Chapter 66

## Sydney Cove, Late March 1789

It was the time of day that Tench enjoyed so much. The sun was just appearing over the trees to the east of the little colony as it began to stir from its nightly slumber. It was also the time of year that he was quickly coming to believe was the most agreeable. The heat and humidity of summer was gone, but the cool, wet days and nights of winter had not yet arrived. Apart from the harsh rations, he was also really beginning to enjoy many aspects of his time in the colony. Working with Arabanoo, although very challenging, was also extremely rewarding when they had a real breakthrough of communication and understanding. He was also excited about his upcoming time at Rosehill, from where, Phillip had assured him, he would have permission to take exploratory expeditions to see what he could discover between Rosehill and the Carmarthen Mountains, which had been identified far to the west of the colony.

Tench had always fancied himself an explorer, and this was the opportunity he had been hoping for since the fleet set sail. Exploring the region around the colony was such an important task. Discovering fertile land or a river could help secure its future, which, given the current parlous state of its food supplies, was vital. He liked the idea of being a part of that, and such sunny ideas filled his daydreams as he strode along that morning. He was, however, about to encounter a storm.

As he approached the government store, he noticed an animated conversation going on at the door between the commissary, John Palmer, and a convict who Tench knew to be a locksmith.

'What seems to be the problem here?' Tench inquired.

'I haven't been able to open this lock, Captain, because there is a key broken off inside it, so I used the other door and discovered there are some goods missing from the store. I have the locksmith here trying to get this broken key out.'

'Goods have been stolen? That's most concerning. How could that have happened?'

'I don't really know, Captain, but to me it would suggest that someone was in rather a hurry to get the key out and broke it off in the process.'

At that moment, the locksmith managed to remove the lock and shake out the broken piece, which fell in the dirt at his feet. He bent down and picked it up before examining it closely.

'I know this key, Mr Palmer. I made it.'

'Really? Who for?' Palmer inquired.

'For one of the marines.'

At that point, Tench cut in irritably. 'Who? Which marine?'

'Ahh, um. Private Hunt, sir,' the locksmith responded.

'Private Hunt?' Tench was incredulous. Hunt was one of Tench's own men, and a trusted one at that.

'Yes, sir.'

'Why would you make a key for him?' Tench probed.

'I was told I 'ad to, sir,' the convict replied defensively.

Tench looked at Palmer, who responded before Tench could speak. 'I know nothing about it, Captain.'

'Leave it with me, John,' Tench said as he hurried away towards Lieutenant David Collins's hut.

Collins was just about to leave his hut as Tench arrived. He quickly apprised Collins of what he had just uncovered and asked for his immediate assistance.

An hour later, Private Joseph Hunt sat in front of Lieutenant David Collins and his captain with his eyes downcast and sweat forming on his forehead despite the mildness of the morning. Hunt was a small, pleasant-looking but rather bookish chap who looked most unlike a stereotypical marine.

Tench came straight to the point. 'Now, Private, can you explain why you have your own key to the government stores?'

'I-I-I haven't, sir.'

'That is a very bad start to our discussion,' Tench said flatly. 'So, let's start again. I suggest you don't lie to me, because there are certain things I already know. Let me start by telling you that the locksmith told me he made you a key for the stores.'

Again, Hunt looked up, but this time with anxiety, bordering on panic, all over his face. 'Did he, sir?'

'Yes, he did.' Tench then made a very reasonable assumption and added, 'And I know you've been using that key to steal from the stores, which you know as well as I do carries the death sentence.'

The blood drained from Hunt's face, and he looked up at Tench as he mumbled, 'Death sentence!'

'If the governor won't tolerate convicts stealing from the stores, he is not going to tolerate a marine stealing from them,' Tench said sincerely.

'But it wasn't just me, sir,' the panic-stricken private responded.

'Really?' said Tench as he glanced over at Collins. 'How many others were there?'

'Six, sir,' murmured Hunt with his eyes again downcast.

A shocked Tench yelled, 'Six?'

'Yes, sir.'

'Who are they?' Tench's disappointment was quickly turning into anger.

'Can't say, sir.'

'Fine, don't tell us. You can hang alone, then.'

There was silence in the room as Hunt continued to stare at the floor and Tench and Collins allowed him some time to think. The sweat from his brow was now running into his eyes.

'If I tell you, sir, will you spare me the noose?' pleaded Hunt as he again looked up at Tench.

'Well, that won't be up to me. It will be up to Mr Collins and the six officers serving in the court, but what do you think, Mr Collins?'

David Collins thought for a moment before responding as Hunt looked at him anxiously.

'Put it this way, Private – if you refuse to cooperate, Captain Tench is correct, you will hang and hang alone. If, however, you tell us who else was involved and the full details of what you stole, we can recommend to the court that they be lenient with you. I must stress, though, that I can give you no guarantees, as this is a most serious offence.'

Hunt thought for a moment, but only a moment, before he responded, 'Jim Baker, Jim Brown, Richard Dukes, Tom Jones, Luke Haynes and Dick Askew, sir.'

Baker was another of Tench's men from the *Charlotte*, and Tench cringed at the mention of his name.

'What did you steal?' Collins asked, naively thinking the thefts were isolated occurrences.

'A few things, sir,' murmured Hunt.

'Like what?' Tench responded sharply.

'Some flour, sir, and some meat and spirits… and…'

'Go on,' Tench demanded.

'And some tobacco and a few other things,' Hunt admitted reluctantly.

'Now, how did the seven of you manage to organise these thefts?' Tench probed.

'Whenever one of us was on guard duty at night, sir, he'd let the others in with the key, and they would get what they needed and leave when he told them everything was clear.'

'Private Hunt, you said *whenever* one of you was on guard duty, so you mean this happened more than just a couple of times?' Tench asked, growing more alarmed.

'Yes, sir,' murmured Hunt.

'How long has this been going on, then?' Collins cut in.

Hunt hesitated, looked up momentarily at his two questioners and dropped his head again as he mumbled, 'About eight months.'

'Eight months!' Tench and Collins repeated in unison as shock exploded across their faces.

They both shook their heads and fell silent for a moment. Tench's mind went straight to thoughts of what Governor Phillip's reaction would be when he was told that, at a time when everyone in the colony was on starvation rations and all were desperately hoping for Hunter's safe return from the Cape of Good Hope, here were seven of the marines systematically stealing from the government stores over a long period. If Phillip's reaction wasn't going to be bad enough, Tench cringed visibly at the thought of what Major Ross's would be.

'What will they do with me, sir?' Hunt asked nervously.

'Well, Private, you'll be damn lucky if you don't hang,' Tench responded, 'but if you don't, you'll most likely be sent to Pinchgut for a time. There you will really learn the meaning of starvation rations.'

'Pinchgut!' Hunt was horrified. The only ones who were usually sent to that rocky island outcrop in the middle of the harbour were the worst of the convicts.

'It will be that or hanging,' Tench snapped.

'Oh, don't let them hang me, please, sir,' Hunt pleaded.

'We'll try, but when Lieutenant Collins and I told you that, we had no idea you had been robbing the stores for eight months. You should be so ashamed of yourself, Private. Here you are, a marine in a position of trust, and you and your cronies are stealing food when everyone in the colony, including the governor, is on such tight rations.'

Hunt had kept his eyes on the floor through almost the entire interrogation, but now, his head sunk even lower, and like a scolded dog, his gaze was fixed on his feet.

\*\*\*

Tench had correctly anticipated the obvious reactions of Phillip and

Ross. Both men were furious, and for once, both agreed. Therefore, the court, made up of six officers headed by David Collins, had little option but to sentence the seven marines to be hanged.

On the morning the hangings were to take place, almost the entire population of the little colony was assembled. Phillip and Ross both believed that all colonists, convict and free, should see for themselves what happened to anyone who stole from the colony's rapidly dwindling stores. There was a feeling amongst some in the starving colony that at least there would now be seven less mouths to feed.

The seven marines, including Private Joseph Hunt, were led out in front of the crowd. Hunt's terror saw him shaking like a gum tree in a southerly gale. Not only had he implicated his colleagues, who now held him in utter contempt as they walked beside him to their deaths, but his betrayal had not even saved his own life.

The first to feel the coarse rope around his neck was Private James Brown, the only married man amongst the condemned. His wife Elizabeth stood at the edge of the crowd, clinging desperately to the arm of her close friend Jane Chapman. A moment later, she sobbed and sobbed as her husband's body kicked and writhed as the life was strangled out of it and he slowly slipped into eternity.

Elizabeth wasn't the only one in the crowd shattered by the sight. Arabanoo stood beside Watkin Tench, who saw the Gamaragal warrior's reaction as his mouth fell agape and a look of horror and disgust overwhelmed him. Tench stood and pondered what a low point this was for the British colonisers. He could not for a moment envisage the horror that was about to engulf the people of his native friend beside him.

*Ref. 59*

## Chapter 67

## Sydney Cove, Early April 1789

It was late in the afternoon as Watkin Tench made his way up the hill to the governor's house. Despite the lack of food, virtually all in the colony had continued to work, and despite its youth, Sydney was beginning to look like a small town. The streets that William Dawes had laid out were taking shape, as small cottages sprung up along them, between the scattered trees that still remained. The Tank Stream's bridge, which had also been built courtesy of Dawes, enabled the eastern and western sides of the harbour to be efficiently linked and was a particularly busy route. Government House, on the eastern side, was set back on the hill, with a large yard and outbuildings, one of which continued to house Arabanoo. On the western side of the cove were the convict camps and the marines' camp, which had gradually been replaced by buildings made with timber and bricks from the kilns at the southern end of the colony.

Tench was about to enter Phillip's front yard when he was approached by Lieutenant George Johnston.

'Captain,' Johnston called.

Tench halted at the gate. 'Yes, good afternoon, Mr Johnston.'

'Captain, the fishing boat that has just returned from down harbour has reported seeing small groups of natives lying dead in several of the coves and inlets they went past. They said they saw a few yesterday, but there are more today.'

'Really? Did they have any indication of what the cause may be? Have the Indians been fighting amongst themselves?'

'No, it would certainly seem not, Captain. My understanding is that these are in small family groups, and they are scattered all around the place.'

'That sounds most alarming. I'm just about to see the governor, so I think you should join us and relay this information to him.'

A few minutes later, Phillip, Tench and Johnston sat in Phillip's office discussing Johnston's worrying news.

'And how many do you think are dead, Mr Johnston?' asked Phillip.

'I don't really know precise numbers, Excellency, but from what the fishermen have said, there must be quite a lot, since they said they saw them in many of the coves to the east. Apparently, there is a family in a cove just to the east of here who are still alive, but they are obviously stricken with some malady.'

'We must try to find out how many there are and what the cause could possibly be. Tell Surgeon White to be ready first thing in the morning, and we'll take a boat to see if we can find this family and any others who we may be able to assist. And we'll take Arabanoo along to act as translator.'

\*\*\*

The next morning, Phillip, Tench, Arabanoo and Surgeon White were rowed by four marines along the southern shore of the harbour to inspect the coves to the east. Phillip had also dispatched Johnston in another boat to check the northern side of the harbour. If they found any natives they could assist, they were to bring them back to the colony to treat if they would come voluntarily. If they found any dead natives, they were instructed to bring the bodies back so they could be examined by the surgeons to determine the cause of death.

Tench and Phillip had done their best to explain to Arabanoo the purpose of the outing, and although he didn't understand all the details, he had understood that some of his people were sick or dying. On Phillip's command, the boat put into the first cove to the east of the colony, where they had immediately seen the family to whom Johnston had referred near the shoreline. When the boat was pulled up onto the sandy soil of the shore, Tench assisted Arabanoo, whose ankles were still manacled, out of the boat before pausing to take in the whole scene. An older man, who was obviously very ill, was lying near a small fire and was being cared for by a boy of about nine years of age. The boy was providing him with water from a large shell. He was drinking some of the water, but the rest, the boy was pouring over his forehead.

Tench looked around the clearing while White and Arabanoo went to assist the young boy, as the man was now being violently ill. In the middle of the clearing was the body of a little girl about six years old. Tench walked over and crouched down beside the child. Her face and torso were completely covered in ugly, pus-filled blisters. Tench knelt over her body and quickly determined she had been dead for some time. He then walked to the edge of the clearing, where he discovered the body of a young woman in the longish grass. She was apparently the children's mother, and she too was covered in sores.

'Excellency,' Tench called to Phillip, who was standing in the middle of the clearing with one of the marines, 'there's another over here.'

Phillip walked towards Tench and paused next to the body of the little girl.

'This is most distressing,' Phillip said as Tench walked over to join him.

'Simply heart-wrenching, sir, but what could this disease possibly be?'

'I don't know. I hope Surgeon White can identify it,' replied Phillip.

'On first examination, it looks like smallpox,' suggested Tench.

'I agree, but it couldn't possibly be. Where could it have come from?'

'I have no idea, Excellency, but it certainly resembles it. Look at the sores all over that poor little girl's face and body.'

'Yes, I would have thought it must be some sort of local disease that strikes the natives from time to time, but from Arabanoo's initial reaction, I'm not sure. He was quite reluctant to go near the old man and the boy. It took Surgeon White's encouragement for him to assist them.'

'He seems to be tending to them very caringly now,' Tench observed as he looked over to where Arabanoo and the surgeon were still assisting the old man and boy.

'Most certainly, but he was hesitant at first, and I may be mistaken, but it appeared to me he had never seen it before.'

'I wonder if that is because of their malady or the fact they are not his people. His people are on the other side of the harbour, and he has explained to us that they are different tribes.'

'You may have a point there, Captain. I know there are plenty of Englishmen who wouldn't be too bothered caring for an ailing Frenchman.' Phillip smiled, despite the gravity of the situation confronting them.

'Indeed, sir, indeed.'

The two men walked back to where White and Arabanoo were still tending to the old man and the boy.

'How are they, Mr White?' asked Phillip.

White looked up at the governor.

'The man is very, very ill, sir, but the boy is fine at this time.'

'What do you think it is?' Phillip asked as concern covered his face.

'Well, it certainly looks like smallpox, sir, but I'd need further examination to be certain,' White replied gravely.

'Let's hope it isn't,' Phillip responded.

'Arabanoo, ask the boy how many days man sick,' requested Tench.

Arabanoo nodded before he spoke to the boy in his soft, lilting tones. The boy replied, and Arabanoo held up four fingers. 'Four, Captain.'

'Thank you.'

'Let's get them both into the boat, Mr White, and take them to our hospital so you can treat them,' instructed Phillip.

Surgeon White and the marines assisted the old man into the boat, and although he didn't have the strength to resist the white men, Arabanoo reassured him and he went willingly. The boy, who was obviously his son, climbed into the boat beside him. Just when they were about to leave, Arabanoo started pointing to the little girl and walked over to where she lay on the sandy soil. He immediately crouched down and began digging a hole beside her with his hands.

'Does he want to bury her, do you think, sir?' Tench queried.

'Yes, it would certainly seem so. Should we go and assist him, Captain?'

'I'm not sure, sir. Burying the dead may be something best left for them, but perhaps I could ask if he wants me to help.'

'By all means, please do, but don't point out the body of the woman. He obviously hasn't seen her. We need to get this other pair back to our hospital as soon as we can.'

Tench walked over to Arabanoo and crouched down beside him.

'Arabanoo, me help?' Tench asked as he performed a digging motion.

Arabanoo shook his head. 'No.'

Tench stood and watched as Arabanoo continued to dig. Given the sandy nature of the soil, it didn't take long for him to complete a hole large enough for the body of the small child, which he lined with grass. He picked her up and gently placed her in the grave before carefully covering her body with more grass and sandy soil, raising a small mound over it. He stood up, nodded at Tench and pointed to the boat.

As they walked back, Tench was struck by the fact that Arabanoo had not provided any sort of prayer for the occasion or any acknowledgement of a greater being. He looked forward to a time when their knowledge of each other's language was advanced enough to discuss such abstract issues.

\*\*\*

When the group arrived back in the colony, Phillip instructed that the building adjacent to the colony's hospital be allocated to the treatment of any of the natives that may be brought in suffering the illness. The man was carried on a stretcher to the house, and the boy, who had told Arabanoo his name was Nanbaree, walked beside him. Tench and Arabanoo followed while Phillip returned to his office.

On arrival at the house, the man was placed on a small stretcher bed, and Surgeon White and Arabanoo continued to treat him before both he and his son were bathed in warm water. When he was laid back on the bed, his health seemed to deteriorate even more rapidly.

'Bado, bado,' he groaned to Arabanoo.

'Water,' Arabanoo translated, and White handed him a canteen. Arabanoo helped the man drink briefly, before he was overcome with a shivering fit, so White directed the convict assisting them to light the fire.

Tench looked on, observing how affectionate and loving the man was to the boy. He continually stroked the boy's hair and tried to smile at him, despite the severity of his illness. It was obvious to Tench that the man knew he was dying and was scared for his son, who was to be left alone amongst these strange white people. The man looked intently at Tench and held his gaze. It was a gaze that Tench was unsure how to interpret, but to reassure the dying man, he responded with a half-smile and a nod as if he understood.

Nanbaree stayed by his father's side as he continued to decline, and shortly after midday, he gave his son's hand one final squeeze and closed his eyes. Nanbaree stared at his father for several moments before he turned to Arabanoo and spoke just one word.

'Boee?'

Arabanoo nodded. 'Boee,' he said, before adding for White and Tench's benefit, 'He dead.'

Nanbaree sat beside his dead father without crying while Arabanoo began speaking to him calmly and soothingly. White walked over and spoke to Tench.

'We should advise the governor of his death. The more I see of this illness, the more I'm convinced it's smallpox.'

Tench was about to hurry out the door to advise Phillip when Arabanoo walked over to him.

'Captain,' he said as he pointed to the deceased native before making digging motions with his hands.

'You want to bury him in the ground... Put him in the ground?'

Arabanoo nodded. 'Yes, Captain.'

'You can. I'll see the governor, and then we will dig a hole,' Tench replied as he imitated Arabanoo's digging motions.

As Tench was about to leave the makeshift hospital, Johnston and his party arrived with two more dead native bodies.

'They're everywhere out there,' Johnston said to Tench, who shook his head sadly.

\*\*\*

That afternoon at the colony's little cemetery, just outside the settlement, a grave was dug by a convict, and Arabanoo prepared it in the same way he had prepared the grave for the little girl's body that morning. When he was satisfied that it was properly lined with grass, Nanbaree's father was placed in the grave, while his son stood by with Surgeon White and Governor Phillip. Arabanoo covered the body with more grass before he and the convict covered it with dirt. Once again, Arabanoo made no gesture of prayer and began to walk slowly away, still greatly restricted by the manacles on his ankles.

Phillip watched him before turning to Tench.

'I think we should take those manacles off poor Arabanoo now, don't you, Captain?'

'Yes, definitely, sir. His behaviour has been exemplary, and given this outbreak amongst his people, we are going to need his help.'

'I agree. Please organise that as soon as you can. The poor chap has been with us over three months, and in hindsight, I think it has probably been rather cruel of me to keep them on him all this time.'

Tench was about to speak, but Phillip cut him off as he held up his hand. 'And yes, I know you and Lieutenant Dawes have mentioned that to me before, so let's just do it.'

'Yes, sir. I'm sure Arabanoo will be delighted.'

'Good. Now, as for poor Nanbaree here, what are we going to do with him?' pondered Phillip.

'I'd be happy to look after the lad, Excellency,' said White. 'William, my servant, can assist. We'll need to keep a close eye on him to ensure he doesn't catch this disease.'

'Thank you, that would be most helpful.'

'And, sir, after I have the manacles removed from Arabanoo, I'll take Captain Ball with me and go back and bury that poor woman we left there this morning.'

'Yes, thank you, Captain. Please do.'

Tench escorted Arabanoo back to the colony and collected the key to his manacles. Tench hadn't told Arabanoo what he was going to do. He thought it would be more interesting to surprise him and to see his reaction. He did, however, want to share the moment with Dawes, who he quickly found at the head of the cove. After outlining the distressing news regarding the disease afflicting the natives, Tench advised that he did have a little piece of good news.

'What's that? asked Dawes.

'The governor has told me to remove Arabanoo's manacles.'

Dawes beamed. 'Oh, that is wonderful. Have you told Arabanoo?'

'No, I thought with the whole communication issue, it might be better to just take them off. Also, I wanted you to see his reaction.' Tench smiled and held up the key.

'Arabanoo, sit down, sit down,' urged Dawes, pointing to a large tree stump close to them.

Arabanoo did as instructed. Captain Watkin Tench of the British marines, like a would-be bridegroom, went down on one knee before the Gamaragal warrior. He inserted the key in the lock of first his left ankle and then his right. As Tench opened the manacles, he looked up at Arabanoo and said, 'You're free, dear friend.'

Arabanoo stared at him incredulously, so, to make the point as clear as possible, Tench threw the manacles away behind him.

Arabanoo bent over and rubbed his ankles, which were red, raw and bloody from the manacles. He looked at Tench, then at Dawes, jumped to his feet and began running around them in circles, his white smile beaming across his face.

'I thought his reaction would be worth seeing,' Tench said to Dawes.

'It certainly is,' came the reply.

When Arabanoo finally stopped running around like what Tench felt was a 'crazy person', he walked over and pointed to the manacles.

'Gone?' he asked.

'Yes, gone, but we don't want you to run away,' Tench explained. 'We need you to stay here and help us. You stay and help.'

Arabanoo walked over to Tench and threw his arms around him.

'Captain, Arabanoo bubana.'

'Yes, I'm Arabanoo's... friend,' Tench replied, glancing at Dawes.

'No, Watkin, it's better than that. He just called you his brother.'

'Really?' Tench looked back at Arabanoo, said, 'Thank you,' and hugged him back.

'What about me?' Dawes said, patting his own chest before holding out his arms.

Arabanoo walked over to Dawes, hugged him and said, 'Will, Arabanoo bubana.'

'Thank you, Arabanoo. You my bubana too.'

*Ref. 60*

## Chapter 68
## Weerong, Early April 1789

The next day, Arabanoo was at the makeshift hospital dedicated to treating the native people. Apart from acting as translator, he was also assisting Surgeon White in providing them with as much care and reassurance as he could. He was standing near the bed of a patient when a man and his younger sister were brought in. The fourteen-year-old girl, who was far less ill than her brother, looked at Arabanoo and, despite him being beardless and wearing European clothes, recognised him immediately.

'Arabanoo,' she said.

He turned and replied, 'Booron, you poor thing. You are sick and your brother too.'

'Yes, we are, but Ngarra is much sicker than me.'

Arabanoo helped Ngarra and Booron onto two of the small stretcher beds. Surgeon White sat beside Ngarra and began examining him, while Arabanoo spoke to Booron with highly mixed emotions coursing through his system. He was delighted and excited to see people from his own mob but deeply distressed that they were ill with such a terrible disease. The first thing he wanted to do, though, was find out about his family.

'How are Weereweea and the children?' he asked anxiously.

Booron hesitated and looked away for a moment before replying.

'I'm so sorry, Arabanoo... They died. So many of our people have died.'

Arabanoo was stunned and sat in silence for a moment.

'I'm so sorry,' Booron repeated.

'I wanted to go back to them, but they had me tied up until yesterday. See,' he said, pointing to the red, raw marks around his ankles.

Booron moved closer to Arabanoo, put her arm around his shoulder and again repeated, 'I'm so sorry.'

Arabanoo tried to regain his composure. No matter how hard he tried, though, he couldn't do so. Finally, he got to his feet, thanked Booron and walked out the door. He walked down to the edge of the cove and along its western foreshore to the point. He stood looking across the harbour to the east, to his own country, as the setting sun painted the sky behind him spectacular shades of crimson and mauve.

'Weereweea,' he whispered before standing for some time, his heart breaking, tears creeping across his cheeks.

\*\*\*

Late that evening, Watkin Tench arrived at the makeshift hospital and was greeted by Arabanoo, but Tench was quickly aware that his 'brother' was very subdued compared to his wild enthusiasm of the previous afternoon. Tench didn't question him about it, though, and accepted that it was due to his concern for his people Booron and Ngarra, who Arabanoo introduced him to.

As soon as he had an opportunity, Tench called Surgeon White aside.

'Mr White, have you been able to confirm that this is definitely smallpox?'

'Yes, so obviously, it would be much better if we could keep all the patients isolated, but given our circumstances here, that just isn't possible.'

'I'm very worried about Arabanoo catching it, and for that matter, so is the governor.'

'I have to admit there is a very real chance of that. I have told him not to touch the patients or their bedding directly, and for the most part, he seems to be following that instruction.'

'That's something, at least, but I'm told that you hold vials of the smallpox virus here,' probed Tench.

'Yes, I brought it out with us in case we needed to use variolation on the children born here.'

'Well, can't you use it on Arabanoo?'

'I could, but there would be absolutely no point whatsoever. To start with, it doesn't give immediate protection, and secondly, he has already been so exposed to it. It would already be in his system if he is going to catch it. As you may know, the incubation period of the disease is ten to fourteen days, so we won't know for a while if he has contracted it. All we can hope is that he is one of those people who just don't catch it for some reason. Look at young Nanbaree. He is perfectly healthy, but he lost both his parents and his sister to this scourge of a disease.'

'Hmmm, it is quite amazing, isn't it? But perhaps we should stop Arabanoo from coming here anymore, just in case he hasn't already caught it.'

'Captain, that is obviously up to Governor Phillip, but he is a huge help to us here. He not only translates for us, but he is a very caring nurse, and the natives take great comfort from having him here to talk to them and soothe them... I think that all we can do is hope and pray that Arabanoo is one of the lucky ones.'

'Yes, well, I certainly hope so.' Tench paused before asking, 'And how are your new patients?'

'The boy is very ill. To be frank, I wouldn't expect him to survive more than a few days.'

At that point, Tench looked over to Ngarra. Booron was sitting on the edge of his stretcher bed, patting his hair, which hung across his blister-covered face.

White saw what Tench was looking at and commented, 'She is amazingly devoted to him, especially when she is quite ill herself. I do expect she will recover, though.'

Tench walked over to Arabanoo, who was stoking the fire, as Ngarra was now having an attack of the shivers. Aided by sign language, Tench said, 'Do you want to come with me away from here?'

Arabanoo shook his head.

'Alright, but don't touch the people who are sick,' Tench added.

Tench wasn't sure if Arabanoo understood, but he nodded and replied, 'Yes, Captain.'

Tench gave him a half-smile, patted him on the back and walked out the door. As he strode around the shore of the cove, he couldn't help gazing beyond the headland to the east in the hope that the *Sirius* may miraculously appear. His stomach churned as he pondered the chaos that now gripped the colony. *Where was Hunter?*

*Ref. 61*

## Chapter 69

## Latitude 44.29 South and 144.30 East, South of Van Diemen's Land, 20 April 1789

The westerly winds of the 'roaring forties' that Hunter had hoped for had appeared only intermittently and had been punctuated by gales and squalls blowing from the south and the north-east, making every nautical mile of the voyage a battle. It was now two months since the *Sirius* had left Cape Town, and the trip had been nothing short of a nightmare for Hunter and his crew. It had left them all exhausted from the need to repeatedly furl the sails and adjust the rigging. To make matters worse, just as Hunter had feared, the *Sirius* had started leaking again, so the crew also had to man the pumps. Even Hunter and Bradley were mentally and physically fatigued, so they were relieved and delighted when that evening, the wind, which had been blowing at gale force from the north-north-west, finally moderated and swung around to the south-west.

After having dinner in his cabin, Hunter returned to the quarterdeck and joined Bradley as the helmsman steered the ship. The *Sirius* was finally under full sail after spending so much of the voyage with the storm sails, and even at times just the foresail, pulling the ship slowly forward. Hunter looked up to the sails and the sky above, where the yellow half-moon they so desperately wanted to see remained hidden, despite gilding the edges of the large clouds that drifted across it.

'Now, isn't that a beautiful sight, Lieutenant,' Hunter enthused.

Bradley looked up and replied, 'You mean, to see her under full sail at last, sir?'

'Aye, and with a lovely sou-westerly behind us... Hopefully, that moon will force its way out from behind those clouds soon,' Hunter said, and being desperately keen to get a reading on their exact location, he rather optimistically picked up his sextant. It had been over three days since they had seen a clear sky.

'It will certainly be a huge relief when it does, sir.'

The two men stood quietly for a few moments before Bradley spoke.

'Let's hope this breeze continues while we get around the south of Van Diemen's Land, because it should be perfect to take us up the coast of New South Wales.'

'Indeed it will be,' responded Hunter.

'We should be home in a few days, then, sir.'

Hunter looked at Bradley, rather bemused, and wondered for a moment if Bradley realised what he had just said. He obviously didn't, so Hunter said, 'Interesting choice of words, there, Mr Bradley.'

'Hmmm, well, I suppose it is all we have for a home at present, sir.'

The two sailors returned their gazes to the sky, where the clouds had now shut out even the tiniest glimmer of moonlight.

'This thick, hazy weather is most frustrating, though,' commented Bradley.

'It is indeed. We really need to obtain a reading to ensure we are well clear of the south cape of Van Diemen's Land before we start our northward voyage.'

'And its ledge of rocks,' added Bradley.

'Aye, exactly.'

As the two men were talking, they became aware that a dramatic change in the weather was starting to hit the ship. The breeze that had been blowing from the south-west had now moved around to the south and was quickly increasing in strength. Hunter looked to the sails above before looking at Bradley with concern in his eyes.

Hunter looked again to the sky above and noted that the glow of the moon remained totally obscured behind increasingly heavy dark clouds. Towards the southern horizon, he saw fierce bolts of lightning, while before his eyes, the swell was beginning to rise.

'Turn her into the breeze,' Hunter ordered the helmsman. He then turned to Bradley and observed, 'This is most unfortunate. If we'd just had that lovely sou-westerly for a little longer, we could have made a fair wind of this southerly to push us up the coast. Now we have yet another battle on our hands.'

He called to the midshipman on the watch, John Harris, 'Mr Harris, have your men ready to furl the sails.'

Harris went to the edge of the quarterdeck and gave the order. Just as the topmen were getting into position at the base of the rigging, *Sirius* was hit by a mighty gust of wind from the south.

'Furl the sails,' called Hunter.

Harris repeated the order, but he didn't have to, for the topmen knew their jobs and had immediately started climbing the rigging. By the time they reached the top, that gentle south-westerly breeze was turning into a full southerly gale, meaning the topmen had to cling to the spars even more tightly than usual as they furled the sails.

'Now let's set a reefed foresail, a balanced mizzen and the three storm staysails,' Hunter told Harris.

'Yes, sir,' responded Harris, who immediately repeated the order to the crew.

The swell began to rise. A few minutes later, the officers on the quarterdeck watched on as a large wave crashed across the ship's bow and tore across the deck. The gale and the seas increased, and rain started pelting from the heavens. Having furled the sails, the topmen immediately retreated to the safety of the deck. More large waves smashed across the bow of the ship and washed across the deck. The *Sirius* began to roll between the waves, and it wasn't long before that rolling increased to more than forty-five degrees as the swell continued to grow.

Another huge wave crashed across the deck, making standing upright impossible for the crew. They knew exactly what to do, however, and began grabbing the nearest available lengths of rope and tying themselves to the rails to avoid being washed overboard to certain death. No sooner had they all done so than the *Sirius* soared, like a breaching whale, over a massive wave before plunging into the trough behind it. The whole ship shuddered as it hit the water.

Over the next few hours, the wind and the seas increased as thunder and lightning rolled across the top of the ship. It was a storm like so many the captain and his crew had been through over their years at sea, but this one had an edge to it, which, when combined with their inability to fix their exact location, left Hunter with a very uneasy feeling. He therefore had Bradley and Midshipman Harris adjourn to his cabin briefly to examine their charts of the southern cape of Van Diemen's land and double-check all the calculations they had made when, over three days ago, they were last able to obtain a clear reading from the skies.

After drying themselves off, the three sailors sat down at Hunter's table.

'Well, gentlemen, are we sure of our position?'

'Yes, I believe so, sir,' replied Bradley.

'Certainly, sir.' Harris nodded.

'Well, Mr Harris, just maintain her on this course, and if you don't mind, I'll try to get a little rest now while I can. I have a feeling this is going to be a long night, because this gale doesn't look like showing any signs of abating. And you should get some sleep too, Mr Bradley.'

As soon as the other two left, Hunter removed his soaking boots, overcoat and blue navy jacket and placed them in front of the stove fire to dry. He then climbed into his hammock, which, given the rolling of the ship in such conditions, was the only suitable sleeping option.

As he lay there trying to sleep, Hunter's brain was racing. He was suddenly more aware than ever of the responsibility that was his and his alone – to deliver the supplies safely to the colony – otherwise, it would be completely doomed to massive loss of life. Although he was conscious of that responsibility when he first set sail and every moment since, it had never been quite so acutely clear as it was now, nor weighed so heavily upon him. It was one thing to lose his own life and those of his crew, but he had a whole colony with women and children depending on him as well.

His mind racing with thoughts of 'home', combined with the chill through every bone in his body, made it impossible for him to sleep, but he did not get up. He just kept staring at the roughhewn ceiling, thinking... *Just this one last gale.*

*Ref. 62*

## Chapter 70

## Sydney Cove, 20 April 1789

It was late morning, and Phillip had assembled some of the senior officers to discuss the colony's perilous position. Tench, Johnston and Dawes were amongst those assembled in Phillip's office, as was Surgeon White. Phillip had, however, avoided inviting the abrasive Major Ross by having the discussion while Ross was away at Rosehill. He was sure it would be a much more constructive meeting without Ross's negative input.

'Gentlemen, I just wanted to discuss with you the parlous state of our colony here and see if we can identify any solutions. Obviously, we have several major issues confronting us at the moment. Firstly, the situation with our food supplies is now so dire, I believe I have no option but to further cut rations. I hate to say that, but I cannot see any other option.'

Phillip paused but was greeted with silence. Finally, Johnston spoke up.

'Excellency, if I may speak, sir.'

'Yes, that's what we are all here for. Go ahead, Mr Johnston.'

'I'd be very concerned if you had to do that. I'd be worried that it could spark an all-out rebellion, not just by the convicts, but by the marines as well. We've just hung seven marines for food theft and had a man starve to death, so I don't know how we could hope to cut rations further without risking a very serious reaction.'

'Well, the man that starved did have underlying health issues, didn't he, Mr White?'

'Yes, Excellency, he did.' White nodded.

'But, Mr Johnston, I nevertheless appreciate your point. Captain Tench, what are your thoughts?'

'Excellency, I don't think we are quite at the point of open rebellion yet, but certainly, it is a major concern. If Captain Hunter doesn't arrive back here soon, and you do have to further cut rations, it may get to that point.'

'Captain, I think you're missing my meaning. I'm not talking about waiting to cut rations if Captain Hunter doesn't arrive soon. I'm talking about cutting them now. The fact is, if he doesn't arrive in the next couple of weeks, we have to be realistic and accept that something tragic must have happened to him. And if it has, we will all starve. It is quite apparent that London is not sending out any store ships to support us, because by now, they believed we'd have plentiful crops grown in the supposedly fertile soil.'

'Thank you, sir,' Tench said. 'I understand, but I'd be inclined to wait and see if Captain Hunter does arrive in the next couple of weeks and then make decisions on rations.'

Phillip nodded quietly as he again stroked the head of his favourite white greyhound.

'Sir, may I suggest we ask Arabanoo more about how his people survive?' Dawes said. 'Obviously, they have been here for many hundreds or thousands of years, so they must have some secrets about what is edible.'

'Mr Dawes, ordinarily I would think that is a good idea, but as you know, I don't want Arabanoo to realise how much we are struggling here. I just fear it may lead to an attack by the natives.'

Tench and Dawes were about to jump in with their replies, but Phillip held up his hand.

'The second point I wanted to raise is smallpox. What can we do about this tragic outbreak amongst them?'

'Excellency, all I can say is I'm glad Major Ross isn't here, because I'm sure he would claim it's a good thing so they are just wiped out,' Dawes said.

Phillip brushed the comment aside. 'Well, I hope not. Now, Mr White, is there anything more we can do for these poor people?'

'Unfortunately, sir, I can't see that in our present circumstances there is anything else we can do. Ideally, we should be isolating the sick from their communities, but we aren't able to communicate that to them out in their camps, and by the time they come in to us, they have infected most of those around them and they're too ill for us to help anyway.'

'It's a most distressing situation.'

The conversation continued for another thirty minutes and went around in circles, without the group coming up with any solutions to either the parlous state of their food supplies or the tragic smallpox outbreak amongst the natives.

Finally, Phillip said, 'Alright, gentlemen, we'll wait a couple of weeks and see whether Captain Hunter returns. So, let's hope and pray that he does, because if he doesn't, I will have to cut rations further, and if that leads to an outright rebellion and we are all murdered, then so be it. I'd rather be murdered in my bed than starve to death.'

## Chapter 71

## South Cape of Van Diemen's Land, 21 April 1789

It was well before dawn when Hunter climbed the ladder near his cabin to the deck. He had tried to sleep and tried to convince himself that there was nothing he could do on the quarterdeck because Midshipman Harris was a perfectly competent sailor, but it hadn't slowed his racing mind. He believed his place was on the quarterdeck, no matter how hard he tried to convince himself it was better to rest.

As soon as he set foot on the deck, though, the fist of tension tightened in his stomach. The gale had now swung around to the south-east and was even stronger. To make matters worse, the night had breathed a foggy haze across the ferocious sea around them, severely limiting their vision in all directions.

Hunter hurried to the quarterdeck and joined Harris.

'When did this wind change, Mr Harris?' was the first question he yelled above the roar of the gale.

'Only a few minutes ago, sir, and it brought this haze and fog with it too.'

'And the sails are all holding?'

'Yes, sir, at the moment.'

Hunter cast a worried eye up to the sails, which were full as the ship tacked to port, desperately trying to make some forward progress into the gale and through the haze.

'I hate sailing blind, Mr Harris.'

'So do I, Captain.'

The two mariners stood side by side, watching the sea and the sails, with Harris helping the helmsman wrestle with the wheel each time they had to tack. The sun was just starting to cast a ghostly glow through the fog when Lieutenant Bradley arrived on the quarterdeck to relieve Harris.

'This gale is even worse, sir,' Bradley yelled as he joined the others.

'Aye, that it is,' replied Hunter, 'and it's now in our faces, with this darn haze to contend with as well.'

As the three sailors discussed their options, the *Sirius* was suddenly hit by an even more powerful gust of wind, which made them all instantly look up. The main sail tore with a gut-wrenching sound as they watched on helplessly. The intensity of the gust continued. First, the foresail ripped like it was a wet London broadsheet, and moments later, the mizzen was shredded as well.

Hunter responded immediately and instructed, 'Set a reefed foresail and a balanced mizzen, Mr Harris.'

The crew frantically carried out the orders while trying to keep themselves safely on the ship as waves continued to crash across the violently rolling deck.

The *Sirius* and her crew battled the tempest throughout the morning and into the early afternoon. During that time, crew members were continuously stationed on the bow, trying desperately to find a break in the haze and checking for any rocks appearing on the ship's course.

Finally, at half past three in the afternoon, as the battle against the raging elements continued, there was a thinning of the haze.

'Land ho!' was the call that sent a shiver down the spine of everyone on deck.

Hunter rushed forward from the quarterdeck to the bow of the ship and immediately asked the crewman, 'Where?'

'Off the port bow, sir,' came the reply as the sailor pointed into the drifting fog.

'How far away was it?' Hunter asked anxiously.

'I don't know, sir, I couldn't tell through the fog,' responded the sailor, before adding frantically, 'Look, there!' as he pointed off the port bow.

Hunter peered through the thinning fog and glimpsed, just for an instant, the last thing he wanted to see... land.

At that moment, Bradley joined Hunter and pointed off the starboard bow. 'Look, sir.'

'Oh no!' groaned Hunter, as he swung around to the starboard side and, through the fine mist, much to his horror, he saw... land!

'We're embayed, Mr Bradley!' yelled Hunter. He rushed back to the quarterdeck with Bradley following close behind.

It was the very worst position for a ship like the *Sirius* to find itself in – in the middle of a gale, surrounded on three sides by land, with unchartered rocks and no room to manoeuvre. As Hunter ordered the helmsman to turn the *Sirius* into the wind, his mind filled with thoughts of being wrecked here in some isolated bay at the bottom of the world where no-one would ever know what happened to them. And with them, the colony's precious cargo would end up at the bottom of the bay.

While those thoughts crashed through his mind like the waves across the bow, Hunter felt almost physically ill. Bradley joined him on the quarterdeck, his face pallid with fear. It was a feeling shared by the entire crew.

'What are we going to do, sir?'

'All we can do, Mr Bradley, is stay calm and do whatever we can to get out of here and back to open water,' Hunter replied, but the calm logic of his words belied his inner turmoil.

Hunter looked through the momentarily clearing haze to port to see massive waves smashing violently against the rocks at the base of a headland's sheer cliffs. Plumes of white spray leapt into the air. Hunter said nothing, not wanting to panic the crew, but only a moment later, one of the men in the bow yelled, 'Land close under our lee!'

Every set of eyes on the ship looked through that haze and saw the same destiny as the *Sirius* was pushed ever closer to the rocks by the relentless gale. It had been under minimal sail to minimise its drift to leeward, but now Hunter made a dramatic change.

'Mr Bradley, other than those on the pumps, let's have all hands on deck, setting every sail they can as quickly as possible,' he ordered.

'Yes, sir,' responded Bradley before repeating the order to the nervous crew.

Hunter turned to the helmsman. 'Wear the ship.'

The helmsman did not even reply as he started turning the ship through the wind. While the crew were in the process of setting the additional sails, the *Sirius* continued drifting closer, ever closer, to the rocks and oblivion.

The crew worked frantically, with the topmen climbing the ratlines like startled monkeys in a jungle. Others hauled on the ropes to set the sails, and those below decks desperately worked the pumps to expel the ever-increasing volume of water that had been inundating the ship since the gale first struck.

Hunter looked through the mist at the sheer cliff and the rocks at its base. His heart sank as he saw the ship was edging slowly but inexorably closer and closer to them. This was to be his fate, then – oblivion at the bottom of the world.

As the dread of that thought gripped his soul, Bradley gripped his arm. Hunter turned his gaze from the rocks to the sails above, which was where Bradley was pointing. The sails were finally set, and almost as soon as they were, the gale began to shift its direction. It was only by forty-five degrees, but it was enough to begin filling the sails.

While the rain battered his face, obscuring his vision, Hunter peered back at the rocks at the base of the cliff and then at the sails above.

'That wind has shifted, sir,' a relieved Bradley yelled above the roar of the storm.

'Aye, it has for the moment. Let's hope it doesn't switch back,' Hunter yelled in reply.

As the wind continued to rapidly fill the sails, Hunter resembled an Easter Island statue. He stood in silence in the raging gale with his jaw set, watching intently as the *Sirius* gradually turned away from certain destruction at the base of the cliff. She was now heading towards the very point of the headland, beyond which was open sea. Hunter knew there was only one last deadly but hidden obstacle between the *Sirius* and safety, and that was the possibility of a rock shelf at the base of the headland. If there was one, how far did it extend into the path of the *Sirius,* and what submerged rocks did it hold? Hunter stared at the water ahead, trying to determine which of the countless whitecaps in the turbulent sea might be the result of submerged rocks and which the result of the wild wind.

With the sails now full, the *Sirius* began to dramatically increase its speed, and Hunter realised it was going to be impossible to steer the ship sufficiently to avoid any submerged rocks, even if he could see them. They were totally at the mercy of the elements.

The cliff at the end of the point loomed menacingly off the port bow as the *Sirius* crashed its way through the churning sea. All on board held their breath, praying they wouldn't hear the dreaded sound of shredding timber or suffer the shudder of a ship beginning its death throes.

The cloud-covered sun had almost set and the sky was rapidly blackening as the *Sirius* battled her way through the huge swell. With the sails full of the power of the gale, it was only a matter of a few fear-filled minutes and they were past the headland. A spontaneous cheer erupted from the entire crew on deck as she reached the relative safety of the open sea.

'We've made it, Captain.' Bradley beamed.

'Aye, for now,' responded Hunter, acutely aware that although the immediate danger was over, while this storm raged, they were still in real peril.

'That was great seamanship, Captain,' Bradley enthused.

'I'd say it was more like divine providence,' Hunter replied, allowing a half-smile to crease his face.

'Perhaps a combination of both, sir.' Bradley smiled.

A few moments later, both men became aware that the wind had shifted yet again and continued with enormous intensity.

Hunter turned to Bradley. 'If that wind had changed any sooner, Lieutenant, our destiny would've been to be smashed against those rocks.'

'That was so fortunate, Captain! Perhaps it was divine providence.'

'Aye, well, I certainly believe so, but unfortunately, while this gale persists, we still have some very difficult sailing ahead of us. We need to get past Maria's Island, and we need to pass to the windward of it, but given our current position and this gale, that is going to be most hazardous.'

*Ref. 63*

# Chapter 72

# Weerong, 1 May 1789

Arabanoo stood outside the smallpox hospital, talking to Booron and young Nanbaree.

'Booron, now you are no longer sick, Mr White has told me they want you to go and live with Mr Johnson, their holy man, and his wife. How do you feel about that?'

Booron shook her head slowly. 'I don't want to. I don't know them. I want to go back to our people.'

'So do I, but you told me most of our people are dead. My family are dead. Your family are dead. So many are sick, and the others have moved away from our country to get away from the sickness, haven't they?'

Booron nodded hesitantly. 'Yes, they've gone to other tribes' country.'

'Where would you go, then?' asked Arabanoo gently.

Booron shrugged. 'I don't know. Somewhere away from here.'

'I'm so sorry, Booron, but I really don't think you should just go wandering around trying to find someone.'

'I don't like it here,' Booron replied sullenly. 'These people are strange. They have very strange ways that I don't understand.'

Arabanoo saw that Booron's eyes were beginning to glisten, so he put his arm around her and hugged her as he gently patted the back of her head.

'I'm sorry,' he said soothingly, 'but I don't know what else you can do. I don't know what else any of us can do, but I promise you it will be alright. They will look after you.'

Booron began sobbing. Arabanoo continued to hug her before holding her at arm's length and looking into her tear-soaked eyes.

'Cheer up, dear girl. Nanbaree will be near you. He is living with Mr White, and you like it, don't you, Nanbaree?' Arabanoo urged.

Nanbaree hesitated momentarily until Arabanoo glared at him.

'It's alright,' he muttered begrudgingly, 'but they don't have enough food, and most of the food isn't nice.'

It was a comment that confused Arabanoo somewhat, as he was still well fed.

'Some of their food is nice. I agree some of it is awful, but Mr White is good to you, and he looks after you, doesn't he?'

'Yes,' Nanbaree agreed.

'See, Booron? They will look after you, and they will be good to you. And Reverend Johnson has cats for you to play with.'

'Cats? What are they?'

'They are soft little animals, like possums, but you can pat them, so that will be good,' explained Arabanoo, clutching at straws.

Booron said nothing but just stared at the ground. Arabanoo gently raised her chin to look her in the eyes.

'Just stay with them for a little while, and I promise you, when this terrible sickness passes, we can all go back to our country and look for our people. Nanbaree and I will come with you. Alright?'

Booron nodded reluctantly before asking, 'Will you?'

'Yes, yes. Definitely. We will all go together.'

'Maybe just for a little while, then,' replied Booron, wiping the tears from her eyes.

'Good girl.' Arabanoo smiled, sure that she still wasn't really convinced, so he gave her another quick hug.

At that point, Tench and Dawes arrived and continued to help Arabanoo reassure Booron. The conversation, with Arabanoo translating, went on for some time before he felt young Booron was truly accepting of her position. In the course of the conversation, Arabanoo finally revealed to Tench and Dawes the reason behind his recent sadness.

'Family boee,' he murmured.

Tench and Dawes looked at each other momentarily.

'Weereweea boee?' asked Dawes, quite shocked.

Arabanoo nodded silently.

'And your two children?'

Arabanoo nodded again as his eyes moistened.

'Oh, I'm so sorry to hear that,' Tench responded as he and Dawes drew their friend to them and hugged him tightly.

'So sorry,' repeated Tench, who wanted to say much more, but the language barrier made it virtually impossible to communicate on issues such as emotions. All he and Dawes could do was hug and pat Arabanoo and repeat their sympathies.

Finally, as the two marines headed back to their homes, Dawes spoke first. 'It's so tragic about poor Arabanoo and poor Booron.'

'It certainly is. What a mess the place is in. We are starving, and the smallpox is decimating the local people.'

'You know, Watkin, it really is such a tragedy that young Booron can't go back to her people even though her family are dead. I really think she would be happier living with them rather than with us.'

'Agreed, but unfortunately, so many of her people have fled this cursed smallpox. How is she going to find them? It would seem that staying with us is the only real option for her. And for poor little Nanbaree as well, for the time being.'

'Yes, I understand that. It's just that I feel there is a certain degree of cultural arrogance on our part, that we believe the natives are better off to abandon their ways and just come and live with us.'

Tench simply nodded. 'Hmmm.'

'Hmmm?' replied Dawes, rather irritated. 'So you're not going to respond?'

'I'm sorry, Will, but in all the current circumstances, I'm just not sure what the best solution is for anyone.'

*Ref. 64*

## Chapter 73

## Sydney Cove, Sunset, 9 May 1789

It was the end of yet another gloomy, depressing day in the colony. The smallpox outbreak amongst the natives continued unabated, forcing more and more of them to seek assistance. Meanwhile, bush rats had eaten the promising corn crop at Rosehill, winter was on its way and there was still no sign of Hunter and the *Sirius*.

A rather unique trio of friends, two British marine officers and a Gamaragal warrior who had just finished his day working in the British colony's hospital, were walking across the bridge over the stream when their attention was taken by a commotion emanating from the headland on the eastern side of the cove.

'What's going on, I wonder?' Dawes commented.

'I have no idea,' replied Tench, 'but let's have a look.'

As they began heading towards the point, they saw others rushing the same way. Those few already on the point were yelling out, but none of the trio could make out what was being said, until all three made out just one word.

'*Sirius*!'

Tench and Dawes looked at each other. Even Arabanoo knew that was a special ship for his captors, but he really had no idea why.

'Could it be?' mumbled Dawes, not daring to get too excited.

Then they heard that word again, this time quite distinctly amongst the cacophony of shouting coming from the point.

'*Sirius*!'

'It is, it is, it's her!' yelled Tench, as he began running towards the point.

A moment later, the three of them joined the throngs of desperate, starving people on the point. As they did, Tench couldn't really believe the sheer relief that enveloped his entire being. He realised at that instant the extent to which the fear of dying of starvation on this remote dot on the globe had been eating away at him beneath his calm, confident exterior.

When they reached the end of the point, they looked down harbour to the east, and there she was. She was battered and bruised, but she was still sailing. She had made it.

It was an amazingly unifying moment for the colonists, as marines joined the convicts and the free in a wave of universal joy. Tench looked at the ever-increasing crowd to see George Johnston doing what everyone else in the crowd was doing – hugging their loved ones, and if they had no loved ones, hugging whoever was close by. Johnston embraced Esther with young Rosie in their arms. Tench turned and threw his arms around Dawes before pulling a confused Arabanoo into the embrace. Johnston spotted them and headed straight over to them.

'That just has to be the most wonderful sight in the world, doesn't it, Captain?' Johnston beamed.

Tench thought that it wasn't only him who had been maintaining a cool exterior to cover his internal fear.

'It most certainly is, Mr Johnston,' he responded before crouching down to Rosie. 'Come here, Rosie.'

The child ran to Tench, who picked her up and pointed down harbour. 'Look, Rosie, a ship,' he said.

Rosie smiled and then put her arms out to Arabanoo, who was standing beside Tench. 'Boo,' she said.

Tench turned and handed the child to the Gamaragal warrior. As soon as she was in his arms, Rosie pointed down harbour and said, 'Boo, ship.'

Arabanoo smiled and repeated, 'Ship,' before adding, 'Nowee.'

Dawes looked at Esther and said, 'Their word for boat.'

Rosie looked away from the ship that was causing so much excitement and to the black man who held her in his arms. Rosie patted the side of his cheek, and he turned his head and pretended to bite her fingers. She quickly pulled them away and giggled.

Tench watched the exchange and smiled before returning to the matter at hand.

'Mr Johnston, if you'd be good enough to stay here to help welcome Captain Hunter ashore – if Major Ross doesn't arrive in time, of course. We'll go up and inform the governor, in case someone hasn't already done so.'

'Certainly, sir,' replied Johnston. 'It will be an honour and a privilege.'

Arabanoo handed Rosie back to Esther and joined Tench and Dawes as they hurried up the hill towards Government House.

\*\*\*

At that same moment, on board the *Sirius*, John Hunter stood on the quarterdeck, watching as crowds of people rushed down to the point and the foreshore of the cove to welcome home him and his ship. It was the end of a long and extremely hazardous voyage. John Hunter, master mariner, breathed a deep sigh of relief to have finally completed the epic voyage. Unknown to him, just eleven days earlier, another British naval captain, William Bligh, and loyal members of his crew had begun an equally epic voyage of three thousand six hundred miles across the south Pacific Ocean in a longboat. Bligh's crew on the HMS *Bounty*, led by Fletcher Christian, had mutinied and cast them adrift.

'A wonderful sight, Captain,' observed Bradley, who, as always, stood beside his leader.

'Aye, it is indeed. It is indeed,' responded Hunter.

'At times, sir, I really didn't think we were going to make it.'

'Aye, well, I was a wee bit concerned myself, I must confess, but this wonderful ship has held together despite the battering.'

'Only just, though, sir,' said Bradley, which caused Hunter to reflect on the damage to the *Sirius,* which, apart from the ever-worsening leaks, included the destruction of all the rails of the head, the figurehead, the rails to which the bumkins were secured, the jibboom and the fore-top-gallant mast.

'Aye, but she made it,' Hunter replied, as his chest swelled with pride. He wasn't sure, however, about its cause. Was it pride in his ship, his crew or himself? As the cheers of the joyous crowds on the foreshore drifted on the breeze and the rays of the setting sun danced across the harbour, Hunter realised it was all three.

It was a feeling he was tempted to embrace and enjoy, but he forced such thoughts from his mind as he set his jaw and his mind on the report he would provide Phillip. He was pleased he hadn't let the moment overwhelm him, though as he glanced at Bradley beside him, he was sure he detected a solitary tear on the cheek of his usually regimented Lieutenant.

***

Tench, Dawes and Arabanoo were ushered into Phillip's office to find his assistant already sitting there, sharing the news of the return of the *Sirius*. Phillip looked up as they entered.

'This is just the most wonderful news, isn't it, gentlemen?'

'It certainly is, sir,' replied Tench and Dawes, almost in unison.

'Yes, Guvna,' added Arabanoo, still unsure as to the real reason behind the enormous excitement.

'On the way here, sir,' said Tench, 'we explained to Arabanoo that Captain Hunter and his crew are very good friends of ours, they have been on a very long and dangerous voyage and we are extremely pleased to see them home safely.'

'Oh, good, good. We are all absolutely delighted to see them return safely,' Phillip replied. 'And I'll immediately organise a welcome-home dinner for Captain Hunter. I think we can safely lift the rations tonight.'

It was a comment that was greeted with enthusiastic agreement and mirth by all, except Arabanoo, whose command of the English language was still very basic, and 'rations' was a word that had never been uttered in his presence previously.

About an hour later, John Hunter, accompanied by Ross, Johnston and Surgeon White, entered the governor's dining room. It was a large, rectangular room with a long table in the middle and a fireplace at the far end, around which Phillip and his guests sat. All greeted Hunter with the warmest of welcomes. Although delighted with the welcome, he was somewhat distracted by his surprise at finding a native of the country dressed in European clothes, sitting beside Phillip and drinking tea from a cup and saucer, which he was handling with the finesse of a London society lady. Hunter saw something antithetical in the fine bone china being held so delicately in his large black hands.

'Aah, Captain Hunter, I must introduce you to Arabanoo,' said Phillip.

'Pleased to meet you,' replied Hunter, extending his hand.

'Arabanoo, this is Captain Hunter,' continued Phillip.

'Captain Hunter.' Arabanoo nodded as he shook Hunter's hand firmly.

'We are teaching Arabanoo English, and he is teaching us the native language and their customs,' advised Phillip.

'Oh, really?' replied Hunter, just a little stunned.

'Now, Captain, please join us for a glass of wine and tell us all about your trip. I have organised a special dinner to welcome you home.'

'Sir, that is very kind, but would you mind if Lieutenant Bradley and Mr Worgan joined us?'

'Bradley and Worgan?'

'Aye, sir. They have been of wonderful assistance to me on this voyage, which I must say has been the most hazardous I have ever undertaken.'

'But of course. Whomever you want. I'll send a messenger down to the *Sirius* to ask them to come and join us.'

'Thank you, sir. And you might tell the messenger to ask Lieutenant Bradley to bring up a few of the bottles of fine wine the governor of Cape Town has asked us to give you.'

'Sounds like an excellent idea, Captain,' responded Phillip, much to the enthusiastic agreement of the others in the room... except Arabanoo, who was more than content with his cup of tea. 'Now, Captain, tell us all about your voyage. I must say, though, you were a little longer than we hoped, because the situation just kept deteriorating here, so we are just so relieved to see you.'

'Thank you, sir, and I am so pleased to be back safely after a voyage like that.'

Hunter was not normally a loquacious man, but he was on a high after completing such a journey. His audience were obviously enthralled and kept urging him to continue as he told the story of the voyage.

Bradley and Worgan arrived just before dinner was served, and both brought a 'few' bottles of the fine wine from Cape Town. The conversation continued unabated over dinner, with Hunter, aided by Bradley and Worgan, telling of their narrow escapes from disasters rounding the Horn and the south cape of Van Diemen's Land, as well as their wonderful reception by the Dutch governor.

'We only had to mention your name, Excellency, and we were treated like kings,' enthused Bradley.

The conversation hit a more sombre note as Hunter advised the group of the disasters that befell the fleet ships returning home – the *Prince of Wales, Borrowdale, Friendship* and *Alexander* – and the massive loss of life they had suffered. The sombre tone continued when Hunter asked about the absence of the natives from the coves and beaches as they sailed up the harbour. When advised of the smallpox outbreak, he and Bradley were both horrified and, like everyone, wondered about its possible origin.

The discussion then turned to updating Hunter and Bradley on goings-on in the colony, including the hanging of the seven marines for theft and the convicts being flogged for their unprovoked attack on the natives. Tench sat there listening and thinking the conversation had turned quite gloomy after it had started off so much fun, celebrating the return of the *Sirius* with the wine flowing over Hunter's gripping stories. He therefore decided to try to lighten the mood a little.

'Captain, I must acquaint you with another story relating to the convicts.'

'Are these the ones from Rosehill, Captain?' interjected Phillip.

'Yes, sir.'

'Oh, excellent. Please tell them that story,' urged Phillip.

'The story, gentlemen, is that a group of some twenty convicts working at the Rosehill farms absconded with their tools and blankets and set out into the wilderness to the north. They were, of course, forced to return due to famine and attacks by the natives. When they were questioned about where they thought they were going, they replied, "China".'

The whole table, especially Hunter, Worgan and Bradley, erupted in laughter. As the mirth subsided, Tench continued, 'But the most amusing part is, they explained that they believed China might be easily reached because it was just some one hundred miles to the north and only separated from New Holland by a river.'

It was a comment that provoked further hilarity before Tench added, 'Now, gentlemen, I trust that no man here would feel more reluctant than myself to cast an illiberal or parochial national reflection, but it is certain that all these convicts were... Irish.'

Once again, all at the table erupted in laughter, including Arabanoo, who, although he understood nothing of the story, had by this time mastered the art of sharing the joy of those around him.

As the night wore on, though, despite the wine clouding his senses a little, Tench noticed Arabanoo, who was sitting opposite him, becoming rather quiet and withdrawn, which was most unlike him in any circumstance, but particularly at the governor's table, where he was always encouraged to tell stories and join the conversation.

At first, Tench thought it may be because all at the table were getting drunk while Arabanoo drank only tea. The more he looked at him, though, the more Tench thought he was beginning to appear unwell. Tench nudged Dawes, who was sitting beside him, and nodded towards Arabanoo.

Dawes immediately asked, 'Arabanoo, are you alright?'

Arabanoo replied, 'No, Will. Bit sick.'

As Dawes got up from his seat to go around the table and check on him, Arabanoo jumped to his feet, rushed to the window and pushed it open before being violently sick onto the verandah outside.

Surgeon White got to his feet and hurried over to Arabanoo. He patted Arabanoo on the back until his nausea eased and then lifted his shirt to check his skin. Given that the only light in the room was from the candles on the table and the fireplace, it was impossible for White to see clearly.

'Pass me a candle, please, quickly,' he urged.

Dawes responded immediately, and as White held the candle close to Arabanoo's skin, the flickering light illuminated the unmistakable rising sores.

The surgeon turned to the others.

'It's smallpox.'

*Ref. 65 & 66*

# Chapter 74

# Sydney Cove, 12 May 1789

Watkin Tench entered the makeshift hospital, expecting to see Arabanoo lying on one of the small stretchers along with the many other smallpox-affected members of his community. There was, however, no sign of him.

Tench immediately asked Surgeon White, 'Where's Arabanoo?'

'He's gone to get some more fresh water for the patients.'

'But he's sick!'

'Yes, but he won't lie down. He just keeps wanting to help care for the others.'

Tench shook his head.

White continued, 'Unfortunately, he has this misplaced trust in us and our medications. Despite the nauseating taste of our medicines, particularly to someone so unfamiliar with them, he has been swallowing any I have given him in the past two days without complaint. He has even allowed me to bleed him to try to remove the infected blood. He believes that we are going to cure him, and sadly, I don't know that we can.'

'Oh, the poor chap.'

'You understand as well as I do, Captain, that if he has a bad dose of this terrible disease, there is little that I or anyone else can do.'

'And you think he does?'

'It certainly appears that way now. I was hoping at first that he didn't, but the sores have really burst forth since you visited him yesterday. You'll see yourself shortly. He should be back soon.'

Arabanoo returned a few minutes later, carrying a water bucket in each hand, which he immediately put down, as he was obviously struggling to carry them. Tench had seen smallpox many times in his life but never on someone whom he cared as much about as he did this gentle warrior. The hideous disease had erupted in pus-filled blisters all over Arabanoo's face. Tench was immediately overcome by a wave of pity and sadness, as well as a degree of anger, but he quickly controlled his emotions and spoke softly to Arabanoo.

'Arabanoo, you shouldn't be working. You should be resting in a bed.'

'I help Mr White. People sick.'

'Yes, they are, but so are you. You sick too. Must rest.'

Arabanoo looked at Surgeon White. He knew the different roles of the white man. They were so similar to those in his culture. The captain was a warrior, and Mr White was a 'cleverman' doctor.

White nodded. 'Arabanoo, the captain is right. You really should rest. Rest,' he repeated, pointing to the only empty stretcher in the small hospital.

Arabanoo held up his thumb and index finger fractionally apart.

'Little rest,' he said, as he virtually collapsed onto the bed.

Tench quickly got a blanket and put it over Arabanoo before handing him a mug of water.

'Now rest, my brother,' he said, as he gave Arabanoo's hand a gentle squeeze.

*Ref. 67*

\*\*\*

As Tench was leaving the hospital, Dawes was just arriving.

'Have you seen Arabanoo this morning, Will?' asked Tench, as a combination of stress and anger marked his face.

'No, but that's why I'm here now. How is he?'

'He's a mess. The pox has really taken hold.'

'Oh, no!'

'Yes, and I'm just so upset and angry about it, because I can't help feeling that we are in some way responsible.'

'Hmmm, I can understand that, and I don't want to upset you further, but...' Dawes hesitated.

'But what?'

'But your feeling may be more justified than you think.'

'Why is that?'

'Let's go for a walk, Watkin. I'd rather discuss this out of earshot of the hospital.'

The two turned and walked towards the cove.

'I was talking to Surgeon White last night about this whole smallpox outbreak and the vials of it we brought out on the fleet ships,' Dawes explained.

'Yes, he had explained to me it was in case it was needed to use variolation on children born in the colony.'

'The point is, however, that variolation may be the reason we have it, but...' Again, Dawes hesitated.

'Will, it is one thing for us to have it and an entirely different matter for us to deliberately spread it amongst the natives, which seems to me to be what you are suggesting.'

'But what other explanation is there? There was no sign whatsoever of smallpox amongst the natives in the fifteen or sixteen months since we arrived. Now they are totally decimated by it at a time we have been having problems with them.'

Now Tench hesitated as anger, frustration and denial wrestled for control of his heart.

'I just don't believe Phillip would ever authorise the release of smallpox amongst them, no matter how many problems we were having with them.'

'He may not have authorised it, but you've told me yourself, the Americans believe we used it against them in their revolution,' Dawes pushed. 'In Boston and Quebec, wasn't it?'

'Yes, amongst other places,' agreed Tench, grudgingly.

'So, the point is, we have a history of using it against our enemies, so don't pretend we're all pure and above that sort of despicable tactic – and perhaps it wasn't Phillip,' suggested Dawes. 'Perhaps it was Ross or someone else.'

'Will, you know what I think of Ross, but I hesitate to think that even he would do something so despicable, and I'm not pretending we're pure at all. Sadly, I know we're not, but surely no-one can believe the natives are our enemies.'

'I certainly hope not, but whoever did it and however it happened, it is quite clear that it came from us. And you must remember that Ross served at the battle of Bunker Hill with a senior officer who had used it against the Americans.'

'Hmmm, yes, I was aware of that,' responded Tench.

'Yes, so, whoever has caused this horrific outbreak, I am sorry to say that all the evidence points to the fact it has come from us.'

Tench looked at Dawes for a few moments as the anger and frustration he felt was slowly replaced by depressed resignation. Finally, as he looked into his friend's eyes, Tench murmured, 'Could we really do that, Will?'

*\*\*\**

Over the next six days, Arabanoo's condition continued to deteriorate, but he fought it like a warrior. In that time, he had many visitors. Tench and Dawes were there every day and sat on the floor beside his stretcher bed while chatting to him. Esther and Rosie also visited him, as did Governor Phillip, the man responsible for his capture and incarceration.

# Chapter 75

# Sydney Cove, 18 May 1789

The drizzling rain that had persisted for the preceding few days had finally cleared as Tench and Dawes entered the smallpox hospital for their morning visit to Arabanoo.

The room was full of the sounds and scents of death. Only the fire, which Joe Wright had burning at one end of the room to combat the morning chill, helped disguise the scents, but nothing disguised the heart-wrenching moans of the dying.

The two marine officers approached Surgeon White to inquire about Arabanoo's condition.

'He is very, very ill,' White explained in a whisper. 'I really didn't expect him to make it through the night, but he has held on somehow. He is in enormous pain, though, as his organs are beginning to shut down. I'm so sorry to say it won't be long now.'

Tench and Dawes looked at each other but said nothing. Their devastated expressions said it all.

'Booron has been tending him, but she just left,' advised White. 'She'll be back shortly. We've moved him into the corner over there.'

'Thank you.' Tench nodded. He and Dawes weaved their way between the stretcher beds crowded across the floor of the little hospital, upon which lay Arabanoo's dying countrymen and women. When they reached Arabanoo's bed in the corner of the crowded room, they both muffled a gasp at the sight of their friend. Although they had seen him just yesterday, he had clearly deteriorated dramatically overnight. The pus-filled blisters that covered his face were no worse, but his breathing was now shallow and laboured and he emitted a low moan with every breath.

Tench and Dawes sat on the floor beside him, and Tench took his hand. This caused Arabanoo to open his eyes, but it was only momentarily.

'Hello, bubana,' Tench whispered. 'Your brothers are here.'

Again, Arabanoo opened his eyes, but again, it was only momentarily. Tench and Dawes looked at each other, and Dawes shook his head. The two war veterans had seen countless men killed in battle, but watching someone you cared about deeply die a slow, agonising death before your eyes was something else entirely. Their hearts bled for their friend.

Dawes picked up the cup of water that sat on the floor beside the stretcher bed.

'Here, bubana, have some water,' he offered. He put his arm behind Arabanoo's head and tilted it as he slowly brought the cup of water to Arabanoo's lips. He was incapable of drinking, though, so Tench dipped his fingers in the water and gently moistened Arabanoo's lips.

Tench and Dawes looked at each other, and this time, they both shook their heads before silently watching their friend struggling to breathe and uttering low moans each time he did. Tench studied him closely and could just discern, between the pus-filled sores that covered his skin, his face creasing in pain with every breath. At that point, Tench looked over to see that young Booron had returned and was with Surgeon White. He motioned for her to come over, which she immediately did.

'Hello, Booron,' Tench murmured, as he and Dawes got to their feet. 'Please stay with Arabanoo.' He pointed to the floor and to Arabanoo. Booron nodded and sat down beside the stretcher.

Tench and Dawes walked back over to Surgeon White, and Tench motioned to the door. As soon as they stepped outside, Tench spoke first. 'Mr White, he is in a most terrible state. There must be something you can do.'

'I'm so sorry, Captain. I've done all I can. There is nothing more I can do.'

'Isn't there something you can give him to ease his suffering?'

'I'm sorry, no. There's nothing I can give him at this stage,' responded White. Tench looked at White, somehow hoping that if he stared at him intensely enough with his piercing blue eyes, White might come up with a solution.

'I'm sorry, Captain,' White repeated to the unasked question.

\*\*\*

Tench, Dawes and White stood on the land of the Gadigal people and gazed across the harbour to the land of the Gamaragal. They were all totally oblivious to the beauty of the scene as the recently risen sun danced across the calm waters. Their minds were all focussed on feelings of sadness and frustration at their total inability to help relieve the horrors of the situation engulfing their friend Arabanoo and his people in the little hospital behind them.

There were no words to express the emotions they knew they were all feeling, so they returned to the hospital, where Tench and Dawes joined Booron, sitting on the floor at Arabanoo's bedside. The Gamaragal warrior's breathing had become louder and more laboured, and the moments between breaths increased. Finally, as they watched helplessly, he drew a deep breath… but he didn't breathe out. Arabanoo's spirit left his mortal body and continued its journey to join the spirit ancestors…

'Arabanoo booee!' Booron murmured as tears began trickling down her cheeks.

Tench took Arabanoo's lifeless hand and, regretting that he had not said it a moment earlier, whispered, 'Goodbye, my brother.'

It was an emotion shared by a devasted Dawes sitting silently beside him.

\*\*\*

An hour later, two shattered British marine officers slowly climbed the hill to Government House to advise Phillip.

'Yes, gentlemen, what is it?' Phillip asked, glancing up from his desk.

Tench paused before he replied, 'I'm very sorry to have to tell you, sir' – he paused again – 'but Arabanoo has just died.'

'Oh, no!' Phillip murmured. 'I'm so sorry.'

Phillip motioned to the chairs in front of his desk and began rubbing his forehead. 'That is so sad. I saw him just a couple of days ago. This terrible disease… it's such a scourge.'

Dawes glanced at Tench, but Tench remained focussed on Phillip.

'It is, sir,' agreed Tench.

'And he was such a wonderful man.'

'Yes, sir, an amazingly gentle, kind soul.'

'And his death is such a loss to our colony,' commented Phillip, as he called his white greyhound to his side. 'He was vital to developing an understanding with the natives and to learning their language.'

The three British officers sat in silence for a few moments.

'Sir, sorry to be pragmatic at such a time, but we will need to make arrangements for his burial as soon as possible,' said Tench.

'Yes, of course. In line with their custom.'

'We are not sure where he should be buried, sir. Lieutenant Dawes and I felt Booron was telling us that he should be buried on the other side of the harbour in his home soil… where he was captured.'

'Yes, sir,' Dawes jumped in, 'that is definitely what she appeared to be telling us, that he should be buried in his home soil.'

'Really, how would you ever interpret that from the girl? She has no English at all, does she?'

'No, not really, but she was making a digging motion, pointing to Arabanoo's body and then pointing across the harbour,' Dawes explained. 'It seemed fairly obvious, sir.'

'Hmmm,' responded Phillip. 'I think I have a better idea. What if we buried him here in the garden of Government House? I'm sure he would be honoured.'

Tench and Dawes hesitated for a moment and looked at each other, before Tench replied, 'If you think that would be better than being buried in his home soil, sir.'

'Yes, yes, I think it would be. I think it's an excellent idea, actually, and would be most appropriate. This has been his home while he's been with us. Please get it organised for this afternoon, gentlemen, and I will attend myself.'

'Yes, Excellency. We'll get it organised,' replied Tench, getting to his feet. As he did so, he noticed the look of frustration and anger on Dawes's face and realised he was about to say something he may regret. Tench tapped him on the shoulder and motioned towards the door.

'Let's go, Lieutenant,' Tench ordered.

Dawes got to his feet and followed Tench, but as soon as they were outside, he pulled the sleeve of Tench's uniform and muttered between clenched teeth, 'It's been his *home*, he says! More like his bloody prison!'

'Exactly,' agreed Tench.

\*\*\*

That afternoon, Gamaragal warrior Arabanoo was buried in the garden of Government House. Attending the burial were Governor Arthur Phillip, Captain Watkin Tench, Lieutenant William Dawes, Surgeon John White, convict Joseph Wright, Booron, Nanbaree, Lieutenant George Johnston, Esther Abrahams and Rosie.

The group stood in silence, quietly praying to their gods as two convicts covered Arabanoo's grave with the soil of the Gadigal people. No prayers or invocations were uttered aloud, as Arabanoo had been seen burying many of his people, and he had never uttered a single word.

Watkin Tench stared at the ground as he ran his thumb along the inside of the white diagonal strap of his uniform. His mind was numb. None of the countless deaths he had seen over the years seemed quite as tragically unjust as this. Here was a kind, gentle man who had been snatched from his family and his people and held prisoner for months before contracting this dreaded disease, and for what? Something about the whole thing disturbed him deeply.

As the final shovelful of soil was thrown onto Arabanoo's grave, Tench's cheek quivered and his eyes glistened, ever so slightly, but the British marine captain refused to allow a single tear to stain his weathered skin.

That was, until he heard little Rosie's voice in Esther's arms beside him. He turned and looked at her as she pointed to the grave.

'Boo gone.'

*Ref. 68*

# Epilogue

# Sydney Cove, 24 December 1790

It was early afternoon when Tench's marines arrived back in the infant colony. They trudged out of the bush beneath a scorching sun burning from the pit of hell. They were exhausted, caked in mud and soaked in sweat and stinking swamp water. They were also empty-handed. They had failed completely in their mission, on which Phillip had dispatched them, to capture or kill local natives.

'I'm certainly glad that's over, Watkin,' Dawes mumbled as they led the detachment into the colony.

'Not half as glad as I am,' Tench replied quietly, before adding, 'I hate failing at anything, but as you well understand, I'm relieved I failed this time.'

'You're relieved? I'm delighted.' The exhausted Dawes smiled.

'Anyway, I had best clean myself up and change into a fresh uniform before I see the governor.'

'Why do that?' responded Dawes. 'If you do, word of our failure will have reached him before you get there – and besides, turning up in your current putrid state at least shows him the lengths to which you went to try to achieve your mission.'

'Actually, I think that sounds like a rather good idea, Will. Thanks.' Tench smiled as he turned up the hill towards the governor's residence.

As Tench sat in front of Phillip's desk, he was neither surprised nor offended when the first thing Phillip commented on was his stench. In normal circumstances, such a comment would have horrified the usually immaculate Tench. After going through the details of their expedition, the governor rubbed his balding head while gently stroking the head of his white greyhound.

'Let me think about what to do next,' Phillip concluded before sending Tench on his way to clean up.

The next day, Tench was summoned to Phillip's office to be told he was to lead another expedition with exactly the same objectives. This time, however, Phillip was sure they could trick the natives by spreading word to Colbee and his kin, who they were on good terms with, that they were heading north to Broken Bay to punish the man who had speared Phillip in September as payback for his kidnapping of Colbee and Bennelong. When they were convinced the locals had received the message, Phillip immediately dispatched Tench back to Botany Bay.

The sun was beginning to set when Tench led his increased detachment of thirty-eight marines into the bush at the southern end of the colony. They had decided to travel beneath the light of the full moon to avoid the heat of the day and to maintain the secrecy of their mission.

It didn't work.

Two days and nights later, Tench and his detachment arrived back at Sydney Cove at nine o'clock in the morning – once again empty-handed. Once again, an exhausted, sweating Tench sat in front of Phillip's desk to report his failure. As Tench revealed the details of the mission, he saw the disappointment etched across the governor's face.

When Tench had completed his report, Phillip did not respond but instead sat in silence.

Tench shifted in his seat a little uncomfortably before filling the silence with, 'I'm sorry, Excellency.'

'Hmm, yes, I can understand you are, Captain,' Phillip said. 'Before you go, though, I should just advise you of an unfortunate incident that occurred here in the colony while you were away.'

Tench replied, 'Yes, sir. What was that?'

'One night, two native men were discovered stealing some potatoes from a garden. They were pursued by marines for some distance to a native camp, where two women were taken prisoner, and unfortunately, one of the men was shot in the back. His dead body was discovered the next morning.'

Tench stared blankly at Phillip as he ran his thumb and forefinger up and down the white leather diagonal of his uniform. He provided no response to the story other than to ask, 'Will that be all, then, Excellency?'

When a slightly surprised Phillip said, 'Oh, yes, certainly,' Tench immediately got to his feet and walked out. He strode down the hill, through the little streets of the colony and up to the headland where Dawes's hut sat in solitude, overlooking the harbour.

'Will,' he called as he approached.

Dawes immediately emerged.

'Have you heard about the killing of this native over the potato theft?' asked Tench.

'Of course I have,' responded an emotional Dawes. 'Simply terrible! Imeerawanyee tells me the man who was shot was Bangai.'

Tench shook his head. 'One day, I'm sent out to hunt the Indians for killing someone. The next, they're being shot in the back for petty theft.'

'A bullet in the back for a potato! That's British justice for you!'

*Ref. 69*

# What Happened to Them?

**Lieutenant George Johnston** was promoted to brevet major in January 1800 and in January 1808 led the 'Rum Rebellion' against Governor William Bligh, installing himself as the colony's lieutenant governor – but that is another story. He survived a court martial for his role in the rebellion and had a successful career as a farmer and grazier, having been granted a total of 4,162 acres of land, with his principal property being Annadale Farm in Sydney's inner west. He died in January 1823 and was interred in the Greenway-designed family vault at Annadale Farm.

**Major Robert Ross** – due to his extremely difficult manner, and to avoid the continual arguments with him, Phillip transferred Ross to Norfolk Island in March 1790. Ross declared martial law there, which exceeded his power, and fought continually with his officers, just as he had done at Sydney Cove. He returned to England in December 1791 and continued his military career but was demoted to captain-lieutenant. He died a few years later in 1794 at age fifty-four.

**Lieutenant William Bradley** – Captain John Hunter's right-hand man remained in the colony and was with Hunter on the *Sirius* when it was wrecked off Norfolk Island. Along with Hunter, he was court-martialled for his role in the shipwreck but was honourably acquitted and continued to serve in the British Navy, rising to the rank of admiral before he retired. Bradley's Head in Sydney Harbour is named after him.

**Joseph Wright** – the young convict to whom Arabanoo was attached in this book did make something of his life. He married Eleanor Gott, a Second Fleet convict, on 19 December 1790 at St

Phillip's Church. He was granted his freedom in 1794 and given thirty acres of land near what is now Pitt Town by the Hawkesbury River. Their neighbours included James Ruses and Henry Kable. Joseph and Eleanor had seven children before he died in 1811, aged forty-four. Please note, for the sake of historical accuracy, that the name of the convict whom Arabanoo was actually attached to is not shown on the historical record – that the author could find, anyway. Joseph Wright has been used simply to give a name, face and personality to that unknown convict.

**Esther Abrahams** continued her relationship with Johnston and bore him seven children. They did not marry, however, until November 1814, at the urging of then-Governor Macquarie. Esther became first lady of the colony when Johnston became lieutenant governor and was highly competent in running the family estates while Johnston was in England fighting his court martial.

**Pemulwuy** led the resistance by Australia's First Nations People against the British invasion of their land. He was a brave warrior who waged a very effective guerrilla war against the superior weaponry of the British. He was wounded many times by British bullets, but because he survived each time, he gained a reputation for being indestructible. He was finally shot on 2 June 1802. His corpse was beheaded and the skull sent to Sir Joseph Banks in London. In 2010, following requests by First Nations People, Prince William agreed to send the skull back to Pemulwuy's people. However, British authorities have not been able to locate it amongst the numerous Aboriginal items in their possession.

**Bennelong** was, of course, arguably the most famous of Australia's First Nations People. After he escaped his original capture by Phillip, he continued to return regularly to the colony to visit Phillip. Ultimately, he had a hut built on the point that bears his name, and which is now the location of the Sydney Opera House. When Phillip returned to England, he took Bennelong and Imeerawanyee with him to 'show them off' to the British establishment. After living in

England for a short time, Bennelong returned to his native land. His wife was Barangaroo, after whom the area on the eastern shore of Darling Harbour is named. Tench said of him: 'Love and war seemed his favourite pursuits, in both of which he had suffered severely.' The proof of this was provided by the scars he bore on his head, torso, arms and legs. Both he and Colbee also bore the scars of the smallpox that had so ravaged their people. He died on 3 January 1813.

**Lieutenant William Dawes** – his strong-minded refusal to follow orders regarding the treatment of First Nations People caused him to have a serious falling out with Governor Phillip. As a result, he returned to England in December 1791, when his strong preference was to stay in the colony. Phillip had offered to allow him to stay if he accepted a demotion to ensign and apologised for his behaviour. He refused. Despite Hunter's request that Dawes return as the colony's engineer during Hunter's term of governor, nothing came of it. Dawes nevertheless had a successful career serving as governor in Sierra Leone and moved to Antigua in 1813 to work for the antislavery cause. He married Grace Gilbert and died in Antigua in 1836.

His work with Patyegerang resulted in him becoming the first European to make detailed records of the local First Nations People's language – records that survive to this day.

Dawes Point, where his house stood, is the location of the Sydney Observatory and the southern pylon of the Sydney Harbour Bridge.

**Captain Watkin Tench** – while in the NSW colony, he wrote two books, which were extremely well received back in England. It is a testament to his skill as a writer and an observer of history that those books were initially published in three editions, were translated into French, German, Dutch and Swedish and are still being published to this day under the title *1788* – over two hundred and thirty years after they were written.

After 'discovering' the Nepean River on 27 June 1789, Tench returned to England in December 1791. He later fought in the Napoleonic Wars, when England was again at war with France, and he was once again taken as a prisoner of war. He was released in a prisoner exchange and returned to England. He married Anna Maria Sargent in October 1792. They had no children, but they adopted the four orphaned children of one of Anna's sisters. He was later promoted to major general and died on 7 May 1833, aged seventy-four.

A large area of parkland and an avenue in the Penrith district near the Nepean River bear his name.

**Captain John Hunter** – after being captain of the *Sirius* when it was shipwrecked off Norfolk Island on 19 March 1791 and being stranded on Norfolk for nearly eleven months, Hunter returned to England, arriving in April 1792. He faced court martial for the loss of the ship, which was in accordance with naval regulations requiring the court-martial of the commanding officer of any wrecked naval ship. He was honourably acquitted of all blame.

He returned to the NSW colony as its second governor in September 1795 and served until September 1800, when he returned to England. His term was marked by some controversy centred on his struggles to control the rising power of the marine officers – the infamous 'Rum Corps'.

He was promoted to vice admiral in July 1810 and died in March 1821. He never married. His name is remembered in many locations in NSW, including a major river, a valley, city streets, and a major hospital.

While in NSW, he combined his love of art and his love of nature to draw much of the country's unique fauna and flora. Of particular note are his illustrations of Australia's platypus. His drawings and descriptions of this unique creature were amongst the first to reach England, where they caused enormous consternation and controversy in the scientific community. Many believed them to be a hoax and were sure that no such creature could exist – a duck-billed, fur-covered, egg-laying amphibian that suckled its young – impossible!

**Arabanoo** was just the first of five local First Nations People to be kidnapped by the British under Phillip's orders. Those captured later included Bennelong and Colbee – yet another story. Arabanoo was instrumental in changing the attitudes of many of the British towards the local First Nations People. Watkin Tench described him as 'kind' and 'of a gentle, placable nature' but 'impatient of indignity and allowed of no superiority on our part... The independence of his mind never forsook him. If the slightest insult was offered him, he would return it with interest. At retaliation of merriment, he was often happy and frequently turned the laugh against his antagonist.'

He was clearly an extraordinary man.

Arabanoo Lookout at Dobroyd Head, overlooking the entrance to Sydney Harbour, is named after him. It provides one of Sydney's most magnificent views and really is worth a visit.

# Acknowledgements

Apart from Tench and Hunter's works, I have used various other primary and secondary source material in writing this book. Full details are provided in the list of references below. Undoubtedly, though, the one that I have relied on most heavily is Rob Mundle's *The First Fleet*. Not only is it an enthralling read, but it has also provided me with so much important detail about the fleet and the people on it. It also provides countless references to various primary source documents, which has repeatedly pointed me in the right direction to find additional detailed information.

Robert Barnes's *An Unlikely Leader* has been very helpful in providing detail on Hunter's life and on his character and values.

*Esther* by Jessica North provided me with another layer to the story and enabled me to introduce Esther Abrahams, her daughter Rosie and Lieutenant George Johnston. It also provided me with the final words of my book, so a huge thank you to Jessica for that, and thank you to our dear friend Karen Pitt, who suggested I read *Esther*. Thanks also to Karen for her very constructive and helpful critique of an early draft of this book.

Thank you to another close friend, Graeme Theobald, for his input and for advising me he had an ancestor on the First Fleet. His name was Joseph Wright, who I have included as the convict Arabanoo was bound to. Graeme also provided me with the wonderful book *To Those Who Came After From Those Who Came Before,* written and published by his relative Wendy Yates, who is also a direct descendant of Joseph Wright. The book contains excellent background information on Joseph and the times in which he lived. Also, a big thank you to another dear friend, Leanne Higgins, for her very constructive suggestions on fine-tuning the structure of the book.

Henry Reynolds's numerous works have always been an excellent source of information and insight into the truth of our shared history in this country. In this case, it was his latest work, *Truth-Telling*, which provided me some excellent historical information that has further enriched this book.

Also, thank you very much to my son Jacob for his very constructive ideas on improvements to the early drafts. Thank you so much to my darling wife Jan for her patience and support over the years of researching and writing this book and for pretending not to be bored when I rambled on endlessly about it.

Finally, thank you so much to the Hon. Linda Burney for being so kind as to write a wonderful foreword for the book. It is enormously appreciated. Also, a huge thank you to my editor from Shawline, Aidan Demmers. Aidan not only has an incredible eye for detail but was also able to provide me with some excellent ideas on how to improve the book.

# FOOTNOTES

Ref. 1: Tench p. 164f & 168f
Ref. 2: Tench p. 170
Ref. 3: Tench p. 171f
Ref. 4: Tench pp. 164–178
Ref. 5: Tench p. 170ff
Ref. 6: Barnes pp. 30–32
Ref. 7: Hunter p. 33
Ref. 8: Hunter p. 34
Ref. 9: Hunter p. 39f
Ref. 10: Tench p. 37f & 42
Ref. 11: Hunter p. 39
Ref. 12: Hunter p. 39
Ref. 13: Tench p. 40f
Ref. 14: Tench p. 38f, Hunter p. 40
Ref. 15: Hunter p. 40
Ref. 16: Tench p. 43f
Ref. 17: Hunter p. 56f
Ref. 18: Hunter p. 57f
Ref. 19: Hunter p. 58f
Ref. 20: Tench p. 75f
Ref. 21: Tench p. 44, Bowes Smyth Feb 1788
Ref. 22: Tench p. 57, Hunter p. 63
Ref. 23: White Feb 30 1788
Ref. 24: Tench p. 58
Ref. 25: Tench p. 68f
Ref. 26: Hunter p. 71, Tench p. 88f

Ref. 27: Tench p. 88f & p. 92f
Ref. 28: Hunter p. 72f, Tench p. 92
Ref. 29: Hunter p. 72f, Tench p. 92
Ref. 30: Tench p. 92, Hunter p. 72
Ref. 31: Hunter p. 78f
Ref. 32: Tench p. 92
Ref. 33: Hunter p. 78f
Ref. 34: Hunter p. 82f
Ref. 35: Hunter p. 81
Ref. 36: Tench p. 92f, North p. 1ff
Ref. 37: Hunter p. 83f
Ref. 38: Tench p. 92f
Ref. 39: Reynolds p. 89ff
Ref. 40: Hunter p. 83f
Ref. 41: Hunter p. 83f
Ref. 42: Hunter p. 85f
Ref. 43: Tench p. 93f
Ref. 44: Hunter p. 85f & p. 98f
Ref. 45: Tench p. 95
Ref. 46: Tench p. 95f
Ref. 47: Tench p. 98f
Ref. 48: Tench p. 107
Ref. 49: Hunter p. 98f
Ref. 50: Tench p. 98f
Ref. 51: Hunter p. 99f
Ref. 52: Tench p. 99f
Ref. 53: Hunter p. 100f
Ref. 54: Tench p. 100
Ref. 55: Hunter p. 101
Ref. 56: Hunter p. 102f
Ref. 57: Tench p. 101
Ref. 58: Tench p. 107f
Ref. 59: Tench p. 102, Swanton p. 2

Ref. 60: Tench p. 102
Ref. 61: Tench p. 105f
Ref. 62: Hunter p. 103f
Ref. 63: Hunter p. 103f
Ref. 64: Tench p. 105f
Ref. 65: Hunter p. 118f
Ref. 66: Tench p. 106
Ref. 67: Tench p. 107
Ref. 68: Tench p. 176f
Ref. 69: Tench p. 176f

# REFERENCES

Robert Barnes, 'An Unlikely Leader: The Life and Times of Captain John Hunter', Sydney University Press, 2009.

Arthur Bowes Smyth, 'A Journal of a Voyage from Portsmouth to New South Wales and China', Edited by Colin Choat, Project Gutenberg Australia, 2020.

Richard Broome, 'Aboriginal Australians', Allen and Unwin, 2010.

Stephen Gapps, 'The Sydney Wars', New South Publishing, 2017.

Jane Harrison, 'The Visitors', Play performed at Carriageworks, 2020.

John Hunter, 'An Historical Journal of the Transactions at Port Jackson and Norfolk Island', University of Sydney Library.

Paul Irish, 'Hidden in Plain View: The Aboriginal People of Coastal Sydney', New South Publishing, 2017.

Grace Karskens, 'The Colony,' Allen and Unwin, 2010.

Douglas Lockwood, 'I, the Aboriginal', Rigby Limited, 1962.

Rob Mundle, 'The First Fleet', ABC Books, 2014.

Jessica North, 'Esther', Allen and Unwin, 2019.

Henry Reynolds, 'Truth-Telling: History, Sovereignty and the Uluru Statement', New South Publishing, 2021.

Bruce Swanton, 'A Chronological Account of Crime, Public Order and Police in Sydney 1788-1810', Australian Institute of Criminology, 1983.

Watkin Tench, '1788', Book 1 'A Narrative of the Expedition to Botany Bay', Book 2 'A Complete Account of the Settlement at Port Jackson', Edited and Introduced by Tim Flannery, Text Publishing, 1996.

Bruce Watt, 'Dharawal, the first contact people', Everbest, 2019

John White, 'Journal of a Voyage to New South Wales', Project Gutenberg Australia, 2003.

Wendy Yates, 'To Those Who Came After From Those Who Came Before'.

Plus numerous other primary and secondary source documents.

Shawline Publishing Group Pty Ltd
www.shawlinepublishing.com.au

www.ingramcontent.com/pod-product-compliance
Lightning Source LLC
Chambersburg PA
CBHW012000090526
44590CB00026B/3807